creative ESSENTIALS

Andy Glynne

DOCUMENTARIES

...and how to make them

creative ESSENTIALS

This edition published in 2008 by Kamera Books
PO Box 394, Harpenden, Herts, AL5 1XJ
www.kamerabooks.com

Copyright © Andy Glynne 2008
Series Editor: Hannah Patterson

A CIP catalogue record for this book is available from the British Library.

ISBN-13: 978-1-904048-80-0

Typeset by Elsa Mathern
Printed by SNP Lefung Printers (Shenzen) Co Ltd, China

CONTENTS

ACKNOWLEDGEMENTS

This book is really a result of the many years I have worked as a documentary producer, director and tutor, and my knowledge has developed from the words and vision of so many people that it would be impossible to thank everyone individually. Nevertheless, there are certain people whose direct contribution has made this book a possibility rather than just a probability. First of all, to all those who I have worked with at the Documentary Filmmakers Group in the UK, who I have known since the beginning and have inspired me to continue on the path as a documentary maker. Of particular note is Kerry McLeod who, as well as contributing to specific elements in this book, has been there as a source of invaluable help. Thanks are also due to all the contributors and filmmakers, who gave their time and words of wisdom. These include (in no particular order) André Singer, Kim Longinotto, Marilyn Gaunt, Emily James, Kevin Macdonald, Al Maysles, Roger Graef, Simon Aeppli, Jerry Rothwell, Sean McAllister, Kevin Hull, Kim Peat, Emma Read, Anton Califano, Russell Crockett, Esteban Uyarra, Phil Cox, Jennifer Abbott, Marc Isaacs, Erik Bäfving, Ben Hopkins, Nikki Parrott, Jonathan Hodgson, Miriam Lyons and Linda Stradling.

THE CONTRIBUTORS

Throughout this book, industry professionals and insiders have kindly lent their words of wisdom, cynicism and expertise. Below is a brief description of who these people are.

KIM LONGINOTTO – Kim is an internationally acclaimed documentary film-maker from the UK who has often provided unique portraits of the lives of women. The award-winning *The Day I will Never Forget* examines the practice of female genital mutilation in Kenya and the pioneering African women who are bravely reversing the tradition. The recent *Sisters in Law* (co-directed by Florence Ayisi), about the landmark achievements of the Women Lawyers Association (WLA) of Kumba, in southwest Cameroon, won the Prix Art et Essai at the Cannes Film Festival.

MARILYN GAUNT – Marilyn is a British freelance award-winning filmmaker, having made over 50 documentaries for most of the major broadcasters and the BBC. Her films include the BAFTA Award-winning *Kelly and Her Sisters*, which looks at three months in the lives of Kelly and her five sisters, six children who live with their mother in poor housing on a run-down estate in Birmingham.

EMILY JAMES – Emily is a filmmaker who studied at the National Film and Television School in the UK. Her first film *The Luckiest Nut in the World* follows an animated American peanut, who sings about the difficulties faced by nuts from developing countries. She has continued to use animation and puppetry in her documentaries, and her most recent current affairs television series *Don't Worry* featured a cast of investigative puppet reporters.

KEVIN MACDONALD – Kevin has made the Academy Award-winning *One Day in September* about the 1972 Munich Olympics. He has also directed *Touching the Void* and the recent award-winning fiction feature *The Last King of Scotland*. Macdonald has been associate editor at Faber & Faber since 1995: he co-edited *The Faber Book of Documentary* (1997), and wrote *Emeric Pressburger: The Life and Death of a Screenwriter* (Faber, 1994, winner of BFI film book of the year and short-listed for the NCR non-fiction prize).

ROGER GRAEF – Roger is a writer, filmmaker, broadcaster and criminologist. In January 2006, it was announced that Roger had been awarded an OBE in the New Year's Honours List. In 2004 he was awarded the prestigious Fellowship of the British Academy of Film and Television, again for his outstanding contribution and achievements. Roger also won a BAFTA in 2003, as the producer of the Flaherty Best Documentary for *Feltham Sings!* Among his more than 80 films, he is best known for his pioneering work in gaining access to hitherto closed institutions ranging from ministries and boardrooms to police, courts, prisons, probation and social work.

SIMON AEPPLI – Simon is an editor and filmmaker who has a background in Artist's Film and Video. He has tutored for University of Wales Institute in Cardiff and the Documentary Filmmakers Group, and has also been a media educator in London at the Institute of Education ARCO PLUS, WAC Performing Arts and Media College, The Place and New Vic College.

JENNIFER ABBOTT – Jennifer is a documentary maker, cultural activist and editor with a particular interest in producing media that shifts perspectives on problematic social norms and practices. In addition to co-directing and editing *The Corporation*, she produced, directed and edited *A Cow at My Table*, a feature documentary about meat, culture and animals, which won eight international awards.

JERRY ROTHWELL – Jerry is a documentary producer-director with a ten-year track record in broadcast documentaries, specialising in programmes about arts, mental health and education. He has produced and executive produced documentary, news and drama for Channel 4, Carlton and the BBC. He is the co-director of the recent feature documentary *Deep Water*, and is currently completing another feature documentary, *Heavy Load*, which documents a year in the life of a punk band, whose members include musicians with learning disabilities.

KEVIN HULL – Kevin is an award-winning filmmaker and series producer for the BBC and Channel 4. His series for BBC/PBS, *Fever Road*, won the One World Award for TV Documentary of the Year. Kevin is resident Documentary Tutor at the London Film School, and a visiting Professor at the National Film School, the Documentary Filmmakers Group, and the EICTV Film School in Cuba.

SEAN MCALLISTER – Sean is widely acknowledged as one of Britain's finest documentary filmmakers. His previous films include *Settlers*, about everyday life in Jerusalem, and *Minders*, an affectionate look at two of Saddam Hussein's Ministry of Information minders. His feature documentary *The Liberace of Baghdad* won numerous awards, including the Jury Prize at the Sundance Film Festival.

KIM PEAT – Kim was appointed as Controller for Daytime, Arts and Religion for the UK's Channel Five in September 2001.

EMMA READ – Emma is the Commissioning Editor, Factual Entertainment and Specialist Factual for Sky One, Two and Three.

ESTEBAN UYARRA – Esteban is an award-winning director, editor and cinematographer of documentary films who has worked for several UK television channels, including the BBC. His recent work includes the award-winning feature documentary *War Feels Like War*, which focuses on the role of journalists covering the Iraq War in 2001.

RUSSELL CROCKETT – Russell is an editor who has worked on many documentaries including Marc Isaacs' award-winning *Lift* (on the DVD).

LINDA STRADLING – Linda has spent more than 20 years in the TV industry, and is an experienced and well-established production manager working predominantly on large documentary series.

AL MAYSLES – One of America's foremost non-fiction filmmakers, Albert Maysles, along with his brother and partner David (1932–1987), has been recognised as the creator of 'direct cinema', the distinctly American version of French 'cinéma vérité'.

Physical Processing		Order Type: **Firm**

Cust/Add: **363610006/01**	**EBOV**	**NEWMAN**
Cust PO No. **NW07001281**		Cust
BBS Order No: **E1302937**	Ln: **34** Del: **1**	BBS
1904048803-28812649		Sales
(9781904048800)		

Documentaries

Subtitle: **and how to make them**		Stmt of Re

PAPERBACK ᴡɪᴛʜ ᴍᴇᴅɪᴀ   Pub Year: **2007**   Vol No.:

Glynne, Andy.   Ser. Title:

Turnaround Publisher Services Ltd

Acc Mat:

Profiled	**Kapco UK**	**Date Due Slip UK**
Tech	**Accession Stamp UK**	**Property Stamp UK**
Services:	**Barcode Label Applicati**	**Security Device UK**
	Base Charge Processing	

Fund: **CREATE**   Loca

Stock Category: **Standard Loan**   Depa

Class #:   Cutter:

Standard Loan

Order Line Notes: **Management report printed - book available fro investigate. 3.6.08 sc**

Notes to Vendor: **3 seven day**
233549,233550,233551

Blackwell Book Services

INTRODUCTION

If you've bought, borrowed or stolen this book, or if you're browsing through it whilst sitting in a bookshop on a long, wet, miserable Sunday afternoon, then it's probably because you're interested in documentary filmmaking. Maybe you are actively making films, and want to read up on some techniques, approaches or tips. Maybe you've never made a documentary film, and you're looking for a good place to start. Or perhaps you're not sure whether or not you're a filmmaker at all, but know that you want to learn more. But whatever stage you're at, I hope this book will prove an invaluable tool, and help you to advance your understanding of documentaries, and how to make them.

The word 'documentary' can refer to many different types of film. From the earliest classics such as Basil Wright and Harry Watt's *Night Mail* through to the latest feature documentaries in cinemas such as *Super Size Me*, the word encompasses as many different types of films as there are people making them. Today, with the clever use of graphics used in historical and nature documentaries, the distinction between fiction and fact has become significantly blurred. And the advent of Reality Television and various other forms of 'Factual Entertainment' have made the definition even broader.

Documentary filmmakers can be a peculiar bunch of people, driven by an amazing drive to tell a specific story, and impart a message. It's a hard slog to make a documentary film, both physically and emotionally, and there are easier, less precarious ways, no doubt, to earn a living. But there are numerous rewards that make it worthwhile. Firstly, as documentarians, we get to completely immerse ourselves in fascinating, hitherto unknown, subject areas. As a result of documentaries I've been involved in, I have learned about the hormones in men, life in women's prisons, missionaries in the Middle

East and unreported wars in West Africa, to name but a few topics. Secondly, we have the opportunity to effect change, or make some kind of difference. A recent survey conducted by the Documentary Filmmakers Group showed that over 80% of documentary filmmakers made films in order to 'make a difference', be that on a global, national, community or individual level. And there are countless examples of films that have either created or contributed to change (see next chapter). Thirdly, we get to observe people. We are the ethnographers of the modern age, meeting a huge variety of individuals, often from all corners of the world; fascinating and sometimes inspirational, they can help us tell stories about unique and interesting subject matter.

There may be many more reasons that compel people to make documentaries, but for me it's primarily about learning. I learn about other people, other cultures and other concepts, and maybe I can share this knowledge or perspective with other people by making a film. Most importantly, though, I learn about myself. Every film I've been involved in has changed me a little bit, given me something and helped me to reflect on who I am.

There is no better time to be involved in documentary filmmaking. In the past few years there has been somewhat of a renaissance in this area, and our televisions and cinemas are now full of hundreds of films that come under the banner of 'documentaries'. We also have much cheaper technology at our disposal, so now anyone in theory can inexpensively shoot and edit their own documentary film. And now with broadband Internet, TV on demand, and the next generation of mobile phones, the possibilities for distributing our work are changing rapidly.

This book talks about the art and craft of documentary filmmaking. But more importantly, it also discusses the ways in which this craft works in today's industry. For example, there is no point in discussing shooting technique on 35mm film, or how to work with an eight-person crew, when such trends rarely exist anymore in the real world. The types of stories we tell, and the ways in which we tell them are also considerably influenced by today's market, and if we want to distribute our films, as well as simply making them, then an understanding of this market is not only invaluable but also essential. Throughout the book, I have often used the term 'independent filmmaker' and this probably deserves some clarification. Many of you who read this book will be at the start of your 'career', if you're even thinking of it in 'career' terms. You will often be making your film independently rather than as part of a Broadcaster's in-house team. Sometimes you might be attached to a small 'Indy' (or Independent Production Company); or you might be on your own. In addition, you may find that you are often working as a multi-skiller, meaning that you are producing, directing and shooting your own documentary – perhaps even sound recording and editing too. As such, you need to keep your costs down, work flexibly and develop skills in as many different areas as possible.

I have tried to break this book into different sections according to the various stages of the production process. 'Section One' deals with the initial idea and how to develop this into a concrete treatment. I then discuss what the fundamental ingredients are for a documentary film, and how one can think about getting various types of funding. 'Section Two' discusses the actual filming process in detail: what equipment you need, and how to use it, along with the important skills of being a documentary filmmaker – interview technique, production management, the art of storytelling and so on. 'Section Three' deals with post-production and how to deliver the finished product (either to television broadcast, cinemas, festivals, DVDs or the Internet). 'Section Four' looks at some of the ethical issues that can affect documentary filmmakers. 'Section Five' is a resources section and details the books, Internet sites, organisations and documentary films that you might find useful. 'Section Six' includes interviews with established documentary filmmakers, with a focus on their process making a particular film (three of which appear on the DVD that comes with this book). The enclosed DVD contains invaluable resources such as a release form, budget templates, sample proposals and lists of commissioning editors, as well as a selection of films that have, in some way, contributed to the current zeitgeist in documentary filmmaking. Put it all together, and you have a comprehensive resource on the core skills you need to go out and make a brilliant, hopefully sellable, documentary film.

An important point to make: if you read through this book sequentially – and really it's a good idea that you do – then all the information included may seem a little bit overwhelming. It does get easier over time, I promise you. A good analogy to hold in your head is that of driving a car. At first, before you set foot in a car, you are *unconsciously incompetent* in that you have no idea how bad you are at driving and how many skills you do not have. As soon as you set foot in that car, and have your first driving lesson, you experience the sensation of *conscious incompetence*, in that you now realise how bad you actually are. After some time at learning to drive, you become *consciously competent*; that is you are aware of things that you can now do – change gear, check your mirror, and use the clutch. The only problem is, it's an awful lot to focus on, and mentally exhausting. But soon you'll reach a stage of *unconscious competence*; i.e. the things you are good at are mostly unconscious and you can drive a manual car almost automatically. The same goes for filmmaking, in that the more you practise, the easier things become, and the less mental effort you need to exert. So, please try to use this book in conjunction with lots and lots – and lots – of practice.

SECTION ONE
PRE-PRODUCTION

1. WHY WE MAKE DOCUMENTARIES

We can go into a high-street shop these days, buy a small DV or HDV camera, and go out and make our documentary. We can then edit the film on our home computers, add a little music, and make it into a DVD. The process might not lead to the highest production values, and our intended audience might only be our mum, dad, or friend, but the very fact that we can just go out and do it is very new. What we now take for granted was not only once novel, but actually incredible.

In the beginning, making a documentary film could often involve a large team and a painstakingly long process. I've tried to give a brief overview below of the history of the documentary, simply because it allows us to see today's filmmaking practice in context, and understand in more detail the tools we have at our disposal. (For those interested in reading more on the topic, I have suggested some recommended reading in Section Five.)

The very first 'documentary films' are a far cry from what we see on our television screens and in cinemas today. At the turn of the century, they were simply a visual and audio recording of an event. No story. No plot. No character development. People would flock to cinemas to see these films, which either reflected contemporary life on the big screen, or, for the first time, showed portraits of what life was like in the far corners of the world (such as Robert Flaherty's classic *Nanook of the North*). In Britain specifically, the early pioneers of documentary such as Humphrey Jennings made films about ordinary people going about their everyday business. Arthur Elton and Edgar Anstey's *Housing Problems* was one of the first times people actually witnessed the experiences of the British working class on film. This powerful look at contemporary society, which had never before been seen in such a way, sowed the seeds of the documentary form as a tool for social change.

Any documentarian will hear the name John Grierson mentioned again and again, often cited as the father of documentary filmmaking, and founder of the Documentary Film Movement in Britain in the late 1920s[1]. He defined documentary as 'the creative treatment of actuality', a definition which has stood the test of time, and a theme we'll come back to later in this book. The Documentary Film Movement produced many classic examples of the emerging documentary genre through several public bodies and corporate sponsors. These include, famously, the GPO Film Unit (which produced *Night Mail*), Shell, and the Crown Film Unit at the Ministry of Information (*Listen to Britain*). The Movement gave us filmmakers such as Alberto Cavalcanti, Paul Rotha, Basil Wright, Edgar Anstey and the now-celebrated Humphrey Jennings. The important point here, though, was the type of documentaries they made, and how this set the context for documentary making over the subsequent decades. Grierson's academic training was as a philosopher, but he also studied the psychology of propaganda, which informed the techniques he used to make documentary films. 'I look on cinema as a pulpit, and use it as a propagandist,' he said, and in some ways it's a legacy that has defined many documentaries we see today (such as Michael Moore's *Fahrenheit 9/11*).

Following World War Two and the advent of television, documentary disappeared from the cinema in Britain to emerge in our homes, where it developed into the television forms we can still recognise today (although increasingly rarely), in current affairs strands such as BBC's *Panorama* and in the work of today's filmmakers such as Marilyn Gaunt and Paul Watson. There were certain fringe movements of cinematic documentaries such as the Free Cinema Movement (1956–1959), which was a series of programmes held at the National Film Theatre in London by a group of filmmakers, including Lindsay Anderson, Karel Reisz, Tony Richardson and Michael Grigsby. They were much more experimental and poetic in form than mainstream fare, and often depicted the working-class experience. Classics here include *Momma Don't Allow*, *O Dreamland*, *Every Day Except Christmas* and *Enginemen*. The screenings ended in 1959, but most of the filmmakers went on to successful feature-film careers and formed the British New Wave, while Grigsby became a renowned documentary filmmaker in his own right.

Meanwhile, outside the UK, the cinematic documentary continued to grow. The transition to more portable 16mm cameras, together with the ability to capture synchronous sound, directly influenced the aesthetics and content of

Figure 1. *Don't Look Back* (1967). Directed by DA Pennebaker. Shown from left (behind the scenes): Bob Dylan, DA Pennebaker. Credit: Pennebaker Films/Photofest.

a movement known as 'cinéma vérité' (Cinema Truth) in France and 'Direct Cinema' in North America. From this movement emerged filmmakers such as brothers Albert and David Maysles, DA Pennebaker (*Don't Look Back*), Chris Hegedus and Frederick Wiseman (*Titicut Follies*) in the US, and Jean Rouch in France (*Chronique d'un Été* or *Chronicle of a Summer*). Both these branches of the movement relied on observational techniques with an attempt to capture real events as they unfolded. Direct Cinema was all about having little or no involvement with the action in front of the lens, with the intention that the camera somehow became 'invisible'; Cinéma Vérité, on the other hand, sometimes sanctioned direct involvement or even provocation when the filmmakers felt it was necessary. Regardless of the subtle differences, this fly-on-the-wall approach had a profound influence on documentaries and, it has been argued, directly influenced the advent of reality television that is so prevalent on television screens today.

Back in the UK, from the 1960s through to the 1990s, the main documentary output was on television, rather than at the cinema. Granada's documentary department produced consistently high-quality documentaries, many of which have now unfortunately been lost to audiences. Highlights from the period include: Michael Apted's *7 Up* series (starting in 1964); Peter Watkins' *The War Game* (1965); Michael Grigsby's *A Life Apart* (1973); Paul Watson's *The Family* (1974); Roger Graef's *Police* series (1982); and John Akomfrah's *Handsworth Songs* (1986). There were many strands and series from the period, including the BBC's *Man Alive*, a social and political documentary strand, which ran from 1965–1981; *Arena* and *Omnibus*, the arts strands; plus Granada's anthropological *Disappearing World*, and *World in Action*, the long-running current affairs strand.

In the 1990s, on both sides of the Atlantic, television saw the advent of video diaries and the docusoap, with series such as *Driving School* and *Airport* creating celebrities of its participants. More recently, of course, we have the formatted derivatives of documentaries (now known as factual entertainment) such as *Wife Swap*, *Big Brother* and *The Apprentice*.

It's this potted history which makes one realise that the term 'documentary' now encompasses a whole range of films. Just as the forms of documentaries are exceptionally varied, so too are the themes. Despite these various forms, perhaps the first intended purpose – to comment on social phenomena or even to effect social change – is one that still appeals to many documentary filmmakers today. And it's this notion of documentary as a tool of social awareness that I would like to briefly discuss.

Throughout my career as a producer, filmmaker and tutor, the vast majority of aspiring filmmakers I have met stated that they wanted to use documentary film to influence social or political change, help inform people, and attempt to make a positive difference. In short, many believed that documentary had the power to change the world.

And this isn't such a far-fetched notion. Many of my earlier films were about mental health. I thought that many stereotypes and prejudices existed about mental illness, and I set out to attempt to dispel some of these. I wouldn't claim that the films made any massive global change, but they did get wide exposure, and not only on television; they were subsequently used in hospitals, community centres, universities and schools as an educational aid. I'm sure, somewhere, some hearts and minds were touched, in which case I've succeeded.

Some documentaries have had a profound influence, and changed the world, sometimes in small ways, and sometimes on a much bigger scale. One such film is Brian Woods and Kate Blewett's *The Dying Rooms*. It tells the tale of the one-child policy in China and the impact that this has had on female babies. We see images of a new-born girl tied up in urine-soaked blankets, scabs of dried mucus growing across her eyes, her face shrinking to a skull, malnutrition slowly shrivelling her small body, and we are told the plight of these children – that literally thousands will be left to die in places that became known as 'The Dying Rooms'. When the film was due to be aired on Channel 4, the Chinese government started to make a lot of fuss; they warned Britain that if the documentary was aired then it would 'poison' relations between the two countries. Channel 4 went on to air the film as planned, and it caused a national outcry about the obvious abuses of human rights. Later it brought international attention to what was happening in China. This resulted in human rights agencies and charities going to China, which in turn led to various reforms of the one-child policy. In addition, True Vision (the production company behind the film) set up The Dying Rooms Trust, which makes various contributions to these charities to help improve conditions in Chinese orphanages. This is just one of countless examples of ways in which, over the course of their short history, documentaries have been instrumental in bringing about change, and the trend still continues today. For example, in Morgan Spurlock's *Super Size Me*, the filmmaker ate nothing but McDonald's food for a whole month. His declining health during that time was seen as a direct result of this unhealthy diet. The film did tremendously well and McDonald's removed 'Super Size' portions from their menus in the US. Roger Graef made a series called *Police* in 1982, in which one episode, *A Complaint of Rape*, filmed police officers interviewing a victim of rape. The footage revealed the harsh and bullying manner in which the police dealt with their questioning, and the film significantly influenced the ways in which the police force in the UK continued such work, leading to changes in policy [see box below].

Roger Graef on *Police: A Complaint of Rape* and the power of documentaries to bring about change

I think it was a direct result of the film coming at the end of five years of debate and two weeks of very intense media discussion. Whether it would have happened without the other two elements I frankly doubt, but that's the way it happened...

It changed the way [the police] conducted their interviews; it shifted the benefit of the doubt towards the woman; it meant that they were more courteous and more considerate and more willing to understand that women don't come in bleeding, screaming and crying when they've been raped. They may actually take quite a long time to come in, and be stunned, and have gone about their business normally for a few days or even weeks. Whereas these cops... they've read the fiction, they've seen the movies, and think rape victims are meant to cry and look like they've been beaten up.

Documentaries can't by themselves change anything. There has to be a recognition and a desire to change. But [as a filmmaker] you can trigger a latent desire to change.

Not all documentaries have an overarching social agenda. Sometimes we make documentaries for other reasons. The BBC's *Walking with Dinosaurs* and *Planet Earth* have used state-of-the-art techniques to give us a view of the world that we have rarely seen in such vivid detail. There are films that inform us of individuals or cultures that we rarely come across, for example the BBC series *Tribe*, and there are documentaries that capture unique moments in history, such as Michael Wadleigh's *Woodstock*. The list is endless and you will find some of the best in Section Five.

Of course the word documentary has now come to encompass reality television and many of the more formatted television shows such as *Wife Swap*, *Survivor*, *Brat Camp* and others. If we apply Grierson's definition here, then they too are documentaries, and despite some of the bad press they get, it is quite probable that they have contributed to the renaissance of the genre. Rather than dwell here on the various merits (and demerits) of this trend, the important point is that the documentary form allows us to now have a window on virtually every aspect of life on this planet, which can be no bad thing.

Why I Make Documentaries

I think [the reason I got into documentary] was just the sense that reality is always a bit more extraordinary than anything you could imagine. I mean, if I had tried to imagine *Sisters in Law* I never could have imagined those amazing characters. For example, Manka, who is only six and yet she's so clever, so resourceful and so dignified. And the man that saves her, this very quiet gentle giant, and a carpenter, it's all kind of so symbolic and extraordinary. And Vera, I never would have imagined a woman like her. I think it's just this feeling that life itself is much richer than you could ever imagine in your head.

Often when I'm filming I'm always thinking this is extraordinary. There were scenes in *Sisters in Law* when if I hadn't been filming I'd have had my mouth open in astonishment. Even down to that divorce at the end, when the men start threatening her and taunting her and saying we'll send you back and he'll split you open, and you just can't imagine people would behave like that. So that's the feeling, that's the delight of documentary: it's also the fear of it. There's

always this fear that nothing's going to happen, it's all going to be boring and that you're not going to find a story. It's double edged really.
Kim Longinotto, Filmmaker (and co-director *Sisters in Law*)

I began making docs because I'm essentially a nosy parker and was terrified of actors. But mostly because the great thing about real life is that nobody sticks to the script, so the journey you go on once you start filming often has detours that take you to a slightly different destination to the one you thought you'd reach.
Marilyn Gaunt, Filmmaker

I chose to get into documentary filmmaking for a number of reasons. I love the challenges, both intellectual and practical. Making documentaries forces one to confront the realities of the real world, rather then hiding away in an ivory tower (as I was doing before I went to film school) or indulging in the egocentrism of fiction film (which is fun, and I'm sure I'll go there again someday). Documentary is not the easy road to take. It's hard to raise the money, hard to get consent, hard to find 'the truth' of a story, and even harder to represent it accurately, but it's precisely these challenges that make it so engaging and the reward in overcoming them so gratifying. But most importantly, a good documentary can change the way people feel about things, open them up to new points of view, and share with them knowledge that they might not otherwise glean. Taken as a whole, documentary films enrich the lives of both the filmmaker and the audiences, so it seems to me to be a worthwhile way to spend one's time.
Emily James, Filmmaker

I went into documentary because I loved being nosy and asking people questions and prying into their lives. I was fascinated by real stories, I suppose. So, I guess it's more of a humanist interest than a political interest. I'm not a hugely political person. I think that a lot of documentary filmmakers have got a real sort of hatred for obvious unfairness and social injustice and can tend to get a little self-righteous, but I'm not actually a really political, political person... I love the fact that you can take little bits of reality and make a story out of them... Life can be overwhelmingly chaotic and over-stimulating and I think we all in some way want to sort of give shape to it. And being a documentary filmmaker, it's exactly what you do as your job, and that's the great pleasure for me.
Kevin Macdonald, Filmmaker

2. DOES YOUR DOCUMENTARY HAVE LEGS?

Documentary filmmakers often carry round with them one or more documentary ideas that preoccupy them to the point of obsession. Many times I have found myself lying awake at night with a documentary idea going round and round my mind. Sometimes, I have to get up, write these ideas down, search the Internet for more information, and then embark on a period of research, often convinced I have stumbled across the most unique, fantastic and amazing idea. I'm convinced that anyone who didn't commission this film would be a fool for not recognising what a masterpiece my idea is. In my early days, my disappointment was counteracted by a huge sense of injustice. I simply couldn't believe that people weren't as enthused and awestruck by my ideas as I was. However, as time went on, and my arrogance dwindled substantially, I realised that objectively my ideas weren't as great as I first thought. Put simply, my ideas simply didn't have legs. In this chapter, I want to talk about what makes a good documentary idea, and how to make sure that such an idea can be realistically transformed into a visual narrative that works, and also one that today's market would be interested in.

WHERE DO IDEAS COME FROM?

Documentary ideas come from everywhere. Often, although not always, they come from somewhere deep within us. Perhaps we are outraged at some social injustice in the world and want to right some wrong. Perhaps we're particularly interested in a specific group of people, or a cultural facet, or maybe we are enthused about something that happened to us, or to our family or friends. I was initially trained as a clinical psychologist, and many of my ideas focused on areas of mental health, which I felt people knew little about; and if they did, they often had certain prejudices, which I wanted to redress. Many of the filmmakers I know are driven by equally personal agendas. The important point here is that, whatever your idea, the first step is to find passion for it. It's often going to be a long, hard slog to make your documentary and unless you develop a personal relationship with the subject matter it's going to be difficult to go through the inevitable peaks and troughs without feeling disillusioned, often defeated, and sometimes depressed. Moreover, only a passion for the subject matter will allow you to make the film the best it can be. Even if we have no choice in the matter (and later on in your career as a filmmaker, you may not have as much choice as you want in the films that you make), it's still important to try and develop passion, or at the very least enthusiasm, for your film.

Essentially what inspires me is the nature of the human condition, how people deal with sometimes extraordinary challenges, but sometimes just dealing with the everyday problems that life throws up can be just as fascinating as the more extreme experiences. For me to want to tackle a particular subject there has to be more than just a good story with interesting characters, there always has to be an underlying subtext, one that makes individual people's experiences reveal wider issues. I have to have a hook to hang it on. What clicks for me? What is the angle/element that most fascinates me?
Marilyn Gaunt, Filmmaker

Ideas can come from a whole host of places. Often they come from a newspaper article or a magazine feature that you may have read, or whilst chatting to your friends you stumble across a character or some anecdote that gets your mind racing. You need to develop your 'documentary radar' here and get yourself into the habit of listening out for ideas that could be turned into films. (Though bear in mind that not every friend's tragedy and every social calamity should become a documentary proposal...!) Seminars, conferences, the Internet – all of these have the potential to inspire.

As a documentarian I happily place my fate and faith in reality. It is my caretaker, the provider of subjects, themes, experiences – all endowed with the power of truth and the romance of discovery. And the closer I adhere to reality the more honest and authentic my tales. After all, the knowledge of the real world is exactly what we need to better understand and therefore possibly to love one another. It's my way of making the world a better place. Some of the best ideas have their source from an early childhood experience, a craving, something personal. The filming should be of ongoing scenes, events that are thus cinematic, not the kind of information better suited to a pamphlet or lecture.

Al Maysles, Filmmaker

IDEAS THAT WORK

So, let's imagine that you've found a great idea. It resonates with you; perhaps it's a story that keeps coming back to you again and again and again. Well, the good news is that you've now embarked on a journey to develop your idea into a documentary, but the bad news is that there are some serious hurdles to jump over before your documentary really has legs.

1st Hurdle – Narrative

Are you telling a story? Is there a journey here? Documentaries, fiction films, novels and plays all work when there is some kind of journey that we follow. Although a character may fascinate you, it is not enough just to assume that living with him or her for a couple of months is going to yield an insightful and engaging film. What is going to happen over the course of these two months? Is the character trying to achieve a certain goal? And if so, what are the obstacles, and will s/he succeed? These are examples of the questions you need to be asking, in order to make a film that is going to engage rather than alienate or bore an audience. And perhaps the most important question you need to ask is whether there is an interesting narrative within your film, or is it just a collection of images, which ultimately lead nowhere? If you can't find the story immediately, it's worth continuing to look, and if you still can't find it, then perhaps it's time to give up and move on to another idea.

As Sheila Curran Bernard states in her book *Documentary Storytelling for Video and Filmmakers*, 'A story is a narrative, or telling, of an event or series of events crafted in a way to interest the audience… At its most basic, a story has a beginning, middle and end. It has compelling characters, rising tension, and conflict that reaches some sort of resolution. It engages the audience on an emotional and intellectual level, motivating viewers to want to know what happens next.'[2]

Does this sound like your film? If not, then you haven't yet managed to jump the first hurdle.

One way of helping you find a story is to consider the *arc*. This refers to the way the plot develops and how characters may change over the course of the film. A man searching for his lost family, finding clues that will eventually help him to meet them, is a definite arc. Or a character who experiences a fall from grace, a man who lost his memory, a businessman who lost everything after going to prison for fraud, or a woman with a fatal illness who wants to die with dignity in her own home – all these are examples of a story with a good arc. Implicit in all these ideas is the idea of a journey, and before we even hear more about the film, we can begin to get a sense of what we might see – the tension, the drama, the loss, the resolution, the personal discovery, or a goal that has either been failed or achieved.

Kevin Macdonald's feature documentary *Touching the Void* is a great example of a compelling and engaging narrative. The film tells the true story of two men, Joe Simpson and Simon Yates, who climbed a mountain in Peru. Yates inadvertently lowered Simpson over the edge of a cliff and, unable to hear him through a storm, uncertain as to his position and gradually sliding down the slope himself, decided to cut the rope that connected them, sending Simpson plummeting to certain death. Miraculously, Simpson survived the fall, and was faced with the prospect of getting off the mountain alone with no food, no water, and a broken leg.

We know, by virtue of the interviews with them, that both men survived, but it's the clever use of dramatised sequences, pacing and story development which makes the film a suspense thriller. There's a definite narrative

Figure 2. *Touching the Void* (2003). Directed by Kevin Macdonald. Shown: Brendan MacKey (as climber Joe Simpson). Credit: IFC Films/Photofest.

here, and as it unfolds it becomes more and more compelling. Will Joe make it? What will happen to him? There are so many turning points in this film that as a viewer the narrative has you on the edge of your seat.

Not all narratives need to contain this degree of suspense. Eric Chaikin and Julian Petrillo's *Word Wars* is a film about the board game Scrabble. At first it doesn't sound like the most compelling subject matter, but the narrative follows four Scrabble players who are all training (yes, you can train for Scrabble) as they get ready for the US Scrabble Championships. Suspense builds as we wonder who will make it to the finals, but what's most compelling here is the characterisation. The characters themselves are interesting, eccentric and extremely watchable, bringing us nicely onto the next hurdle.

2nd Hurdle – Characterisation

Not all documentaries involve characters, but since many of them do, it seems fitting to include this as a hurdle – if your idea doesn't involve characters, then you can move onto the next hurdle.

Characters, subjects, protagonists, contributors – whatever we choose to call them – can be essential to the telling of your story. Documentaries can often fall into two camps – either subject driven, or character driven. Both can often involve characters, but it is the latter that we are really concerned with here – we'll return to the first type later. With character-driven documentaries, if you don't have a character that can carry the story and its various themes, then you've got a dull film that even a good narrative can't rescue. It will meander along, sluggish, insipid, wearisome and colourless.

I think it's a mistake to think that someone who you find interesting in life will be interesting in your film. A documentary audience is at best harsh, and at worst unscrupulous, and they expect to be immediately engaged, often entertained, or at the very least find some kind of connection or resonance with the people in your film.

So, then, what makes a good character for a documentary film? This is answered in part in *Casting Contributors* on page 50, but, as a rule, it's people who give us real windows into human experience or whose particular dilemma makes us think or reflect on our own human-ness that make good characters.

You need to also think carefully about the current and future relationship you have with your subjects. A difficult or conflict-laden interaction does not auger well for the future (with a few exceptions) and you need to consider how open they are to you filming them and, more importantly, how much they are going to let you into their life, whilst knowing that much of what they say and do might end up in a film which hundreds, thousands, or even millions of people may see. There are ethical considerations here, which you need to consider such as:

- Do your subjects know what your film is really about? Are you misleading them in any way?
- Are you in agreement with your subject as to how long you will be filming them for, and have you agreed what kinds of things you will be filming?
- Have you clearly defined the parameters of their editorial involvement in the film? Most directors, when asked, tell their subjects that they will not be able to sit in on the edit, and will not have 'final say' regarding the film. You would really need a strong reason to say otherwise, as it could land you in all sorts of trouble, for obvious reasons.

3rd Hurdle – Is my Idea Really a Documentary Film?

Can you visualise the story? Is it better suited to radio, a fiction film, or a magazine article? This may sound an odd thing to say, but it is an extremely common mistake to make. Many of us get very excited by an idea, which in all honesty might not work best as a film, but instead would make a fantastic article or radio documentary. There is a quick test you can do here to make sure: think of your film, and ask yourself whether you can visualise it. Are there visual sequences that come to mind, or could your film only be achieved with a ludicrously expensive budget, or is it dependent on levels of access that are simply impossible to achieve? If you can think of visual sequences, are they actually going to be sufficiently interesting? Again, if it's not going to work as a film, let it go and move onto a different idea.

4th Hurdle – Access

In my role as a producer, I am continually approached by filmmakers who have access-driven ideas, without actually having the access in place. It's all very well wanting to make a film about Evo Morales, the Bolivian president, or a religious cult in Texas but can you actually get proper access to the subjects, or is it just a pipe dream at this stage?

Even though films can be made about a subject matter without relevant access – by using archive, for example – it's increasingly rare for the industry to be excited by this, as access-driven documentaries are becoming ever more popular and in demand. So, you need to make sure that you can get access AND that the subjects will be okay with being filmed. There are also ethical concerns here. For example, vulnerable contributors can potentially be exploited by their inclusion in your film – see Chapter 18 on ethics. You also need to ask yourself whether you might be putting your subjects in any danger if you were to film them. I have seen numerous documentaries that have identified specific individuals in countries where their safety would be at risk if authorities knew what they looked like or where they lived, so do consider this.

5th Hurdle – What the Industry Wants

Is your idea what the industry wants? Documentaries aren't made in a vacuum. We make them so that people watch them, and in order for them to be watched they have to be seen somewhere – either on television, in cinemas, on DVDs, online or in festivals. And that means that someone somewhere has to want your product in order to fund or distribute it. Although you might find a topic really interesting to you, it might not have a broader appeal. More importantly, it may simply not be something that is 'in fashion' at the moment. Awful as this sounds, it is the reality and you really need to keep this in mind if you want anyone to see and/or fund your film.

Specific details of what the industry wants can be found in Chapter 6 of this book. But, for now, it's a good idea to consider two important points which will help your chances of making the kind of film that people will actually end up seeing:

1. Watch television and go and see documentaries in the cinema. You need to see what is actually being made. Not only will this give you a sense of the kinds of documentaries that are being commissioned and distributed, but it will also stop you trying to pitch something that has been made recently. Again, I am frequently approached by filmmakers who haven't bothered to see if the idea they are developing has already been made. If it has, there is little chance that it will be picked up by a broadcaster, unless you can justify bringing a new perspective or something novel to the subject matter. All it takes is some simple research to find out if your idea has been made in recent years – an Internet search will often suffice – and help you avoid the ensuing disappointment.

2. Find out specifically what the industry is looking for. Many broadcasters and funding agencies have websites that outline the kind of film they are prepared to invest in. This is discussed more in the chapter on funding. Without wanting to be repetitive here, you can't simply have an amazing idea for a film, and try to find someone who wants to fund it. You have to target your idea so that it fits the remit of specific funders.

You may have to compromise over how your subject matter is handled, but it's an important skill to develop.

IDEAS THAT DON'T WORK

If you do manage to jump over the various hurdles outlined above, it's a good start. If not, then persevere, let your idea breathe and possibly find a new angle or perspective. It's also worth pointing out here that there are some ideas, which may pass all the criteria above, but still not work for other reasons. Michael Rabiger, author of many fantastic books on documentary filmmaking, suggests staying away from:

- Worlds you haven't experienced and cannot closely observe
- Any ongoing, inhibiting problem in your own life (see a good therapist; you won't find any solutions while trying to direct a film)
- Anything or anyone that is 'typical' (nothing real is typical, so nothing typical will ever be interesting or credible)
- Preaching or moral instruction of any kind
- Films about problems for which you already have the answer (so does your audience)[3]

I would add to this 'Complicated issues that you don't fully understand'. Don't be over-ambitious in trying to make a film about something that is way over your head. For example, investigative documentaries (such as those seen on the British TV series *Panorama*) involve specific journalistic and investigative skills that you may not possess, at least not yet. Try to pick an idea that you can get your teeth into, but not too big that you can't chew it.

SIMPLE IDEAS ARE THE BEST

The best ideas are always the simple ones. There is a tendency – especially for documentary filmmakers at the beginning of their career – to have an over-complicated thesis for a film: trying to explore multifarious themes and complex issues in a film, or trying to explore a simple issue with a convoluted narrative. I was recently involved in making a series of films in India, all of which looked at the theme of Independence (it was the 60th anniversary of independence from the United Kingdom). Now this theme could be explored in lots and lots of different ways. You could make a historical documentary looking at how India has changed over the past 60 years. This could involve interviewing politicians, civil servants and journalists in India. Such a film would probably be quite heavy in commentary, and with such a vast issue you're probably going to make a film that is quite dry, potentially boring and way too didactic. Audiences prefer to be shown rather than told. One of the filmmakers in this series went to a tea plantation, and made an observational documentary, following the managers of the plantation who still lived their life as if it were 60 years ago, wearing colonial uniforms, drinking tea, celebrating Christmas with carol singing and rarely going outside their land. The film captures a bygone era; it's about a place stuck in time and through its simplicity says far more about Indian Independence than a long, commentary-driven, interview-based film could.

3. RESEARCHING YOUR DOCUMENTARY

Once you have come up with a documentary idea, and you feel that it really does work as a documentary film, you need to start doing some detailed research. Research is an ongoing process and, depending on the specific nature of your film, may involve vast amounts of time spent trawling through libraries, documents and articles, and speaking to people from all over the world. This may continue throughout the entire production of your film but, at the very least, the starting point for research is to try and get to know the subject area as well as possible. It's the beginning of a journey that will take you from the general to the specific, and will help guide you to set the foundations for developing your idea into a workable documentary film (see the next chapter, *Developing Your Idea*). Cast your net wide, and find out as much as you can about a given topic. Although no one expects you to be a world expert in an instant, you do need to be the next best thing: as well informed as you can be.

There are several reasons for this. Firstly, if you don't know much about your subject area, then you simply won't be able to make a good film; with not enough preparation, your film will not have the necessary focus or substance it needs. Secondly, the more you do know, the more you are likely to facilitate engagement and rapport building with your subjects. Thirdly, if you want this film to receive funding, you need to show you are well informed on the subject matter. Often, certain types of funding require you to describe the subject matter in vivid detail, and the more you know at this point, the better your proposal/application will be. Finally, throughout the process of research, you are collecting images in your mind that will help you to script your film, and give it its own visual sense. This is really important, as so often when we start out making documentaries, it's easy to forget that film is a visual medium and we need to *show* as well as *say*.

So, this is the time when you will at least start thinking about what the visual substance of your film may be. They will just be thoughts or images at this stage, sequences that would help tell the story, or observational footage, or a particular use of archive. Whatever the images, they will help form the visual vertebrae of the film.

KEEPING A JOURNAL

One of the best ways to get to grips with your subject matter is to keep some kind of journal or scrapbook. This may simply be ideas that you have, or information that you may come across – press clippings, articles, notes you have taken and so on, or it may be full of sketches, thoughts and preliminary interviews. One filmmaker I know keeps an extremely detailed journal with drawings, storyboards, and notes of every aspect of the subject matter. It is littered with different ideas and thoughts – some of them methodically thought out, others jotted down at some moment of nocturnal inspiration. One of the things to note is that, at this stage, your film could take many different paths, and it is only through a great deal of thought and research that the story starts to take shape. For those who have written a long essay or a thesis, the process is not that different. At first you collate as much information as you can, and as you start looking through all this, some kind of form or narrative starts to take shape.

Compiling scrapbooks has been an integral part of my filmmaking practice from the beginning. These books are made from scraps of photographs, photocopied and found images, newspaper clippings, written fragments, quotes, letters, lists and my own notations.

The process of keeping scrapbooks is a vein of activity that runs continuously from day to day, from project to project. I use them as a way to collect my thoughts and record whatever catches my interest or sparks an idea. Maybe it's because my ideas stay on paper for such a long time that I have found it necessary to keep the research process as rich and tactile as possible. There is a physicality to keeping scrapbooks that throws up new ideas, associations and narratives.

Often I have looked over my books and wondered whether these collections of fragments, scribbles, starting points and dead ends are actually my main body of work and the films are by-products of that process. This brings me back to one of the first things I learnt at art school – the process is the product.

Simon Aeppli, Filmmaker

THE INTERNET

The Internet is both a blessing and a curse. It's full of a whole wealth of information; as you know, you can literally find something about absolutely anything and everything. In that respect, it is a good starting point. Be careful though: often some of the information can be misleading, so it's important to check the primary source. Also, there are much more subtle pieces of information, and personal anecdotes and stories which simply aren't on the Internet. It's usually these stories that are the most interesting and the most unique. As well as using standard search engines (such as Google), there are also specific searches that can help make your research more robust, for example, the LexisNexis resource, which catalogues news articles from print media around the world (www.lexisnexis.com). The AskCharity (www.askcharity.org.uk) website is also a great resource allowing you to search hundreds of charities based on a simple keyword search.

BOOKS, ARTICLES AND JOURNALS

These sources often go into a lot more depth than a simple Internet search, and have the added bonus of usually (though not always) being more reliable. Use your local library, and if you need more information, then try to get access to university or specialist libraries. Browse bookshops, and you may not only find a book that covers the area you want to research, but you may often find information that opens up your film. Many times I have started to research a specific area, and then found more information which opens up the film, allowing it to be something much more relevant and with much more depth. The same goes for newspapers and magazines, which often have details and depth that other sources don't have.

A word of warning here though: many production companies, especially the larger ones, will regularly go through all national and regional newspapers looking for a story that might form the basis of a good documentary. Chances are that if you stumble across an amazing story, so too have other producers, so don't put all your eggs in one basket here.

VISUAL ARCHIVE

Visual Archive can include moving image, still photographs, articles, journals, letters and documents. Researching visual archive will not only help you learn more about the subject area, but may also help you find invaluable material for possible inclusion in the final film. Some films rely heavily on the use of archive for their films. For example, Mark Achbar, Jennifer Abbott and Joel Bakan's *The Corporation* uses archive in a particularly interesting way, juxtaposing old US public service archive with modern-day news footage – all edited together to create slick, engaging, often satirical accompaniment to the interviews that have been shot:

We had an amazing archival researcher named Paula Sawadsky who sourced the archival footage for us. We would ask for all archival footage she could find related to different themes and she dug up many gems. Sometimes I wouldn't know how a particular clip would be used, but while editing the film I would draw on bins and bins of footage I had collected and organised from the 100 or so hours of archival footage we accessed.

One of my goals as a filmmaker is to make the familiar appear strange and working with archival footage is one of my favourite ways of doing this. By casting a different light on what we encounter daily, archival footage can have a wonderfully subversive effect on the reified social order. Archival footage of say a SPAM commercial that shows ham and jello salads betrays the food we eat as a

social construct. By using archival footage with the intent of calling into question contemporary norms, we layer a film, adding to, not just illustrating content.
Jennifer Abbott, Co-Director and Editor, *The Corporation*

Using Archive in the Feature Documentary *Deep Water*

Deep Water tells the story of Donald Crowhurst, an entrant in the first non-stop single-handed round-the-world sailing race, who after a long period of radio silence seemed to be at the point of successfully completing the fastest ever circumnavigation of the globe.

In July 1969, Crowhurst's boat was found in mid Atlantic with no one on board. Crowhurst had vanished, leaving his uneaten dinner, a 25,000-word tract about God, computers, cosmic beings, apes and time travel, his tape recordings and films of the voyage and a set of logbooks showing that his record-breaking voyage was a fabrication.

Deep Water was always going to be a film that didn't use just archive to tell a story – the archive (tapes, films, logbook) was itself part of the story, a central player in events, holding crucial clues to the mystery of Crowhurst's disappearance.

Early on in the development of the film we gave ourselves a rule that we wanted to tell this story as much as possible through first-hand witness – either footage or material taken at the time or interviews with those who had been involved in Crowhurst's voyage or in the race he entered. This meant no expert outsiders to the story and no actor reconstruction. It also meant that the archive research was critical to the kind of story the film would be able to tell.

Many of the nine sailors involved in the race had taken cameras with them and we started by trawling all the major archives to recover this material. Database and web searches led us to particular kinds of footage – principally finished films and news broadcasts.The problem with the database-driven culture of contemporary archive is that if something isn't entered on the database, it's as though it doesn't exist. We found some crucial first-hand material from the race, and tantalising sections of Crowhurst's own footage that had been cut into other films, notably a 1970s documentary made shortly after his voyage. But Donald's original films and tapes (made on equipment given to him by the BBC) seemed to have disappeared.

Spreading the net to other sources with the help of a specialist researcher yielded richer material: the Sunday Times archive contained over 1,000 stills, cuttings and correspondence about the race; the sailors' families and friends held more personal material, in particular extensive footage taken by Crowhurst's co-competitor, Bernard Moitessier. Appeals to local film clubs and museums uncovered some eyewitness Super 8 of the sailors' leaving or returning to port, and finding filmmakers who had specialised in yachting films in the sixties led to 16mm of the competitors at sea.

Our aim was to find footage that could bring the story alive. Documentary – and particularly the documentary feature – needs events to unfold in the present, to play out a story in front of an audience in a time-limited experience. The challenge is to use material in a way that isn't just illustrative (playing a supporting role to interviews or voiceovers) but enacts events in the way a drama might, with the images leading the story rather than following it.

Documentary archive, however, especially news or diary material, rarely in itself contains the story beats you need onscreen. Instead, you hope to build them out of a jigsaw of sounds and pictures, reinterpreting material, which has often been shot for a completely different purpose.

As with any archive from the 1960s, the footage we found presented a series of technical challenges. Sometimes the mute picture would be discovered in one archive, with the sound turning up in another archive weeks later. The material used a bewildering array of different formats and aspect ratios. Different versions of the same film would crop up in different collections, presenting complex rights issues. Selecting archive was a long process of juggling cost against quality. Our strategy was always to try to get as close as possible to the original rushes, ultimately persuading the BBC to give us access to negatives for scanned transfers from some of the archive.

How quickly material could be cleared was also a factor. Where the ownership of material was disputed or unknown we had to weigh up the time and cost of complex negotiations with the different parties against the needs of our schedule.

After two years of searching we still hadn't come up with Crowhurst's original tape recordings or rushes, and began to believe that they had not survived the culls of BBC archive that took place in the 1970s. If you're looking for something specific, you need to be meticulous about your detective work, talking to anyone who might have been involved in the original productions, trying to establish the trail of its last known whereabouts. Eventually, noticing some anomalies on film can numbers given to us by libraries led us to Crowhurst's original reversal films (mislabelled in the wrong cans) along with a host of other news footage of his preparations and departure. A chance follow-up conversation with

BBC staff uncovered nine hours of Crowhurst's quarter-inch tape recordings in a box buried in a warehouse. We'd had the good fortune of finding some diligent archivists to help us in the search, and they were able to take us to the places that databases couldn't.

Rediscovering Crowhurst's original footage didn't solve the mystery of what happened to him, but what emerged was a fuller picture of the man: a sustained half hour of audio recorded whilst drunk, deliberately ambiguous descriptions of life at sea, repeated takes of scenes on board his boat. The new material humanised him, showing him variously as playful comedian, confused victim of circumstance, artful dissembler, deep thinker, down-to earth pragmatist. Finding this material changed the narrative of the film, enabling us to focus the story much more closely on Donald. The ambiguity of the recordings – made by our central character in some of his most desperate moments – gives the film much of its power, pushing the audience to scrutinise them for evidence they unsettlingly refuse to give.

Some thoughts for anyone embarking on a similar search… Work out what you need that's unique (generic footage is cheap and easy to find). Weigh up cost, technical quality, the time spent to find and clear material and its importance for the film. Be persistent. Don't believe what the databases tell you. Approach the task like a detective. And hold on to the belief that the material you're looking for is out there somewhere.

Jerry Rothwell, Co-director, *Deep Water*

WORKING WITH PEOPLE

It's really astonishing the amount of proposals I have received that are based on vague Internet research or a newspaper article which caught the fancy of some hopeful director. These proposals are often superficial and fail to convey a real understanding of the subject matter, as well as failing to give any kind of unique or fresh perspective. The main reason for this is that the filmmaker has simply failed to talk to people, and therefore is unlikely to get a real understanding of the topics being researched. There is no substitute for, where possible, talking to people about the various themes that will form the backbone of your film. If, for example, you are making a film about the experience of living in a particularly violent housing estate in Glasgow, no

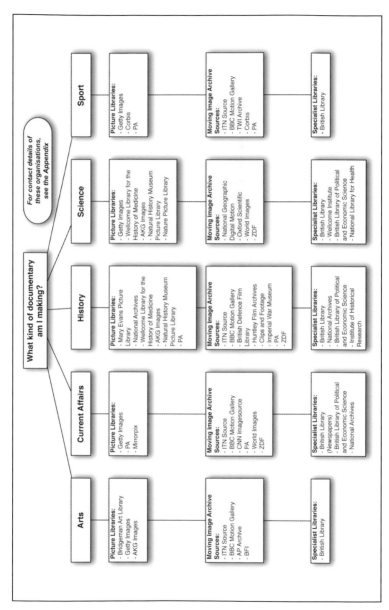

Figure 3. Table showing research sources: UK

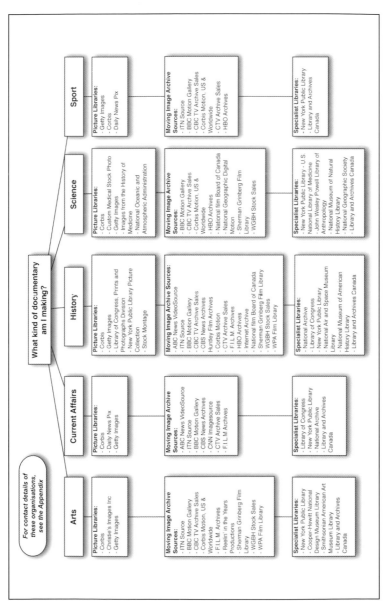

Figure 4. Table showing research sources: North America

amount of reading on the sociology of urban living, or the working classes of Glasgow, will give you a real understanding of what it is like for people to actually live there. You can, of course, speak to people on the phone, talk to various experts, academics or politicians, but there would be something lacking if you did not go to the original sources – the people themselves who are living on this housing estate. Nothing is ever as good as going there in person, meeting people, and getting a strong sense of what's really going on, and who these people really are.

CASTING CONTRIBUTORS

Meeting and talking to people at this stage not only helps you become increasingly informed about the subject matter and themes of your film, but also – if your film is character-based – then this is an important time to consider casting: that is, who is actually going to appear in your film.

Although you may think that 'casting' is something that only happens in fiction films, it's equally as important in documentary. Just as a fiction film needs actors who can best bring alive the vision of the writer and director, so too casting in documentary is about finding characters who can be representative of the arguments, thesis, or themes in your film, and can also engage the viewer. Finding these characters is not as easy as you may think. There are some people whose extraordinary lives may make compelling reading, but who simply appear dull on film, and will not help to convey the themes you are trying to explore. Conversely, there are also people who are entertaining, compelling and fascinating, but may distract the viewer from the main focus of your film. Some people open up in front of a camera, some become incredibly shy, and others 'act up' so that any authenticity is lost. Whoever you want to be in your film, you need to ask yourself why you want them there, what function they serve, and in what ways they contribute to the overall aims of your film.

Some films rely on a single character to carry the narrative. An example of this is Sean McAllister's *The Liberace of Baghdad*, which focuses exclusively on one character, a pianist, who lived in Baghdad throughout the recent war. All these films work because the character is someone whom we find likeable and identify with, or at the very least empathise with, and it is this empathy that proves essential if we are to feel engaged with the film, rather than alienated from it. In addition, such characters often have specific, sometimes urgent issues – an emotional journey they have undertaken, a stand they are trying to make in the world, a personal obstacle they are trying to overcome, or some eccentricity which in itself can make compelling viewing. It is this latter theme which has been a recent trend in British documentary filmmaking – characters who are 'extraordinary' due to some physical or psychological trait. Examples of this include *The Boy with the Incredible Memory*, *The Girl with X-Ray Eyes* and so on. The filmmaker Kevin Hull (see pages 53-4) talks about the importance of anti-charisma:

> It's said that contributors must be clear, articulate and concise, and empathetic; that they must be moderately outgoing and friendly and easy to identify with. Dream on! The contributor who will make your film work will most likely lack all these fine qualities; instead they will radiate a kind of anti-charisma – a dark-star quality. They will be inordinately ugly, charmless and rambling – but they will just be so shockingly alive and surprising that they choose themselves for the documentary.

Character-based documentaries that involve several people bring another element to the issue of casting. Here, not only do your characters have to work by themselves, but you also need to consider the ways in which they work together. This becomes an issue of balance and counterbalance. If, for example, I am making a film about the experience of offenders being released from prison, to pick subjects who all end up re-offending within five weeks, or all end up on the street and taking drugs, not only offers a skewed perspective, but is in danger of being dull or clichéd. It also lacks integrity. It is therefore important that we try, as filmmakers, to portray a balanced perspective. It's also important that we find counterbalance within the film, focusing on characters who all cope with leaving prison in different ways, thus adding much more depth to the film as a whole (and much more credibility to you as the filmmaker).

Figure 5. *Liberace of Baghdad*

What Makes a Good Character?

I think a good character determines a good film. What lets most documentaries down for me is weak or dull characters. This can often be poor filmmakers who fail to know how to communicate with people or ask the right questions or more often than not filmmakers who have nothing to say about the world and shouldn't really be holding a camera.

But what makes a good character for me is usually someone I can relate to, someone who is either like me, or if I were in a similar situation to that of the 'character' I would be like them. I think I have to find some personal investment in who I film. The 'character' has to have a screen presence. I think we 'cast' in a similar way to fiction directors. We require them to look good and have charm, be funny, be engaging. Ultimately, they have to turn me on, get me out of my bed every day, make me want to film them. Maybe my characters need to be in some political context that reflects the world we live in – they need to be suffering in some way. A character trait of that I like is 'outsiders who are within the mainstream, but marginalised' – often by their own making.

I guess the character has to want something. They have to be contradictory, unpredictable, keep me guessing and constantly surprise me. In a way the perfect character reflects the imperfections of myself and of all my friends back home in Hull. When I choose a character in Iraq or Israel or try to find one in Japan, I am looking for someone my mates would relate to; someone who will take them into their world, often a political conflict they have never engaged in before, but through common things like drink problems and money problems, this character engages them in a political world they would not normally engage in.

Character is everything. Without a strong, complex, engaging character you don't have a film in my opinion. But finding them is a fucking nightmare. I spend more time looking for them than filming them.

Sean McAllister, Filmmake

SOME POINTERS TOWARDS A GOOD CONTRIBUTOR by Kevin Hull

A good contributor:

- Will further the narrative. Often an engaging potential contributor will have to be stood down, if they do not 'fit' – i.e. they don't help the story.
- Will be credible, relaxed and trustworthy. Your documentary HAS to be believable, and a good contributor will enhance the feeling that the film has authority.
- Will have a magical charisma. Unlike that of an actor in the fiction film – it usually involves a kind of 'anti-charm' – a disarming, raw nakedness or spirit that survives the shrinking of the lens.
- Will surprise you and the audience
- Will have stamina to withstand filming, which normally takes longer than people expect.
- Will be on their own journey of discovery, which energises your film.
- Will be able to express points in a way you had not considered, and in a clearer, more concise way than other potential candidates.
- Knows something that no one else in the film knows and hopefully would have expertise beyond other candidates.
- Is not too keen to appear in a documentary!

- Although the reluctant contributor is often the best, they cannot be so careful that they will not be able to speak freely and openly when the time comes to be filmed

During research for filming of *Einstein's Brain* for BBC's *Arena*, I was missing a main contributor for the filming in the USA. After three months of searching through contacts, books and papers, I had drawn a blank because I could not find someone who had the charisma I needed, was on their own journey of discovery and would further the narrative. I met many experts and many interesting people, but they would not carry the film. I found the right person eventually, not in the USA but in a university in Osaka, Japan: Kenji Sugimoto. I had to fly him out to the USA for filming. He was so passionate and engaged; he regarded the documentary as his film – a film that he was making with my help. He chose himself through his energetic commitment to both my subject and the film.

CASTING EXPERTS

Sometimes you may want experts in your film to talk about a particular topic. They may be academics, politicians, psychologists, psychiatrists, or even people who witnessed a specific event. There are several points to bear in mind when selecting an expert. Firstly, there is a tendency to go for the most well-known, high-profile, or published expert in the belief that this may add credibility to your film. However, such people aren't always the most articulate, and may often fail to offer a more interesting, and perhaps less orthodox perspective. Secondly, there is a tendency in documentary filmmaking (and one that you really need to be aware of, so you can avoid it) to pick those experts who will support the thesis of your film, and avoid those who don't. This is bad practice. There will always be 'evidence' that supports one view above another, and even the most 'scientific' theories are surrounded by dissension, counterpoint and alternative approaches. Put another way, you need to be careful not to make a film that just supports your perspective exclusively, especially if there is clearly more than one side to the argument. Even if we accept that documentaries are subjective and unavoidably loaded with the values (or bigotry) of the filmmaker, it's good practice to try to present balance, if not for any other reason than trying to engage, rather than alienate, an audience. Only selecting the evidence or information which fits your theory is really no different than propaganda. A film like Michael Moore's *Fahrenheit 9/11* is, in my opinion, a prime example of this: we are presented with information that suits Moore's polemic, and anything which may offer a different perspective or explanation is omitted.

4. DEVELOPING YOUR IDEA

So, let's do a quick review of how your documentary idea is developing…

First of all you've come up with an idea – perhaps due to a burning desire to make a film on a certain topic, or a person you've met with a unique story that you think needs telling. Secondly, you've checked the idea has legs, and that it works – in principle – as something that could make a good documentary film. Thirdly, you've done your research, and can bore yourself and others stupid with what you now know about this subject area. Now you're ready to actually develop the idea into something resembling a documentary film. And this, in some ways, is the biggest challenge you face as a documentary filmmaker, for it's at this point you need to start being able to provide answers to the two following related questions:

What is my film actually about? ←→ What is the style/approach of my film?

Each of these questions gives rise to some further considerations:

What is my film actually about? ←→ What is the style/approach of my film?

What is the duration?
Does it have a beginning,
middle and end?
Who are the central characters,
and is there a journey
(physical or emotional) that
they are going on?
Why is it interesting?
Who is the intended audience?

Observational
Authored
Archive based
Drama-documentary
Animated
Investigative
Presenter-led

WHAT IS MY FILM ABOUT?

Both of these questions will play an important part in shaping your film. We have dealt briefly with describing what your film is about in Chapter 2, but now you have to give your idea much more substance. The true test to making a documentary film is to be able to answer the question, 'What is my film about?' at each and every point during the production process. Remember, earlier on in this book we talked about the difference between the general and the specific; it's all very well wanting to make a film about human rights abuses in the Turkish Mental Health System, but this is not a description of what your film is about. It's too general. You need to be much more specific now, and be able to answer questions such as:

- Who are the characters in my film?
- Where will I be filming?
- What is the actual story here?
- What happens to my characters?
- Is there a beginning and an end here?
- Is there a journey that my character(s) will be taking?
- Am I just filming a variety of interviews to camera, or is there more to my film than this?

These are just some examples of the kinds of questions you need to start asking, and answering.

For instance, in the above example, there are an infinite number of ways to cover the same topic. You could interview a number of mental health professionals in Turkey who could talk about ways in which some institutions abuse basic human rights. You could also talk to various human rights organisations, which might be more forthcoming about some of the abuses that are going on. You might focus on one family who can talk about the experiences of their son in a nearby institution. All these are valid ways of approaching the subject matter. The only thing is that they are limited both in scope and duration. There are only so many people you can interview until you have made your point; after that, it just becomes repetitious and more suitable, probably, for a short news piece. If you want something with narrative, that sustains an audience's attention, then you need to be more creative here. Perhaps this would involve telling the story of one individual, and his life before, during and after his incarceration. Anecdotes from his family, the use of photographs and other archive can help give the sense of a passing of time, and we get to see someone who has been changed and affected by his four years inside an institution, when he was subject to beatings, electro-shock therapies and degrading treatment. Perhaps he is mounting a legal case against the institution and the film is contextualised by this. As you can hopefully intuit here, we can begin to 'see' this film; it becomes more than a collection of facts; instead it is an examination of these facts *within the context of* a personal story, through a character with whom we can engage and identify. In doing so, we have a much greater emotional connection with the subject matter of the film.

Another example... Let's imagine that you want to make a film about the increase in knife crime in your city. You have done a lot of research into the topic and found that most of this knife crime is committed by young teenagers.

So, what is your film going to be about? Is it going to be an investigative documentary about knife crime, with a presenter? During your research you identify two families who live on the same housing estate. One family has lost their child due to knife crime – their 12-year-old son was killed. The other family have their 15-year-old son in a Youth Detention Centre, because he was convicted for wounding a 26-year-old woman with a knife. Does your film focus on either one of these families, or possibly both of them, interweaving two narratives within one film? Do you focus on the families, or do you make the film about the perpetrator in prison? Or do you try to get access to a gang who all have knifes in order to see how they think and feel? Eventually, after more preparatory research, you decide that you are going to follow both families over the course of one year: the first family as they adjust to the loss of their son, and mount a legal case against the perpetrator, and a parallel story of a perpetrator as he opens up on camera, explaining the gangs he was part of and what drove him to commit this act. Two sides of a similar story.

Hopefully, by now, you can see that the idea not only has legs, but is beginning to take shape and form. It's a film that you can begin to visualise in your mind. There are characters who we can develop a relationship with over the course of the film. There is a definite journey here, and by making a film about this specific situation, we're looking at the bigger issue of knife crime, the judicial system and gang culture.

WHAT IS THE STYLE OF MY FILM?

Once you have an idea of the substance of your film, and a sense of the narrative, you need to now consider your style or approach. This is a difficult decision to make, because it's often dependent on numerous factors, such as who is funding your film (see Chapter 6), what budget you have available, what your personal style is (even if you don't know this yet, it will evolve over time) and what approach the subject matter lends itself to. There are many different documentary styles, including ethnographic, experimental, science, historical, nature, mockumentary, docudrama, and so on. Today, many documentaries use a blend of different styles, although it's worthwhile considering the components of the main ones, which are discussed below. Describing in words the unique nature of these approaches is not an easy task, and therefore I would encourage you to watch as many of the films mentioned as you can.

Observational

Observational documentaries – or *Obs Docs* as they are sometimes known – have their history in the Direct Cinema and Cinéma Vérité movements of the 1960s. As the name suggests, they involve no intervention, no commentary and no re-enactment, and in essence try to observe the action as it happens and unfolds. Although many films may have observational sequences in them, wholly observational films have a distinct aesthetic, often preferring to use small crews (often a single director/cameraperson) and handheld camera. Classic observational films include Frederick Wiseman's *Titicut Follies* (1967) (which showed some of the abuses which went on in the psychiatric facility in Bridgewater State Hospital, Massachusetts) and Richard Leacock's *Primary*, a film which followed the primary election between John F. Kennedy

Figure 6. *Titicut Follies*

and Hubert H. Humphrey for the United States Democratic Party nomination for President of the United States.

Authored

In some ways, this is a misleading description, as all documentaries, by their very nature, are authored. However, this category refers to those films in which the filmmaker has either made himself part of the film, has made a film about himself, or has put, at its core, a specifically and explicitly subjective viewpoint. For example, Nick Broomfield often includes himself in the film, both in terms of narrating it and actually appearing in frame (often in his dual role as director/sound recordist). Many contemporary documentaries from the UK and USA use this approach, including Michael Moore's films (*Roger and Me*, *Bowling for Columbine* and *Fahrenheit 9/11*). Morgan Spurlock not only appears in his film *Super Size Me*, but also puts himself through the gruelling challenge of eating nothing but McDonald's food for the one-month duration of the film. On the other hand, Adam Curtis' *Power of Nightmares* can be described as authored in that it is a very personal and specific thesis (i.e. not a popularly accepted view) about a certain topic – in this case the way in which governments have deliberately tried to instil paranoia into their citizens as a way of driving forward certain political agendas.

Archive-based films

Many films use archive, but some documentaries are specifically built round archive. An obvious example is the historical documentary, which uses news-reels, old film footage and photographs as a reference to some specific event in history. Jeremy Isaacs' 26-episode *The World at War* is a classic exponent. Other films might use archive in different ways. *The Corporation* by Mark Achbar, Jennifer Abbott and Joel Bakan uses archive footage from the 1950s and 1960s in order to make irreverent and often comic statements about contemporary multinational companies. Whatever your use of archive, it's important that you don't use it as a substitute when you can't get real access to a character. So, for example, if you are making a film about a living pop star, just using archive because you can't get proper access, it's likely to lead to a second-rate film, and in today's industry would probably not be well received.

Reconstruction, Re-enactment and Drama-documentary

These synonymous terms refer to recreating sequences in the absence of having an actual record of the event. You will no doubt be familiar with the use of reconstruction in television shows such as *Crimewatch*, where we see the dramatisation of a scene so that the viewer gets a better sense of what happened. This trend has become prevalent in documentary filmmaking, especially for historical programmes, where we can see Elizabethans, Crusaders, Alexander the Great and even dinosaurs parading around our screens in High Definition. It's also used in films with a more contemporary theme, such as the BBC's *The Secretary Who Stole £4million*. However, the terms drama-documentary, docu-drama, faction and documentary-drama are often used inter-changeably to refer to documentaries with dramatic sequences, dramas based on fact, and fake documentaries (or mockumentaries) such as Peter Watkin's 1965 Academy award-winning *The War Game*, which tells the story of a nuclear war and its aftermath in 1960s Britain. The film appeared so 'real' that the BBC delayed its transmission until 20 years later, stating that 'the effect of the film has been judged by the BBC to be too horrifying for the medium of broadcasting'.

Animation

It may sound odd to include animation as a documentary style, but increasingly filmmakers are making animated documentaries, in which the voices of characters are real, but animation is chosen as the visual form. I made a series of four animated documentaries called *Animated Minds* for Channel 4 television, in which each film had one person narrating their personal experience of mental illness. It was felt that the use of animation would help by visually representing these individuals' inner experience, in a better way than 'talking heads' or observational styles could do. Other documentary filmmakers have also chosen to use animation to deal with sensitive subject matters, such as Orly Yadin and Sylvie Bringas's *Silence* (1988) or David Aronowitsch, Hanna Heilborn and Mats Johansson's *Hidden*, which uses an interview with 12-year-old Giancarlo, who lives as a hidden refugee in Sweden. Jonathan Hodgson's *Camouflage* uses a combination of live action and animation over people's testimony about growing up with parents who have mental illness.

Figure 7.
Jonathan Hodgson's
Camouflage.

There are other styles of documentary filmmaking, such as reportage, investigative and expressionistic. Many films use a blend of different approaches and styles. The important thing is to consider which style best suits your film, and whether the same style suits your skillset and preferences as a documentary filmmaker.

5. WRITING THE PROPOSAL

At this stage, you may be wondering why you need to write a proposal. Surely, after researching, developing, thinking, visualising, ruminating, and researching again, you could just get on and start making the film. Well you could, but writing a proposal of your idea is an extremely useful thing to do.

Firstly, it allows you to clarify, for yourself, what your film is about. A proposal should be no longer than a page or so in length, and writing it down gives you a slightly more objective way of seeing if your film works, even as an idea on paper. It's a good exercise to pass such a proposal to colleagues and see if they 'get' the film, or whether you have become too involved to have an objective sense as to whether the idea really 'works' as a documentary.

Secondly, as I mentioned earlier, documentaries are not made in isolation, and often require the involvement of a broadcaster or other funding body. In the first instance, such funders or commissioning editors want to read a proposal so that they too can see whether your film is something they would want to invest in. There is a particular style in writing these kinds of proposals, and specific bits of information, which need to be presented.

Thirdly, often during your research stage, some individuals and organisations would want to see a proposal in order to give you access, either to themselves, their offices or their archives. A one-page proposal clearly outlines what your project is, and also gives it some credibility, and is therefore a useful resource to have at your disposal before filming commences.

Proposals for each of the purposes outlined above may all differ slightly in content. However there are some principal points that they all have in common. For the purposes of this chapter, we will look at the proposal you would send to a commissioning editor or funding body; this is the most common reason to write one.

THE TITLE

These days the title is everything. Particularly with commissioning editors in the UK, the title needs to sum up the programme and be catchy too. If you watch a lot of documentaries on television (and if you don't, you should) then you will notice a trend towards tabloid, slightly sensationalist programme titles. Broadcasters justify this by saying that in order to compete in a multi-channel environment, the title has to immediately *say what the film is* and appeal to a wide audience. Although I don't particularly condone this trend, it is a reality, and one that you are unfortunately going to have to play along with. For example, a recent film about an individual with high-functioning autism becomes *The Boy with the Incredible Memory*; a film about a young girl in Russia who has the alleged ability to diagnose illnesses in others, without even touching them, becomes *The Girl with X-ray Eyes*, and a film about someone who has a rare skin cancer and has little time left before he dies becomes *The Boy Whose Skin Fell Off*. Such titles do little to convey what are often great films, and this trend has caused much controversy. But, you have to play this game too, so make sure you have a title that can both capture the attention of the audience and sum up what the film is about.

Next to the title, it's a good idea to put the length of the film. Different broadcasters work with different length programme slots, so do your research here (for example, one-hour slots often mean a 52-minute film). Is it a feature-length 90-minute film, a one-hour-long programme, a series, or a one-off half hour? Don't just guess, or try to cram a two-hour film in a half-hour slot. The running time needs to reflect the type of film that you want to make.

THE OPENING PARAGRAPH

Commissioning editors and other funders receive literally thousands of documentary proposals a year. It goes without saying that they rarely sit down and read each and every one from start to finish. Often they may read the title and the opening paragraph, and if their interest is captured then they may read on. Essentially this means that you need to capture their interest straight away, and once the title has tickled their interest you need to really convince them in the next six or seven lines; or else your proposal will find itself in the trash with a cursory rejection letter, and your one chance of getting them interested in this film has gone. Forever.

Your opening paragraph needs to get straight to the point. Briefly contextualise the subject matter of your film, then go on to describe what is specific to your film (i.e. what it is about). It's best here if there is a seamless relationship between the two. One way of writing this is to avoid academic, essay-style rhetoric, but instead imagine that you are reading this as a TV billing in your local newspaper. And the acid test would be: would you want to watch the film? If so, then you're on the right track. If not, then how can you expect to interest a commissioning editor (and a potential audience) if it doesn't sound interesting to you? There is a skill to doing this; you need to familiarise yourself with as many proposals as possible (some are included on the DVD with this book), but also try to stay away from the tendency to be over-academic, or verbose. An example is a series of short documentary films I produced for Channel 4 about the children of Christian missionaries. Both the director, Miriam Lyons, and I were interested in the way in which these children coped, as teenagers, when they returned to the UK, after many, many years overseas. We felt that the films would provide an interesting perspective on contemporary British culture, but also windows into the complex and often contradictory themes of alienation and belonging that these children experienced.

Now, whether you or I find this interesting is secondary to how it reads. A proposal that talks about 'windows into the complex and often contradictory themes of alienation and belonging' is interesting, but it's not enough for a commissioning editor. It doesn't allow us, in a quick glance, to see what the film is, and even though it might be interesting to you and I, it has to have (for this particular TV channel) a much broader appeal.

Therefore, the title and first paragraph ended up looking like this:

Mish Kids

Imagine spending your childhood in a place where you always stand out and are treated as a foreigner. Yet you learn to make friends, grow to love the country and think of it as home. Then suddenly, as you enter your teens, you're brought back to Britain. Back home. But it's not home. You may now look like everyone else again but your accent's changed. You don't wear the right clothes or say the right things. Everyone thinks you're weird. And you are. A global nomad, you have experienced several cultures but belong to none. This is how 'Mish Kids' feel: a group of children of British missionaries who, having grown up overseas, suddenly find themselves forced to start a new life in the UK. Dishwashers, Tube stations, S Club 7, Topshop, getting drunk, Big Brother, DVDs, asylum seekers and small talk are all part of what for them is a bewildering world. Wrestling with their convictions and struggling to find out where they belong, this series (4x3') of short documentaries offers a fascinating glimpse into the strange no-man's land that these children inhabit.

The title has a nice ring to it, and it's what the kids in the film actually call each other. Today, the title is most probably too oblique for British television, and would more likely be called *Teenage Missionaries* or something similar. The series got commissioned because it described a world that is familiar to all of us, but seen through different eyes. And the opening paragraph succinctly sums up this main theme.

CHARACTER AND NARRATIVE

The next couple of paragraphs you write will talk about both the narrative (what's going to happen) and the characters (who it is going to happen to). Assuming you have captured the interest of a commissioning editor, you now need to describe what it is that we will be seeing in the film. The example below from *Mish Kids* describes three of the characters. Since each film is only three minutes long, there is no need to really go into narrative here. For longer films, you need to discuss narrative in much more detail.

Paul

Paul can't fit in. He hasn't got the right trainers, doesn't like Hollyoaks and can't understand why he needs a mobile phone. He's left his friends behind in the Middle East to join a comprehensive school in Middle England where most friendships have already been formed and he's the outsider. Before term started, Paul went on a summer camp designed to help Mish Kids integrate and so now knows how to use the Tube, what a Dyson does and who the Blazin Squad are. But somehow it's still not enough

Emma

Emma has pledged her virginity to God. She wears a ring that her father told her she must wear as a constant reminder of that promise until the day her future husband replaces the ring with his own. Growing up in Ecuador and schooled in an American Academy, this was fine. But now in her South London college, all the girls want to talk about is boys and all Emma wants to do is fit in. Blonde, pretty and popular – especially with the boys – Emma looks like she's part of the 'in' crowd... Keeping that promise will be very difficult...

Sarah

Sarah's friends think she's weird. She doesn't know how to act around boys. As a conversation starter, she'll ask them things like, 'In life, what makes you sad?' Small talk wasn't necessary in the Yemen where Sarah grew up and being home-schooled meant not having any peers, let alone peer pressures. Men and women were segregated for everything, even in the home, so Sarah never met any boys. The freedoms of college life in the UK have come not only as a shock but also as a challenge.

THE OTHER BITS

If you are writing a one- or two-page proposal, then you need to quickly put some other important bits of information in here.

- **Style:** You need to describe the approach to this film. Is it presenter-led, authored, archive-based, drama-doc? Ideally, this would become obvious from the way you write the first paragraph but, if not, you need to put it in the proposal.

- **Cost consideration:** Although you don't need to specify the budget you are looking for at this stage (you will need to address this in the pitch, though – see Chapter 6), you shouldn't deter the commissioning editor. So, if any of the content of your proposal sends alarm bells ringing (filming underwater, on 35mm film, in 15 different locations etc.) then you need to show an awareness and justification of extra costs, or else leave it out.

- **You:** You need to put a little paragraph in about who you are. A commissioning editor will want to know this information so that they can see your experience, get a sense of why you are interested in this subject matter, so if you have some relevant personal experience, or a PhD in the specific subject area of your documentary, then put it in.

- **The Company and Executive Producer:** As we will discuss further later, whenever approaching any funding organisation for your film, you usually have to go through a production company. This is so that someone giving you a big cheque feels confident that there is a company that knows how to budget properly for a documentary (and stick to this budget), but there is also an executive producer on board with the project who will ensure that you deliver a high-quality film.

PROPOSALS, TREATMENTS AND DIRECTORS STATEMENTS AND SCRIPTS: WHICH ONE DO I USE?

A proposal is usually defined as a one- or two-page document which outlines the main concept of the film. It is an initial document to get the interest of a commissioning editor or funding organisation. If a film is commissioned, or it is assigned some development money, then the next stage is usually to write a treatment (sometimes called a script), which is a much lengthier document that outlines, in more detail, the narrative of your film. This may sometimes include a Director's Statement, which outlines the director's personal motivation for making the film. Just to confuse matters, sometimes these words are all used interchangeably, and someone demanding a proposal actually wants a treatment, or vice versa. As a rule, it's always best to write a proposal first; if someone wants more information from you, then they can always ask. Better to do it this way round than spend weeks writing a long treatment which no one is particularly interested in. Having said that, you will – at some point during the production of your film – have to write a treatment, even if it's just to clarify for yourself the shape that the film is taking. Some examples of treatments can be found on the DVD with this book.

6. FUNDING AND PITCHING YOUR DOCUMENTARY

There may come a time when making documentaries becomes more than a hobby or pastime. Many people I know are so enthused about making documentaries that they may take months off from their job to go overseas to shoot their subject, devoting evenings and weekends to making a film. This is all very well, but at some point many of us want to earn a living doing the thing we love. It is extremely unlikely you will ever become rich as a documentary maker, so you need to have realistic expectations. If you still want to embark on this career, then read on...

I want to discuss funding this early on in the book for numerous reasons. Firstly, it's important to be aware of the various options available to fund your documentary, primarily because it's better to be able to feed yourself whilst doing something you love. Secondly, when any of us make a documentary we want people to be able to watch it; funding usually helps here, particularly if you want to put your film on to television or into cinemas. And thirdly, if you want money to make your film AND want it to be seen by as many people as possible, then this affects the kind of film you make. You can't just go ahead and make whatever documentary you want in the hope that someone, somewhere, will buy it. The television, film and distribution business is both complicated and often quite prescriptive, and you need to think carefully about the aesthetic, style, narrative, length, and overall look of your film to make it an attractive proposition to a buyer. Throughout the production process (described in the next section of this book), you need to be aware, at all times, who this film is for and where you want it to be seen. That's not to say that your film can't still be great if it's made without any funding or plans for exhibition, but if you were an architect who wanted to make a theoretical house, in order to actually build it you would need the finance in place, planning permission, the help of engineers to make sure that the building would work structurally, and so on.

I am going to describe funding in the sections below. The first deals with the television system of funding as it works in the UK, North America and Australasia. Next I will consider the process of European financing and feature film funding of documentaries. Thirdly, I want to briefly mention other sources of funding. However, it's important to note that these 'categories' are quite permeable. Something that is funded by US television can easily end up as a feature film in the cinemas, and something that is part funded by the UK, could end up having French, British and Australian broadcasters involved, as well as money from a regional film agency, private equity and grants. I have nevertheless tried to simplify it as much as possible.

Towards the end of the chapter, I'll talk a little bit about the importance of pitching and the taster tape.

TELEVISION FUNDING IN THE UK, NORTH AMERICA AND AUSTRALASIA

I have grouped these territories together, because they work in a similar fashion: the main way to get your films funded is through a commission by a television broadcaster.

So a television broadcaster (for example Channel 4, or SBS Australia, or PBS in the USA) will commission a film based on an idea put forward by a production company. The important thing to understand here is that many of these channels have specific strands or slots, and therefore you need to target your idea to the right strand and broadcaster. There is no point trying to sell an 80-minute music documentary on your favourite band to a commissioning editor who only has a 52-minute slot for religion or current affairs. So, before you even approach these commissioning editors you need to know exactly what they are looking for, and more importantly what they have already made. There is nothing that can do more damage to your reputation (and your pride) than approaching a commissioning editor with an idea that either doesn't fit their specific slots, or on a subject that they made a film about two weeks before. So, how do you find this out? Well, the first thing you need to do is watch lots of television. This will give you a strong sense of what kind of films are being made, how long the slots are and whether films are grouped together in specific strands. In addition, most broadcasters have specific areas of their website which regularly update producers on what they are looking for. (See Section Five on how to access these.)

For example, at the time of writing, Channel 4 has a strand called *Cutting Edge*. The strand is seen as the channel's 'gold standard documentary strand' and seeks 'films with authorship, wit and invention…for strong narratives and… a mixture of observational and past-tense stories. The strand will focus on the personal and domestic, but there is always room for more journalistic and international pieces' (Meredith Chambers, Commissioning Editor, Channel 4.) Therefore when trying to get your film commissioned you need to make sure it fits the remit of this strand. If not, then you either need to rethink your film, so that it does fit with this remit, or else start to look elsewhere. In addition, different channels commission different types of documentaries. A Channel 4 documentary is often poles apart in terms of style and content from one on ITV or SBS. The Discovery Channel will probably be looking for very different content from, say, BBC3. You need to become an expert on who is looking for what.

In the UK, we have become exceptionally spoilt by the many, many channels that commission documentary ideas outright. Often the process can be very simple: you write a one-and-a-half-page proposal, pitch your idea to a commissioning editor and, if you are lucky, then – voilà, you are given money to go and make your film. In reality, it's a little more complicated than that but it is much easier than the system that exists in Europe. The situation that exists in the UK, and to a lesser extent in other, non-European countries, has its advantages and disadvantages. Although it's a relatively simple process, it's also extremely competitive. There are literally thousands of individuals and production companies who are all fighting and competing for the same limited slots, and often they will have the edge over you. Big production companies have large development teams whose job is solely to write proposals and develop ideas for domestic television. Rather than attempt to compete with them, you need to have something that they don't. This could be access to a subject matter that the big companies don't have, or to a specific character who the film is based around. This would mean that no one else can make this film apart from you.

The other thing to note is that many of these production companies concentrate on making series rather than single, one-off documentaries. Why? Well, from a purely business point of view, it makes much more sense to make numerous films at one time because it brings in more money. As an individual or a small production company it's harder to make a documentary series – you don't have the experience or the resources to deliver it. But here's the thing: developing a single one-off documentary is your domain. If you have a good story and amazing exclusive access, it can be a really good way in.

TELEVISION FUNDING IN EUROPE

Another thing that might give you the edge over many of the domestic production companies is access to the European market. Due to the reasons mentioned above, the larger production companies often don't think about accessing this market. On the surface it's a much more complicated way of accessing funding, but if you do the maths then your chances can often be higher than just trying to get an outright commission from your national broadcaster. The essence of European funding for television is trying to get different broadcasters in different countries to put in little bits of money. It's a time-consuming process, and one that often involves negotiating with many diverse partners.

Another good reason to try and access this market is because the types of documentaries which European television is interested in are often very different from the channels mentioned above. The UK and the US often want a specific type of documentary, one which may have mass appeal, often with a liberal use of commentary, and stylised in a way which some filmmakers might find limiting. If you watch TV in the UK, you will notice that there is a strong tendency for a certain type of documentary. It's often 'formatted', meaning that its structure is often set to predefined rules, possibly limiting creativity. The themes tend towards the sensationalist and away from the subtle, and exposition is achieved with the heavy use of commentary. European broadcasters are also interested in this type of film but consider a much wider breadth of subject matter, and allow for a more 'creative' approach to the film.

Europe is made up of lots of little broadcasters and a few larger ones. This is the territory of co-production, which means that two or more broadcasters put funding into one documentary. Furthermore, this is also the land of the pre-sale, which means that even more broadcasters put small pots of money into your film. Your skill here is to manage to get some of these broadcasters to invest in your film. Once you have a couple of co-producers involved, other smaller broadcasters might become interested in your film, which then means an extended period of negotiating, pitching and hopefully getting your film funded.

The Jargon of Documentary Finance

The financing of films can be quite complicated, but these are a few terms that you will repeatedly come across, so it's a good idea to know a little bit about what they each mean.

A commission. This is the easy one. This means that a broadcaster (or other funder) effectively pays you money to make the film. In the UK, for example, getting a television broadcaster to pay for you to make your film is the most common way of funding a documentary film. It's usual for one broadcaster to invest in your film 100% of the costs.

Co-production. A confusing term. From a broadcaster's perspective, this is when one or more different broadcasters become involved in funding a single film. This happens less in the UK, but is the usual manner in which funding operates in Europe. The main reason that broadcasters choose to partner together like this is a financial one: both can part with less money and still end up with a finished film. From the producer's perspective, the term can mean something different, and refer to two or more production companies partnering on a film. Again, the main reason for this is often financial, and different production companies in different countries can access specific finances. But it can also be a great creative partnership, in which each company brings something different to the film.

Pre-buy. Also known as a pre-sale, this is when a broadcaster (or other funder/distributor) buys your film before it's finished being. They are, in effect, guaranteeing to buy your finished product for use in their specific territory or country. Unlike a commission, they are investing much less in your film, have no involvement in the editorial process, and are effectively paying you a licence fee to have limited use of your film on completion.

Acquisition. This is when a broadcaster or distributor buys your completed film. The documentary may have been funded by another broadcaster (for example, Discovery) and you are selling it to someone else (for example, the BBC), or it may be a film that you have self-financed, and are now hoping that someone will buy it. Examples of the latter category include Esteban Uyarra's *War Feels Like War* (which is discussed in more detail in Section Six of this book).

There's not room here to go into the in and outs of European co-production, although there are numerous helping hands which make the process easier. To access this information, the European Documentary Network (EDN) publishes a fantastic resource called 'The EDN Television Handbook', which lists every single commissioning editor of documentaries in Europe. It has their contact details, and also information on what kind of films they are looking for in terms of subject matter, length and format. It also clearly explains whether each broadcaster is interested in commissioning, pre-sales or acquisitions.

Making documentaries can often be more about who you know rather than what you know. As an emerging documentary filmmaker you are a small fish in a very, very, very large pond, and it's really important that you develop relationships with commissioning editors. This is particularly important for Europe. There are various events at which such meetings are possible, and more is discussed about this in the chapter on festivals in the third section of this book. However, some specific training initiatives deserve a mention here, which exist to help you learn the nuts and bolts of European funding as well as giving you an opportunity to meet, pitch to, and speak with commissioning editors. EDN offers such training courses, which are scattered around Europe. You can find more information on their website (www.edn.dk).

These courses are project based, which means you bring a documentary idea to the training sessions. They usually last a few days and have three main elements. Firstly, they introduce you, in far more detail than I have, to the art of European funding for documentaries. Secondly, you spend time working on your written proposal and verbal pitch. Thirdly – and this is the best bit – you get to pitch your proposal in front of fifteen or so commissioning editors. This is a formal pitching event, and commissioning editors fly in from all over Europe (and sometimes beyond). Not only do you get to practise pitching in a very real environment, but there is also the possibility that they might be interested in your film, and may even put money on the table. Perhaps most important though is that this is also an invaluable opportunity to start building specific relationships with the key players in the European world of documentaries, relationships which will last for many more years.

Another way of accessing European funding and expertise is through an organisation called MEDIA (www.mediadesk.co.uk for the British site). This is an organisation set up by the European Union to fund training, production and exhibition within the audio-visual sector. They offer part-funding for production, both for established production companies, and for 'New Talent'. Of particular interest here are some of the MEDIA-approved training courses such as EURODOC (www.eurodoc.fr) and the Discovery Campus (www.discovery-campus.de). These are like the EDN courses mentioned above, but involve two or three weeks study over the course of a year, and therefore offer an opportunity to develop your project in much more detail. As with the EDN courses, they end with a Pitching Forum. Places on these workshops are quite competitive, but it's an invaluable way of learning to access the market.

When to Direct and When to Let Go

So far we have covered the various pathways to obtain funding for television. Much as I hate to be the bearer of bad news, there is something that you should know at this point. If you are a first-time director – meaning that you have never made any kind of documentary before – then it's extremely unlikely that you will get to direct your first broadcast film. In some ways this is understandable, as large sums of money are involved here (a typical one-hour documentary can cost anywhere between £40,000 and £120,000), so it's a big risk for a commissioning editor to take if they have no evidence that you know what you are doing. So, this begs the question: 'How do I get to direct something for television, if I have never directed anything before?' Well, there are several answers to this, discussed below:

- **'New Talent' Strands** – Some broadcasters, particularly in the UK, offer various opportunities for what they call 'New Talent'. For example, Channel 4 have a strand called *3 Minute Wonder* which, as the name suggests, is a three-minute documentary that immediately follows the Channel 4 evening news. There are other strands that the main channels offer specifically for new and emerging filmmakers, and full updates on these strands and similar initiatives can be found on the relevant broadcasters' websites as well as the DFG website, www.dfgdocs.com. There is, however, an unfortunate catch here. The term 'New Talent' does not really mean 'New'. The assumptions are that you have either made some films, even if they were non-broadcast, or you have some experience working within the industry – for example as an assistant producer or editor.
- **Fight for Your Right** – If you feel you really should make your film, and you think you know what you are doing, then you should fight for your right to make the film. You stand more chance if you have amazing access to a subject, and a showreel or 'taster tape' will be invaluable here. Remember that this is effectively your big chance, so there is no point trying to bluff your way through your first commission if you don't feel up to it.
- **Working with Production Companies** – It's a fact that broadcasters prefer filmmakers with an established track record. It's also a fact that they prefer working with production companies with whom they have an ongoing relationship. This is because they know that the executive producer can deliver a good film on time, and on budget. So it's going to strengthen your case in either of the above scenarios if you build a relationship with an established production company. In order to do this you need to watch the kind of films that you enjoy, and see which com-

pany made it, then approach them directly with an idea. A full list of production companies (along with descriptions of the specialities) can be found in the Pact Directory (see www.pact.co.uk). Even if you are not going to direct your film, a decent production company will develop your idea and, if it gets commissioned, will make you part of the production team, either working as a researcher or perhaps an assistant producer. Don't snub this: it's a fantastic opportunity to learn a lot about the production process, and even though you are maybe letting go of control of your idea, there'll always be a next time.

FEATURE FILM FUNDING

The funding of feature documentaries can be quite complicated, not just because of the complex financial structure, but also because of the ambiguity in what defines a 'feature'. The usual definition – a film that has a theatrical release in cinemas – doesn't quite fit here, as many of the European films that we see in cinemas (for example, *Être et Avoir*) were funded by television (as were some North American documentaries, such as *The Corporation*). Therefore, to write about feature funding also involves an understanding of the television market, as well as specific funds that are uniquely for feature documentaries. A working definition of a feature documentary defines it as a film that exceeds 60 minutes. In the UK and the US we often refer to 'feature' documentaries as those which are on cinematic/theatrical release and are clearly different in structure and form to television documentaries. In Europe they often use the term creative documentary, and although these are largely funded by television, they are the same kind of films as those we would call feature documentaries. Confusing?

There are many, many ways of getting your documentary funded as a feature film, although these can broadly be put into three categories. Firstly, one can try to get funding through broadcasters, as described above. Secondly, you can apply to the plethora of funding bodies that invest in feature documentaries, and many of these are described in Section Five of this book. Thirdly, you can take the approach of fiction-film feature financing, using a variety of grants, funds, deals with distributors, tax breaks, sale as leaseback, private equity and gap financing and so on. Since this approach is really the exception rather than the norm, I won't focus on it here. However, there are numerous books and resources that describe this process in more detail, and I have mentioned a couple in Section Five.

ALTERNATIVE SOURCES OF FUNDING

Sometimes, either because you lack a track record or because you want to make the type of film that won't attract the usual motley crew of broadcasters (either due to its length, style or subject matter), you might want to pursue alternative sources of funding. Your film may still end up on television or in cinemas, but might not be initially funded in this way. Depending on which country you are living in, you will be able to access particular funds that can be used to fund (either explicitly or implicitly) a documentary film. Many countries have their own national film fund, and some have regional film funds too. There are various charities, non-governmental organisations, trusts and other grant-giving bodies who might all be sympathetic to your subject matter. The key here is to think creatively, and be persuasive in order to get people and organisations to part with their money.

For example, you might be making an observational documentary about an ageing immigrant Jewish couple who live near you; you want to look at their interesting lives, how they left many of their family behind in Poland and Lithuania, never to see them again. There are Jewish film funds in many countries that have a large Jewish population. There might also be local Jewish organisations that would give some funding to the film – even, perhaps, the local synagogue. A film about children with Polio in India may get funding from UNESCO, as well as various NGOs such as Christian Aid, Médecins Sans Frontières or OXFAM. A film following a group of teenage missionaries (as in our example earlier in this book) may be funded by various Church or Christian organisations, and a documentary following a group of extreme sports people doing the most dangerous bungee jumps around the world might be sponsored by a sports label or a sports magazine. The main thing you have to worry about from any sources of funding is the issue of editorial control. Under no circumstances can the local church dictate what goes (and what doesn't go) into your film about missionaries, the sports label shouldn't really insist that your subjects wear a certain sports item of theirs (unless you make this explicitly clear in your film).

Put simply, you mustn't take money for your film if the moneylender can seriously influence the editorial integrity of the film. Sometimes this is simply a moral decision that you must take. At other times, if your film is ever to hit a television screen, then there are national (and international) laws governing accepting funding from certain sources – most notably tobacco companies and the pharmaceutical industry.

SELF-FINANCED DOCUMENTARIES

As the name suggests, this means going off and making a documentary on your own, with no formal financing in place. At one extreme, this means a 'credit card' film, and at the other it means getting private sponsors on board.

There are advantages and disadvantages to funding your own documentary. The advantage is that you have more or less total freedom and therefore total control over your film. The disadvantage (apart from obviously not having much money in your wallet) is that there is no guarantee that you're going to make your money back – or, in the case of private sponsorship, someone else's.

If you are going to go ahead and self-finance your own film, then you really need to keep a number of factors in mind. Firstly, it's important that you keep costs to a minimum. This might mean self-shooting, and it definitely means no lavish hotels, no personal assistants and no large crews. But the second and most important factor is that you still need to make a film that an audience will want to see, and that a broadcaster or distributor will want to buy. There's an irony here, as your film might be self-funded because no one else is interested in it; and, if no-one else is interested in it, then they might not want to buy it once it's finished. So unless you have unlimited dispensable income, if you are going to make a film on your own, then still make it with broadcasters and buyers in mind. Think about which channel you can imagine seeing your film on, or whether you can see it in a cinema. And always make the film with these factors in mind, otherwise all your hard efforts will have gone to waste, with an empty bank balance, and some rather disappointed, if not angry, private investors. There are numerous examples of filmmakers who have successfully self-financed and distributed. For example, the filmmaker Simon Chambers made *Every Good Marriage Begins with Tears* with his own funds, managed to get the film into some of the top documentary festivals, and then it was bought by the BBC's *Storyville* strand.

Oh, and just a quick word about private investors – if they are your friends, or family, or family's friends, then you need to consider how they are going to feel if they don't get their money back. Documentaries rarely make a lot of money, and even the big blockbusters can often bring little return. I find it's always the best thing to be honest with your funders; often they might invest in your film because they believe in what you are trying to say, rather than being motivated by profit.

THE PITCH

Pitching is a unique skill and quite disconnected from the craft of writing a proposal. Proposals serve a very useful function – they get you noticed, and they bring attention to your project. If written well, then they can inspire a commissioning editor to want to know more about you and your project. And if it gets to this stage, then you need to be able to pitch it. Although the written proposal is seen as invaluable for pitching forums and various funding agencies, it's really the pitch that's going to get you a commission, as it's the face-to-face encounter that's going to either impress or alienate a commissioning editor, distributor or other financier.

There are three principal skills to pitching your idea. The first is to be able to sum up your idea in a few sentences; the second is to be able to inject passion into your project. I have seen so many commissioning editors swayed by a passionate pitch – to see that you really care about your idea is worth so much, and can convince a funder that you are really going to work hard on this project. And the third, and perhaps most important, is to be able to second-guess the kinds of questions that a broadcaster will ask. They don't just want to know what the film is about – it would be easy if they did – but commissioning editors are business people, and they want to know if they can afford your idea, and if it's going to work for their channel or fund. So, here is the secret guide to wooing a commissioning editor:

- **Know your broadcaster, and know the slot you are pitching for.** We've touched on this theme earlier on in Chapter 2, when we discussed how your idea has to be related to industry needs. But now you need to know much more detail about who you are pitching to. Firstly, why are you pitching to that specific channel or funder? Why would they want your film, more than any other funder? Is it uniquely a History Channel type film, or something that the Sundance Fund is likely to fund? More importantly, if pitching to a television broadcaster, try to envisage exactly when you would see your film: would it be a nine o'clock slot? Would it fit within one of their current strands? Is it really the kind of film that this channel funds? The only way to really find this out is watch lots of television, paying attention to various strands and slots, attend any open days or conferences in which commissioning editors discuss what kind of content they're looking for, and seek out extra funding information which can usually be found on the broadcaster's or fund's website (see Section Five for a list of these).
- **The duration of the programme.** Here, you need to know how long you want your film to be, but also whether it fits into the channel's slots that they have available. You may be pitching a 90-minute film that simply has no place in the channel's schedule as it's more appropriate as a feature documentary to be screened in cinemas. Or, you might be pitching your film for a half-hour slot, when it simply isn't the kind of documentary that can fit into a half-hour – the breadth of it simply requires a longer film. Also, you need to know that 'one-hour slots' and 'half-hour slots' rarely exist. Due to advertising and in-house promos on a channel, a 'half-hour' can range anywhere between 20 and 30 minutes and an 'hour' can be anywhere from 45 minutes to 60.
- **Has it been made before?** Many good ideas evoke some sense that it must have been made before. Sometimes it has, and sometimes by the very channel that you are pitching to. So, you're going to look really

stupid pitching an idea for a film that was broadcast by that very channel a couple of months ago. Sounds silly, but I know of many producers who have made this mistake. Again, do your research and avoid such embarrassing moments.

- **Who is making it?** This is really important. You need to talk about the talent involved in making this film. Who is the director? Who is the executive producer, and who is the production company housing the film? The answers to these questions are extremely important – rarely is a film commissioned for a new director with no named talent attached. Commissioning editors are, on the whole, risk-averse creatures and don't want to give thousands of pounds or dollars to a project without having the assurances that it can be delivered by a good director, a good producer, a great executive producer and the back up of a trading production company. If there is on-screen talent, such as presenter, then here's the time to say who it is (make sure they can actually do it, as it would look a bit silly if you said, 'Oh yeah, and John Cleese is going to present this,' if you have made no contact with him and have no idea if he would do it).

- **How much will it cost?** Time and time again I know producers and directors who confidently walk into a pitching meeting, only to completely fall apart when they are asked about cost. Most of the time, they simply haven't thought about it. There's two common mistakes that are made here: the first mainly comes from new producers and directors – they are so desperate for a commission that they give some ludicrously cheap estimate – say £10,000 for a one-hour film. This makes you look ridiculous and is a sure way to sabotage your chances of gaining a commission, or at the very least raises doubts about your competence. The other mistake is to present an idea which is going to cost a fortune, and way more than most broadcasters can afford. So try to avoid pitching an idea which involves filming on the International Space Station! As a guide – and a very rough guide at that – single, one-hour documentaries range from £40,000 to £100,000. Any estimates below or above these amounts, and you're entering dangerous territory. Try to cost your film properly and, if you don't know how, then get a producer or production manager to help you out. In Chapter 14 on Managing Your Production there are some tips on how to budget for your documentary.

- **When are you going to make it?** You need to be realistic here. Some commissioning editors may have a slot available in three months time, and you need to know if you can make it within this time frame. Be honest if you can't, but you do need to give a realistic time frame here.

The Role of the Commissioning Editor

One of the key challenges is not to begin to believe your own publicity... Commissioning editors occupy the role of buyer in a market that is over-supplied by sellers; this means that all independent producers want to be your friend and are always happy to buy you a drink/lunch etc and laugh at your jokes. Being a commissioning editor also means you are always open to being pitched to, wherever your path crosses that of an indie; the 15-minute pitch one Sunday morning at our local Lido is not a fond memory. The good and unique far outweigh the bad, however; you get to work with a wide range of hugely creative people, whose own passions, if you are lucky, can combine with yours to create something where the whole is definitely greater than the sum of the parts. And the unique element is that you can have a real impact on people's lives, whether it's the contributors through life-enhancing constructed-reality documentaries (The Singing Estate etc) or the viewers by inspiring them to find out more, or simply by prompting an emotional response.

Kim Peat, Controller of Daytime, Arts and Religion at Channel Five

A commissioning editor is a hugely privileged and creative role on the front line of television. The best thing about the job is the endless access to talented people and the chance to flex the imagination and brain every single day. I never resent going in to work. Commissioning editors are the people who create the landscape of television from the genesis of an idea to transmission and that is extremely exciting. To be a successful commissioning editor I believe that the most important thing is to understand the audience inside out and be able to spot ideas which will instantly connect with the public. Commissioning editors have to have vision and a common touch but they also have to be able to guide producers through the production process to create excellence – clarity of vision and thought are key. But with the position of commissioning editor comes huge exposure to risk and constant analysis of your work. It's a fine line balancing innovation and creativity as you try to realise the channel's brand and ambitions – too many failures and innovation can quickly start to look like lack of vision! It's not for the faint-hearted. I receive hundreds of great ideas and it's tough saying no to good ideas and talented producers who have worked hard on a proposal. However, it's essential to be rigorous in selecting ideas that work specifically for your channel or no one wins.

Emma Read, Commissioning Editor, Factual Entertainment, Sky

What makes a good pitch?

The best pitch is when the producer has done you the great good service of watching your channel and your output and thought through how their proposal might be shaped to deliver what you want; who seems to get what you are trying to do and has thought ahead about how to evolve your approach to the genre (it's rare, but it does happen). All commissioning editors like to be flattered by producers having a good knowledge of their programming and it certainly helps overcome the commissioning editor's most hated pitch which is, not surprisingly, for the idea that went out on your channel (or indeed, a competitor, it doesn't really matter...) only six months ago. Second most hated pitch is the one that starts, 'I've come with a fantastic list of ideas, I'll just run through each of them...'. The best ideas tend to come from talking around broader themes and invariably the 'must have' idea is the one that comes up just as the producer is standing up to leave and is often entirely unrelated to anything you've spent the past hour discussing.

Kim Peat, Controller of Daytime, Arts and Religion at Channel 5

When a producer can sum up an idea in a sentence or a paragraph – if you can't then it probably needs more development and thought. I want to feel that a producer is passionate about an idea but it's essential that they are pitching an idea which they believe people will watch on my channel and not just an idea they want to make!

The worst mistake any producer can make is revealing ignorance about the channel they are pitching to. Why would any commissioning editor give money to a producer who can't be bothered to watch their channel? As a commissioning editor on a non-terrestrial channel I have to work hard to persuade producers to bring me their best ideas and many ideas start in channel or through discussion with producers rather than from unsolicited proposals. So it's a good idea to try and build a relationship with a commissioning editor and just brainstorm.

Then I have three golden rules about ideas:

1. Strong PR hook that will win the programme lots of media coverage.
2. Engaging subjects which viewers are already interested in.
3. Do we care about the characters and the outcome of the programme?

Above all, be relaxed and be prepared to enter a dialogue and collaborate with the commissioning editor on any idea. Most great programmes are the result of collaboration between producers and the channel.

Emma Read, Commissioning Editor, Factual Entertainment, Sky

THE TASTER TAPE

A taster tape is effectively a short selection of rushes which adequately illustrate the film that you are pitching. It's more and more common now that broadcasters and other funding agencies want to see some visual evidence of the film you are pitching, before they commit to giving you any money. A taster tape does not need to be a well-edited short film; on the contrary, sometimes it can just be some roughly shot footage of one of your principal characters. What's important is to give the commissioning editor some sense of what your film will look like and who the main characters are. If you're trying to pitch a character-based documentary, no matter how enthused your pitch is, and no matter how much you go on about how interesting your character is, no one these days is going to put money on the table without seeing the character. Production values needn't be overwhelmingly high here (I have seen films commissioned based on poorly shot footage from a hand-held consumer camera); what's important is that you convey the substance of your film.

SECTION TWO
PRODUCTION

7. THE NUTS AND BOLTS OF DOCUMENTARY FILMMAKING: WHO DOES WHAT?

When some of us have an idea for a documentary film, we get passionate, almost obsessive, and want to rush out and make it as soon as possible. The easy access to cameras, sound equipment and editing equipment has made it increasingly easy to be a lone ranger, travelling to other countries as a one-man band to make our independent feature documentary. And although this role is becoming increasingly common, it's also true to say that in the world of broadcasting and feature film funding it's rare that you will ever truly be that alone. Part of this is due to the nature of the business – there are distinct roles within the documentary filmmaking industry – but also working as part of a team can be an extremely rewarding endeavour, and often lead to a film-making process that is less stressful and a film that is richer in content. I want to spend some time in this chapter explaining what these roles are, and then talking about the new emerging role of the 'multi-skiller'. Most of these roles, with the exception of the commissioning editor, come under the umbrella of an independent production company.

THE COMMISSIONING EDITOR

Some might think it odd to include this role in a list of production roles of a documentary film, but more often than not, it is the commissioning editor who has given you the money to make your film. Most, but not all, documentary films these days are made for television and it's the commissioning editor who decides what gets commissioned and what doesn't. Even on the big screen, there are still people in a similar role that will decide whether or not to fund your film, and as such will have ultimate control over the film.

Commissioning editors are a mixed breed. Some of them have a long history as documentary directors or producers, others have come by different routes. They are interested in documentary films and will definitely play a role in helping you make a great film. However, they have another agenda – to ensure that the films they commission also bring in an audience. So, it's not just a question of whether you have a good idea for a film or not. They take into account the needs of the broadcaster, viewing trends, costs of the production, and of course whether there are any legal risks if your film is made.

THE EXECUTIVE PRODUCER

The executive producer is, effectively, the overall boss of your production. He or she usually runs the production company that you may be attached to. They oversee the whole production and often act as the interface between the filmmaker and commissioning editor; they often have the unenviable job of trying to please both groups of people, even though they may often have polarised views of how they want the film to be. Executive producers are often the people who get a film commissioned. They may come up with the idea and look for a director to make the film, or they may be approached by a filmmaker and help get funding for the film. If you have a good executive producer (often known simply as 'Exec' or 'EP'), then this is the person you turn to when you are having moments of crisis, want advice, are concerned about the script or just need someone to tell you that you are doing okay. They also have a wealth of knowledge about media law, including issues of compliance, copyright, finance and commissioning. They will be involved in your production at various stages, often have vast experience, and will help you make your film work. Productions are, in theory, hierarchical, although in practice a good production team works in an egalitarian way. But just so you know, the executive producer is the boss.

THE PRODUCER AND DIRECTOR

I've put these two roles together because, depending on which country you are making films in, and what kind of films you are making, they can often be the same role. In the world of feature documentaries, there is often a separate producer and director, and the same goes for the documentary industry in mainland Europe. But in the UK, North America, Australia and some other countries, there is a growing trend that the two roles of producer and director are undertaken by the same person. On documentaries with a small crew this is actually a benefit, as the director becomes directly involved in the day-to-day running of the production, rather than two people constantly overlapping.

In larger-scale productions, the producer effectively acts as a manager of the production, co-ordinating the finance, the crew, the shooting schedule and general day-to-day business of the production. Producers vary from film to film: some are much more hands-on and are a driving force behind the look, feel and narrative of the film; others stay much more in the background and deal with the business side only.

Directors are responsible for the overall creative look of the film. They are responsible for the story or narrative, the way it is filmed, the script and commentary. Directors will work closely with the producer and executive producers, as well as with the cameraperson, sound recordist, production manager, researcher, editor, and other members of the production team.

ASSOCIATE PRODUCERS AND ASSISTANT PRODUCERS

As the names suggest, these two roles involve working under the producer (which, of course, may also be the director, but let's not confuse things). In small crews, the associate producer (or 'AP') will help organise shoots, as well as maybe doing some of the interviewing and camera work. They may also double up as a researcher, if appropriate. On large-scale productions, they may be the primary contact during production, will liaise with subjects, arrange shooting and will assist and co-ordinate final delivery of the film. Assistant producers will usually work on a specific aspect of the production and will work under the associate producer, often taking on a research role.

PRODUCTION MANAGER

To me, a good production manager is the backbone of the production team. They will examine all aspects of production including budget, production schedule, and legal issues arising, crew contracts, insurance and Occupational Health and Safety. Any query as to whether one can film in a specific location, how much the crew need to be paid, what types of insurance are needed and whether the film is on budget – all these are down to the expertise of the production manager.

Being a production manager is the most fun you can have with your clothes on. If the job suits your skills and abilities – you need to have a feel for figures and be anal about details – it's the best job in the world. When you get up in the morning you never know what the day is going to bring. Will you become an expert in spitting snakes in order to do a risk assessment for the crew going off to shoot in Africa, or will you be fluent in pidgin French so that you can track down and order a brace of helicams in Toulouse?

I couldn't believe my luck when I got my first job in TV and on my first day at LWT I was sent to Harrods with a large wad of cash to pick up a luxury lunch hamper for a crew filming for a documentary about the return of eels to the Thames. And even though those spendthrift days are over, the fun, camaraderie, hard work, new challenges and learning curve continue unabated.

OK, I know that sometimes it's hellish and you want to smack the arrogant director and knock heads together and shriek – but when it all threatens to get too much hopefully a sense of humour and repeating the holy mantra, 'It's only telly, it's only telly,' to yourself somehow gets you through it.

You should be getting reasonably well paid (you deserve it!), you may get to travel all over the world and you will have a degree of autonomy that many others can only dream of. You meet a variety of different people, you see your name whiz up the TV screen, there's a new challenge every time you start a new project, and, perhaps, after you've sacrificed a year of your life to bring the series or programme to the screen, your best friend – when you ask if she enjoyed watching your 'baby' when it went on air the previous evening – says, 'Oh, was it *last* night?!'

What other job could be so satisfying? Building a good team and getting them to work together, and having fun doing it, organising recces and shoots so that nothing (well, hardly anything) goes wrong, or if it does you think on your feet and put it right, bringing the project in on budget – or a little bit under so you can throw a decent wrap party... it all makes up for the long days, worked weekends and sleepless nights. Who wants to retire? Bring it on.

Linda Stradling, Production Manager and Producer

RESEARCHER

There's a common belief that researchers are the most junior part of the production team and, whilst it's true that they may often be little more than glorified runners, a lot of the time researchers are an invaluable and much needed part of the production. They often liaise directly with the producer/director and not only hold a lot of information in their heads about the subject matter of the film, but often may add creative input into it as well. Some researchers have specific specialities, such as archive or historical research, and they are often integral, giving weight and accountability to a documentary.

RUNNER

A runner does all the odd jobs from making coffee to assisting on a shoot. They might sometimes do research, they will undertake administration tasks, and they will also help lug equipment from one place to another. It sounds a fairly boring and menial job, but, to be honest, you can learn a great deal in this role – especially if it's with a nice and friendly production team. Many people who started as a runner on films I have been involved in later went on to work as an assistant producer and director. Another bonus is that the production company might let you use their resources (edit suite, cameras etc) in 'downtime'.

CAMERAPERSON AND SOUND RECORDIST

A production is nothing, of course, without the crew. The main two roles here are a cameraperson (often known as a 'DP' or director of photography) and a sound recordist. The skills involved here will be discussed in much more detail further on in this book. Both sound recordists and camerapersons are often freelancers; they are brought in for the duration of the shoot and then they will go off and work on other projects. A good DP will not only bring technical excellence to your film, but will also be able to help bring life to it. Likewise, a good sound recordist is worth their weight in gold; it is often one of the most important, and overlooked, areas of the filmmaking process.

EDITOR

Editors, when they are good, are as important as the director in post-production, bringing structure and narrative to a bunch of rushes. Both the director and editor are going to be spending a long time together locked in an edit suite, so the relationship between the two is really important here. Most editors work on one of two software suites – either AVID or FINAL CUT PRO – but again, we'll discuss this later on in the book.

JACK-OF-ALL-TRADES

Within production companies, tighter budgets often mean the teams are becoming smaller and smaller so there is often significant overlap between roles. It's not unusual on a small production for the one person to be the producer, director, cameraperson and sometimes more. There is also a trend, recently perpetuated by the BBC documentaries department, for directors to do a rough edit of their film. This means that we are becoming multi-skillers, which can also translate as being jack-of-all-trades and master of none. Whereas a cameraperson may have been trained for years at film school, and an editor the same, now we are often required to do both these roles, and more. This leads to a different kind of filmmaking, and this is most noticeable on the various documentaries we can see on television. Also, there are both distinct negative and positive aspects to this. The negative is obvious – we lose the professional expertise of dedicated, skilled craftspeople, and potentially make our job much more stressful. The good side, however, is that we can now make much more intimate films with a level of control that we previously might not have had. If we are filming overseas, or filming sensitive subject matter, we can effectively be a one-man crew, which not only keeps costs down, but also can make us much more flexible, because we don't have to book in crew for specific times.

On Multi-Skilling

For a few years I have been making films on my own, something into which I fell by need more than by choice… For years I convinced myself that this was the easiest, most practical and best way to get close to those intimate and truthful moments that all documentary filmmakers aim at. And clearly the benefits of this approach outnumbered the potential deficits; or so I thought.

Recently, while making a film in Iraq about the trial of Saddam Hussein, some of these preconceptions have been challenged by specific situations I have encountered.

Let me explain: from my personal experience, there are two different situations for a filmmaker wherein the 'on your own' approach will have different results.

The first one is when recording a purely 'observational' situation. In this case this approach has great benefits, as you take the role of a 'stills' photographer. Flexibility of movements and becoming unobtrusive are key factors when covering this kind of scene in the best possible way. On the contrary, having a crew with you could make you more visible and not allow you to follow your subjects accordingly. The only problem in these situations is the recording of sound, as in most cases you won't be able to stick a radio mic on your subject/s and then you are left with the sound from your camera mic. So, following conversations or trying to film from behind or faraway can become difficult. This is a gamble I take myself and try to cover the scenes from vantage points where I know the sound will be good enough, thus sacrificing some camera positions for the benefit of capturing good sound. Normally I will try to capture the other types of shots (like reaction shots) during moments where I feel a given conversation is not relevant to the final film. But overall working alone and handheld in these situations has more benefits than problems.

The second situation is one-to-one interviews. I have always assumed that this approach gave me the opportunity of achieving a level of intimacy with my subject that I couldn't achieve if accompanied by a crew. Again, I found that in specific intimate moments, it was extremely beneficial to be alone, and that the subject would open up in ways they wouldn't do if surrounded by people. I normally put this down to the fact that they felt comfortable with just my presence and that somehow my approach made the camera 'invisible'. But this is not completely true. In fact, in many cases, the fact that I was the sole operator of the camera and that I had to place the camera in between me and my subject drew more attention to the camera than, let's say, if I (as the director) was making eyeline contact with the subject while a cameraperson filmed from right behind me. So in this approach the camera becomes more visible (and obstructive regardless of the size) than if there was a two- or three-person crew, since the camera is normally placed on the line of vision where the eyes of the director and the subject should meet. On some occasions I overcome this problem by placing the camera on an angle, down looking up, so that I can still meet my subject's eyes, or from a side, so that my subject hopefully forgets about the camera's presence. Furthermore, on occasions you will find yourself losing concentration on the subject as your focus moves to technical considerations such us exposure, framing or focus. And you will miss key developing moments in your exchange as your priorities are to get a good image/sound. For this reason, I even take a bigger gamble, and leave as many automatic set-ups as possible. I understand the potential problems of this approach, but if you are aware of them, you can get an overall good picture by only controlling the focus manually, and just be aware of any strong lights behind your subject so that the exposure of your camera doesn't close down and darken your subject.

At the end of the day, you have to put all these elements in your 'melting pot' and decide for yourself what you gain and lose by working alone. For good or bad, you need to think of all these pros and cons, as working alone is not just a practical issue but will affect your style immensely.

Esteban Uyarra, Filmmaker

8. THE BEGINNER'S GUIDE TO CINEMATOGRAPHY: PART 1 – THE TOOLS OF THE TRADE

Now we've talked about your idea, it's time to discuss how to actually execute it, and that means using various pieces of equipment. This can cost a few thousand pounds or a few hundred thousand, depending on your budget and, of course, the specific requirements of your film. Whatever your film, you always need the two important basic pieces of equipment: a camera and a microphone. In this chapter, we'll describe both of these as well as some important peripherals, which you might also consider. Don't worry if you don't understand all the technical terms I've used; this is intended as a quick introduction to run you through the basics. The next chapter will look in more detail at how to apply them.

THE CAMERA

I'm not going to get too technical here, but it is important that you understand some of the fundamental principles of how a camera works, as it will inform your camera skills no end. At its most basic, a camera is a simple device to record light. Light hits a lens, leading to an image, which is focused on a photosensitive surface – either film, an electronic tube or electronic chip (or CCD – charge-coupled device) – which records onto a tape or hard disk.

Most cameras that you might come across operate in the same way: they allow you to focus on an object (using the lens), determine the amount of light it lets in (aperture) and then record this image. All the other aspects and functions of a camera are merely ways to enable this to happen.

There was a time when documentary filmmakers used film cameras, either 16mm or 35mm film, but the costs of processing and developing have now made such equipment largely prohibitive, especially due to the low cost of shooting on video.

With the advent of video in the 1980s, there was somewhat of a minor revolution in documentary filmmaking. It suddenly became much cheaper to produce a documentary, even though analogue video never looked as good as film. Then, in the 90s we were given digital video, which not only led to lower costs, and higher production quality than analogue, but allowed picture information to be stored in the form of numbers (like a CD), which means that it can be copied and edited without the loss of quality you get when editing VHS tapes. Also, because it is a digital format, it allows editors to cut the film in a non-linear way (more about this in Chapter 16). This, if you didn't know about it already, is really good news!

If you go into a store that sells cameras, you will be bombarded with manifold technical terms. You may be thinking of buying a high-street camera, or your ambitions (and your wallet) may be far grander. The most important point here is to consider who you are making the film for. If it's a home video, then a simple, cheap DV camcorder would suffice. But if you want to make something that would be good enough to be broadcast on television, or for theatrical release, then you need to start thinking more seriously. As a general rule, cheaper cameras often rely on in-built automatic functions where the computerised technology makes decisions for you (and not always good ones); the more expensive cameras often rely much more on manual functions and, as such, give much greater control to the cameraperson, and the aesthetics of the picture. Other considerations include the format that you are recording on, the aspect ratio, the lens, and the robustness of the camera.

Cameras come in many shapes and sizes, and in many different formats. A brief overview of these different formats will help you understand why you often see varying picture quality and production values on documentary films, and may help inform your choice of camera.

DVCam, MiniDV and DVC Pro

These are words you will constantly hear, and they refer to three tape formats that are collectively known as DV (or Digital Video) formats. As the name suggests they are all digital, which means they record the data as a series of 1s and 0s, and they can be directly digitised into a non-linear editing system.

There are subtle differences between the three formats. MiniDV and DVC Pro are almost the same, except each format is used by a different group of manufacturers (for example Sony embraces MiniDV, whilst Panasonic embraces DVC Pro). All three utilise the same compression method called DV25 (which is sometimes just referred to as DV compression). The same data is recorded onto each format, with the difference between the formats being how the data is physically recorded onto the tape. DVCam allows more information to be recorded onto the tape, and is therefore the most robust format of the three. It's important to realise that these descriptors relate to the way in which the camera records, and not the tapes themselves. Just to complicate matters slightly, MiniDV is also used to describe a type of tape. This means that MiniDV, DVCam, DVC Pro and HDV can all be recorded onto MiniDV Tapes. But more on this later...

Betacam and DigiBeta

These are formats that are used by the larger (and more expensive) cameras. The term Betacam refers to a family of half-inch videotapes developed by Sony. As with DV above, the term is now used loosely and refers to both the tape and the camera. Betacam (or the later and better Betacam SP) is an analogue format. Although the format itself may not be better than DV, the cameras are much higher end, with better lenses, better CCDs, and more professional features. DigiBeta is seen as the gold standard of all standard definition formats, and is correspondingly very expensive. Many high-end television programmes (drama, documentary and news) are filmed in this format. Often though, for documentaries – and especially documentaries made by independent filmmakers – the costs and size are too prohibitive, with many preferring to use the smaller DVCam and HDV formats.

HD and HDV

In the last couple of years you may have heard the word 'Hi-Definition' (HD) bandied around as if it were the Holy Grail itself. Hi-Definition means there are far more pixels than standard definition, which in turn means a much sharper picture. Even Hollywood films are starting to use HD. Broadcasters both in the US and UK are actually starting to transmit certain films in HD, and are increasing demands that programmes be delivered in this format. There is a distinction between 'true HD' and HDV, which you need to be aware of. The latter refers to a highly compressed version of the format, which is usually recorded onto MiniDV tapes (using MPEG compression). However, even HDV is far better than DV and most of the analogue formats.

Tape and Tapeless

At the time of writing, most cameras still use tapes – either MiniDV, Beta, DigiBeta or specialist HD tapes. However, within the next few years it's my guess that tape-based cameras will become largely obsolete, and be replaced by on-board hard disc recorders. (Some cameras, like the Panasonic HVX200 have both tape and hard-disc capabilities.) This has already started happening with cameras such as Sony's XDCAM. The advantage to this is that there is minimal risk of dropout or loss of data, and the footage can be digitised into a computer instantly for editing, rather than having to wait to capture the footage from a tape. The disadvantage is that the discs are currently prohibitively expensive, although costs are likely to come down significantly as the technology becomes more widely accepted.

If you are buying your own kit, most of you will probably be shooting on MiniDV tapes. Many manufacturers of tapes will try to convince you that you need to buy either MiniDV, DVCam or HDV tapes depending what format you need to shoot on (i.e. MiniDV, DVCam or HDV). However, the truth is that there is little difference between them in terms of the chemical components of the tape: in many ways it's little more than a marketing gimmick. Granted, a low-end MiniDV tape is probably inferior to a high-end HDV tape, but in essence they are the same. So, if you find yourself shooting in DVCam or HDV format, just buy a good MiniDV tape and there will be no real loss of quality – you'll save money, too. The only thing to be aware of here is that if you buy a 60-minute MiniDV tape and use it in DVCam mode, then you will only have 40 minutes of recording time. This is because the tape goes past the tape head slightly quicker in DVCam mode so that it can store more information.

Many of the documentary filmmakers I know choose to shoot on a hand-held professional camera, such as the Sony HDR-Z1E (or simply Z1 for short) or the JVC GY- HD100U. These cameras are relatively affordable, robust and compact (and therefore travel well), and are astonishingly good in picture quality, considering their price and size. What's remarkable about these cameras is that they are capable of shooting in a Hi-Definition format, something that, until recently, would have cost a fortune. These cameras cost around £3,000/US$6,000 and can record onto MiniDV tapes. They also have the added benefit of being able to shoot in true 16:9 aspect ratio (see below), and DVCam mode too. They are easy to use, reliable and sturdy, and have a great combination of automatic and manual features, so they are easy for the beginner to use and flexible enough for the consummate cinematographer.

Figure 8. Z1 camera

ASPECT RATIO

The aspect ratio refers to the relationship of the width of the screen to the height, and is usually referred to as a ratio, for example 4:3 or 16:9. Older television screens used the original standard, the 4:3 aspect ratio, whilst later televisions use 'widescreen' or the 16:9 aspect ratio, which is more similar to a screen you will see in a movie theatre. Since all new televisions are 'widescreen' most broadcasters now want the film to be delivered in the 16:9 format, and this has important implications for the kind of camera you buy or use. The older cameras, like for example the Sony PD150, only shoot natively in 4:3, which means the computer chip that the light hits (the CCD – see next Chapter) is 4:3 in shape. This is a problem, because it means that your film is natively 4:3 rather than the preferred 16:9. These older cameras have a function within the menu, which changes it into 16:9, but you must *never ever* use this function, as it digitally changes the image leading to a loss in picture quality. It's much more preferable to use a camera that films in native 16:9. Older cameras, like the Sony PD170, do not shoot in 16:9, but most new cameras do shoot natively in 16:9.

LENSES AND FILTERS

It's always helpful to have some extra lenses and filters with your camera. If you're only going to invest a tiny amount, then make sure you get a Wide Angle lens for the camera. For some cameras, especially the 'prosumer' (somewhere between a consumer and a professional camera) cameras like the HDR-Z1E, you cannot change the lens, so instead you need to get a wide-angle adaptor. A wide angle allows you to have more of the scene in the shot, and if you are shooting with a handheld camera, it means the shot will look much steadier too.

In terms of filters, a Neutral Density filter (ND) is invaluable. In the event that your image is too bright, or over-saturated, an ND filter can reduce the amount of light that can pass through the lens. Many cameras, especially at the higher end, come with built-in ND filters, which are often more than adequate. An ND filter aids your creativity too, and allows you to be much more flexible in specific circumstances.

THE SOUND EQUIPMENT

Sound is probably the most overlooked aspect of documentary filmmaking, and yet can be one of the most important, as it contributes to at least half of your film and, if it's done badly, then your film can be ruined. Many cameras (especially the low-end consumer and 'prosumer' models) come with either built-in microphones or a standard microphone. These mics are poor quality and should be avoided at all costs. This means that you need to invest in an arsenal of microphones and peripherals, which can cost you anywhere from £300 to around £3,000. We'll discuss the various models available later in this chapter.

Balanced vs. unbalanced audio

The cheaper cameras also don't have balanced audio, meaning that they use a 3.5mm stereo jack input, like the type found on an MP3 player. Using these inputs is problematic for two reasons: they fall out and get disconnected easily and they are also much more prone to 'noise' from electrical interference. Far more preferable is using a camera that has balanced audio, which has sturdier three-pin XLR sockets and is much more robust in general, with virtually no 'noise' at all.

Bidirectional, omnidirectional and unidirectional microphones

If you are really interested in the technical aspects of this, then you can read numerous books (which are referenced Section Five). What you really need to know at this point is the three basic patterns in which microphones pick up sound: bidirectional, omnidirectional and unidirectional. Bidirectional mics are not often used in documentary filmmaking; they are really only used in formal studio set ups. Omnidirectional mics, as the name suggests, pick up sound evenly from all directions. It's good to pick up general sound within a given location. For example, if you wanted to record the general 'chatter' in a bar, then you might choose this microphone, or if, for some reason, the microphone had to stay in the same place, whilst the action (and sound source) was moving around. The third type of mic, unidirectional, is the most common to documentary filmmaking. They pick up sound only from the end of the microphone. They vary in how 'targeted' they are to a specific sound source, with the supercardioid microphone (or shotgun mic, as it's usually known) being the most highly directional. It will specifically pick up one of your subjects, for example, whilst rejecting sound from other directions. If you are only ever going to buy one microphone then get a good shotgun one. Also, make sure you buy a decent 'fluffy' or windbreaker, which will help get rid of any handling sound or wind noise.

Headphones

This is perhaps obvious, but I cannot over-emphasise the importance of having a good set of headphones. By wearing them, you will be acutely aware of what the microphone 'hears', rather than what you hear. Noises that you have managed to tune out in your mind can become exceptionally noisy when you really listen to what the microphone is picking up.

Battery Power vs. Phantom Power

Some microphones run off batteries (usually AA ones), but others do not come with their own power supply and rely on being powered either by the camera or by an external power module. These are called phantom-powered mics, and you need to make sure that your camera can generate phantom power (most good ones can), otherwise you might find you are lugging around bulky battery packs and it will become quite irritating after a while. The good shotgun mics, like the Sennheiser 416, can be phantom powered from a camera.

Lapel or Lavalier microphones

These are the very small microphones that are usually attached to a person, usually around their chest area. They are commonly called 'radio mics' although this is, in fact, a mistake as any microphone can be attached to a radio transmitter and become cordless. However, lapel mics are usually used wirelessly and therefore are more commonly associated with the term. The microphone itself is attached to a transmitter, which the subject would usually carry in their back pocket. The receiver is usually attached to the camera and can pick up a clear signal from your subject, even if they are some metres away. Lapel mics allow you to follow a subject that is moving around, and will allow you to put some distance between your crew and your subject – for example if you are filming him walk off with someone else, or if you want a wide shot of the action, but don't want a boom or mic to be in frame.

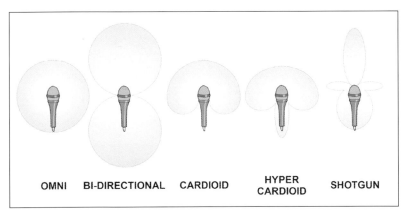

| OMNI | BI-DIRECTIONAL | CARDIOID | HYPER CARDIOID | SHOTGUN |

Figure 9. The basic pick-up patterns of microphones

TRIPODS AND OTHER CAMERA SUPPORT SYSTEMS

Also known as 'sticks' (for obvious reasons), tripods are essential for those smooth pans and tilts and for fixed shots, although there are some styles of documentary (especially observational documentaries) which often rely on handheld camera alone. Again, as with microphones, it's a bad idea to skimp on costs here: cheap tripods mean a cheap-looking film. A good tripod can set you back anywhere between £250 and £1,000, and are made by companies such as Vinten, Manfrotto and Miller. The important components of a good tripod are:

1. A sturdy frame, with adjustable legs. Don't go for lightness here; you want something that is quite heavy so that it is going to put up with the abuse it's going to get over the years.

2. A spirit level, which helps you to make sure that your camera is properly horizontal and/or vertical.

3. A fluid head. Many tripods have different mechanisms to ensure that the pans and tilts are smooth. However, you will only be guaranteed good results if you buy one with a fluid head, which has separate pan and tilt frictions.

4. A quick-release hot shoe. This allows you to get the camera on and off the head quickly.

Over the years, various other systems for mounting your camera have been designed. Many of you have probably heard of a *Steadicam*, which refers to a camera stabilisation device that isolates the movement of the camera from that of the cameraperson, providing a very smooth shot even when the operator is moving quickly over an uneven surface. Steadicams are very expensive pieces of equipment (even to hire) and are most often used in fiction films. Many documentary budgets wouldn't be able to afford it, especially those made by independent filmmakers. There are cheaper alternatives to the Steadicam, such as the DV Rig Pro (see www.dvtec.tv), which offers the same kind of camera support, although it's far inferior to the Steadicam. Some filmmakers swear by such systems, whilst others prefer to do decent handheld shooting. The choice is up to you – it's a good idea to try to borrow one from a friend, or ask if a shop can lend you one for a day, and see how it feels.

There are other camera support systems, such as a 'dolly', which looks like a little car and runs on tracks (like a train) so that you can have really smooth tracking shots. Again, it can be an expensive piece of equipment, and many independent filmmakers improvise by using, for example, a wheelchair, which can still give smooth tracking shots with a cameraperson and camera sitting on it.

LIGHTS

Sometimes you need to have lights for your shoots, although a lot of the time documentary filmmakers try to make the best use of natural available light, especially if they are filming in multiple locations, with a small crew, or doing observational sequences in which people are moving around within a given space. Lights are quite heavy and unless you are doing lots of filming which requires them, I find it is always best to hire rather than buy, because I rarely use them, and the costs and maintenance will be too prohibitive. In addition, some hire companies will deliver the lights to your shooting location, which saves you having to lug heavy lights around with you.

How to use lights is discussed in Chapter 10. For now, it's important to just get a sense of what lights you need to consider for your shoot. Many different types of lights are used in filmmaking, and the main difference between them is their wattage. The lights in your house are between 40W and 100W. Lights for filming start at around 800W and can go up to 18,000W. The most common lights that a documentary filmmaker will use are called 'Redheads' which range from 650W to 1,000W (although they are usually 800W). Redheads are usually used in an interview set up, and tend to come in packs of three. They allow for a basic lighting set up, although won't allow you to create the advanced lighting set ups that you might need for dramatised sequences in your film. 'Blondes' are basically bigger versions of Redheads and range from 1,000W to 2,000W. They are more powerful lights and are used for lighting large areas.

Regardless of whether you are using natural light or a set of redheads, you need to have a reflector with you, as it's a cheap and invaluable way to control light. The best ones to use are the portable, fold-up type, which are white on one side, and silver on the other. You can use it to reflect light back on to the subject and control the places where light – either natural or artificial – falls.

CABLES AND BATTERIES

No filmmaker should travel without a bag of cables and extra batteries. Extra XLR cables (for microphones) are very important, as they sometimes can become damaged and that means you cannot record sound properly. You should also carry extra batteries around for your camera, microphone (if needed), radio transmitters and any other equipment that requires them. Nothing is more frustrating than being on a shoot, having all the right equipment, but suddenly running out of charged batteries.

THREE POSSIBLE KITS FOR THE INDEPENDENT FILMMAKER

The list below gives three possible combinations for buying or renting kit. It assumes that you are multi-skilling (i.e. directing, doing camera and sound), or working in small crews of two or three people. It's by no means an exhaustive list, but helps to give you a sense of what you need and what you can afford. If you are using a sound recordist, they will often bring their own kit (including SQN mixer, boom pole etc) so some of this equipment has not been included here. Remember – many parts of a kit can be hired if you're not going to be using them a lot. At the very minimum, try to buy yourself a camera and a decent microphone and set of headphones. It's often easier to justify hiring rather than buying the more expensive cameras.

The Basic Kit
Approximate Price (inclusive of VAT/SALES TAX) £4,000

	Kit	Comments	Price
Camera	Sony HDR-Z1E	A good, sturdy all-round camera, allowing you to film in DVCam and HDV mode. 1080i picture.	£3,000 + VAT
			$3,000 - $5,000
Batteries	Extra Long-Life Batteries X 2	Really important to have extra batteries. Each one will give around five hours of life.	£99 each
			$300 each
Microphone	Sennheiser ME 66 + K6 Shotgun Microphone	Good, all-round mic.	£400
			$480
Headphones	Sennheiser HD 201	These are good entry-level headphones.	£15
			$29.95

Accessories	Rycote Softie Mount & Handle (Medium Hole)	Fluffy and pistol grip to fit ME66.	£77
			$229
	Camera bag	Portabrace Camera Case.	£180
			$300
	XLR Cables - short		£6
			$13
	MN755 MDeVe	An entry-level Manfrotto tripod. Made entirely from aluminium which makes it versatile and cuts down on weight.	£148
			$278
	Raincover	Kata CRC-13 rain cover.	£72
			$55

All Round Kit
Approximate Price (inclusive of VAT/SALES TAX) £7,000

	Kit	Comments	Price
Camera	JVC Camera GY HD100 (HD101 in Europe)	A great camera, that allows HDV and DV filming, using 720p. The big selling point here is a detachable lens, meaning that you can buy or hire excellent additional lenses.	£3,500 - £4,000
			$4,500
Batteries	53 WHr batteries for JVC GY- HD101 X 2	Fits to camera and replaces supplied BN-V428U batteries.	£116 each
			$330 each
Lenses	WCV-82SC Wide Angle Converter	Offers 18% wider angle of view and no loss of light in picture occurs.	£375
			$769
	Hoya 82mm Circular Polariser Glass Filter	Removes unwanted glare when shooting surfaces like glass and water and improves the picture's colour saturation.	£65
			$116
Microphone	Sennheiser 416 Shotgun mic	A much better all-round shotgun microphone.	£800
			$1,450
Radio Mics	Sennheiser Radio mics EW112PG2	Important for interviews and observational documentaries. Good entry-level radio mics, but fine for broadcast.	£350
			$835
Headphones	Sennheiser EH2200	Good, durable headphones.	£51
			$140

Lights	Lowel GO Intro Kit		£940
			$1,115
Accessories	Rycote Softie and Softie Mount & Handle Kit (Small Hole)	Fluffy and pistol grip to fit 416.	£149
			$229
	Petrol PCUB-HD Camera U-bag HD	Made especially for the JVC GY-HD100/HD101.	£175
			$220
	XLR Cables - short		£6
			$13
	MN755MF3 MDeVe	Similar to the entry-level Manfrotto tripod but with larger leg diameter and greater weight capacity.	£290
			$479
	Reflector		£10 - £70
			$16 - $90
	Raincover	Kata CRC-14 rain cover.	£86
			$60 - $80

The Platinum Kit

Approximate Price (inclusive of VAT/SALES TAX) £25,000

	Kit	Comments	Price
Camera	Panasonic AG-HPX500 P2	Shoots in 32 high definition and standard formats, including 1080i and 720p. Latest in tapeless recording systems, records onto removable P2 memory cards.Interchangeable lenses, variable frame rates. 2/3" 30 CCDs.	£9,995 + VAT
			$14,000 - $20,000
Batteries	Anton Bauer dionic batteries X 2	Industry standard for high-end HD cameras. Lasts over six hours.	£210 each
			$417 each
Lenses	Canon KH10ex3.6 IRSE super wide angle HD zoom lens	Boasts the widest angle view possible for portable HD cameras. Lens designed specifically for emerging HD camera technologies.	£12,000
			$19,000
	Tiffen 4X4 Ultra Circular Polariser with white HD glass	Achieves the same effect as the Hoya polariser but with higher-quality glass.	£100
			$230
Microphone	Sennheiser 416		£800
			$1,450

Radio Mics	Sony UWP C167HR		£600
			$1,100
Headphones	Sennheiser HD 25, 70 Ohm	Top-of-the-line headphones used by audio-industry professionals.	£150
			$260
Lights	Dedolight KDS31S Standard Kit	High-end kit includes universal dbl Aspheric lens, barndoors, dim transformer, halogen lamps and soft case.	£2,100
			$4,000 (US equivalent standard Dedo kit)
Accessories	Rycote Full Windshield 4 Kit		£320
			$629
	Petrol PCUB-3	Made for cameras of substantial size and weight.	£220
			$275
	XLR Cables - short		£6
			$13
	MN351MVCF	The premium in Manfrotto tripods. Can carry weight of large HD cameras. An excellent tripod head and lightweight materials allow for easy manoeuvring.	£450
			$765
	Reflector		£10 - £70
			$16 - $90
	Peli 1510 Travel Case	Important hard-cover case for use when travelling with camera. This particular case is waterproof.	£120
			$140
	Raincover	SHAN-RC700 (Compatible with camera).	£90 - 150
			$250

9. THE BEGINNER'S GUIDE TO CINEMATOGRAPHY: PART TWO – THE CAMERA

Now that you understand a little about the tools you are using, it's time to understand how to actually use them. In this chapter, we'll deal principally with the camera, and in the next we'll talk about sound and lighting. As always, theory can only take you so far, and you need to go out and practise as much as possible. If you cannot afford the various bits of equipment, try to borrow from friends and colleagues – even if it's only for a day or so. It's through the various mistakes you make, and re-reading this section of the book, that you will eventually, over time, become much more fluent and competent in the art of cinematography.

As mentioned in the last chapter, most professional or semi-professional (often known as 'prosumer') cameras share the same fundamental features and shooting principles, which are discussed below. For the purposes of this book, we will look at the Sony HDV-Z1 camera, as this has become one of the most common cameras for independent documentary filmmakers. Its relative affordability – around £3,000 – robustness, small size and ability to film in either DV or HDV, has made it the camera of choice for low-budget documentaries, by both broadcasters and filmmakers alike.

THE MAIN FEATURES OF THE CAMERA
– WHAT YOU REALLY NEED TO KNOW

The first thing to say is this: don't become overwhelmed by all the buttons and dials on your camera. It can really seem that there is too much to get your head around, and although all these buttons are designed to make your job easier, it might not seem that way at first. If you are just learning to use a camera, then all you really need to understand are the principal functions described below.

The Principal Functions of Shooting

Focus

Focus can be defined as the point at which an object must be situated with respect to the lens in order for an image of it to be well-defined. So, images which appear clear and sharp are said to be 'in focus', whereas images which appear blurred or distorted are said to be 'out of focus'. Most of the time, as a filmmaker, you want images to be in focus, although there will be times that you will want to experiment with this in order to create a particular effect or atmosphere. There are three ways in which you might want to focus your camera. The first is to do it manually, by using the focus ring on the lens. Turning this round will bring the picture in and out of focus, and will yield better results than using auto-focus. Auto-focus, as the name suggests, is when you let the camera do the work for you. Although today's cameras are usually pretty good they can often make mistakes, particularly when you are either shooting an individual who is not centre-frame – the camera's auto-focus is likely to try and focus on something else – or you are moving the camera around (for instance, whilst shooting fly-on-the-wall with a handheld camera) as the camera will get confused as to what it should, or shouldn't, be focusing on. A third way is to use a function called 'Push Auto' which is a combination of both the above techniques. In this scenario, you are using manual focus, but when you change the frame of your shot, you can press the Push Auto button, which will automatically put the shot in focus and then return to manual mode. I use this when I am directing and filming at the same time using fly-on-the-wall filming with a handheld camera; with so much to think about it helps to be able to push a button to get the picture in focus. On the whole, I would recommend you use manual focus when you can, but it does take practice to get it right.

Exposure

Exposure controls the amount of light that is exposed to the camera. It's controlled using both the aperture and the shutter speed. An aperture – or iris – is an opening that allows light through the lens, which in turn strikes the film (or in the case of a digital camera, the computerised chip, known as the CCD). The greater the size of the opening, the more light comes into your camera, and you modify this by controlling the iris, in the same way that the iris in your eye enlarges or shrinks depending on the amount of light in the environment. The iris is often a dial or small 'wheel' on the camera. Just to confuse you slightly more, the variable size of the iris is measured as an 'f-stop' number, and confusingly the higher this number, the less light it is letting in. It takes time, and practice, to get the exposure right. In simple terms, you need to increase the exposure (a lower f stop) in dark or low light conditions and decrease it (a higher f-stop number) where there is ample light. Changing from one f number to the next – either opening or closing the aperture – doubles or halves the amount of light passing through.

A quick note here: there is no such thing as the correct exposure. Your personal preferences, style of film and environmental conditions will dictate what exposure you want. As with focus, many cameras (and the Z1 camera mentioned here) allow you to turn on 'auto-exposure'. Although I wouldn't recommend using this function whilst shooting, it can serve as a helpful reminder as to whether you are 'on track'. All you need to do is quickly look at the f-stop number that the camera has picked in 'auto' mode and then see if your manual estimate was close. If there is a substantial difference between your estimation and the camera's, then this might mean you're doing something wrong.

Shutter speed is the speed at which a mechanism within the camera opens and closes between frames. A fast shutter speed means that the shutter is opening and closing many times within, say, a second, meaning that you are letting in less light, whereas a slow shutter speed conversely means it's opening and closing less, and therefore letting in more light. Shutter speed is also altered when you are filming fast-moving objects (like, for example, people playing sport), where a fast shutter speed is needed to prevent the action becoming one big blur. Slow shutter speeds are used when you are filming a static object, probably on a tripod, where you need to allow maximum light into the camera.

Although the aperture and shutter speed settings are both used to modify the exposure, it's the aperture which you are going to play with more, especially if you are a beginner and want to keep things simple. The shutter speed will usually stay at a constant (1/50 for PAL, and 1/60 for NTSC – see below for an explanation of PAL and NTSC), unless there are specific circumstances which dictate altering it. This might include shooting fast-moving objects, but could also include things like filming computer monitors; these usually flicker at a different rate, and you might need to alter your shutter speed accordingly.

White Balance

White Balance is a way of getting your camera to see white objects as truly white, not as a tint of another colour. You are, in effect, telling the camera *what is white*. In our day-to-day experiences we see things as white that are not necessarily so, as 'white' can change depending on the environment we are in. Our brain makes the necessary adjustments for us. For example, we see snow as white, or a sheet of paper as white. Cameras don't have this ability, so we have to tell it what white is – if we don't, then it can get confused, and you will get a tapestry of strange colours in your film, where people's faces look blue, and an outside shot lit by street lights may accidentally make everything look pink if the white balance has not been set properly.

Cameras such as the Z1 do have an automatic white balance setting, and for the most part they are fairly reliable. However, if you are mixing two sources of light – for example artificial light (known as Tungsten) with normal daylight (natural light) – then the camera can get confused, and it's best to set it manually. In fact, as a rule, I would say set the white balance manually whenever you change location. To do a manual white balance, put a white piece of paper in front of your lens so that it fills the frame and hold the white balance button down until the symbol (usually two triangles) stops flashing.

Focus, Exposure and White Balance are the main aspects of camera functioning that you need to bear in mind, each time you start the camera recording. A good exercise is to go out and practise filming in different situations and locations, and experiment with these functions, seeing how fluent you can become.

OTHER IMPORTANT ASPECTS OF THE CAMERA

If you want to delve a little bit further into cinematography, then it is helpful that you understand the following concepts.

Gain

There are some situations, especially when you are filming in the dark, without any available light, where your camera is not receiving enough light for a picture to be clear, even when the lens is fully open. The gain function is a digital method for amplifying the signal, making your picture look brighter. The only problem here is that there is a trade off in quality; by artificially boosting the signal, your camera also amplifies unwanted video noise too, leaving an image that can look really grainy – an undesired effect most of the time. Resist using the function, unless the shoot really demands it and there is no way to have extra lighting. If a scene is mildly under-lit, it's best to film it without gain, and try to correct this in post-production (see Chapter 17).

Zebras

Zebras refer here not to a striped animal, but to a mechanism built into your camera which lets you know quickly what areas within your frame are exposed or over-exposed. Most cameras have this function and, when turned on, it superimposes a number of striped white lines (hence the name) onto your LCD or viewer on the over-exposed areas. This, in effect, is a quick way of seeing which areas within your image are over-exposed, allowing you to quickly change the exposure and correct the problem.

Time code

Often overlooked, time code is the way in which the camera measures the passage of time on your tape, in the same way that you have a counter on your DVD player (or cassette recorders for those old enough to remember them). The only difference between the two is that your DVD player will work in real time (hours, minutes and seconds), whereas time code on a video camera works a little bit differently.

Often you will have shot your film on numerous tapes (let's say you have shot 20 x one-hour tapes for a half-hour film. When you begin to put your tapes (or rushes as they are often called) into the computer for editing, it's really helpful if the editing software can distinguish one tape from another. Therefore, time code is really important for being able to identify where your specific images are on your tape, but it is also invaluable for the edit.

Now the way in which your camera records, or lays down, the time code will differ depending on what kind of camera and what standard (e.g. PAL or NTSC – see below) you are recording on. It's important to know which standard you are using, as this will dictate how you read time code, when it comes to editing your film.

PAL, NTSC AND SECAM

This is another important, and often overlooked, element of cinematography. Different countries have a different way of recording footage in terms of the 'Frame Rate' or the number of frames per second. They also differ in terms of Colour Signal, Field Frequence and the Horizontal (Scan) Lines they use. This is known as 'Broadcasting Standards' and refers to the ways in which different countries choose to broadcast (and, by inference, record) video footage.

Each country in the world uses a different broadcasting standard, and, just to make matters really easy, none of them is compatible with any other! So, something recorded on PAL format in the UK is, in theory, incompatible with the NTSC format in the USA. Many cameras will only record in one format or the other. So, if you are recording on a PAL camera, then it will not work when you try to edit and play it back on an NTSC monitor or television. Although you can theoretically convert a finished film from one standard to another, you can't really ever convert the actual way in which it was recorded, and therefore it's a good idea to choose one format for your camera, deck and so on.

The USA, Canada, Mexico and Japan all use NTSC, which stands for the National Television Standards Committee. Sometimes this has been called 'Never The Same Colour' due to its problems maintaining colour consistency. Most of Europe, Australia and Asia use PAL, which stands for Phase Alternating Line. There are various technical differences between the two, but, for your purposes, you need to know that NTSC records and plays back at 30 frames per second (fps) – actually it's 29.97 fps, but it approximates to 30fps – whereas PAL records and plays back at 25 frames per second. There's a third system, SECAM, but, since this records at 25 fps, it's easily converted from PAL.

INTERLACED VS. PROGRESSIVE, AND 24P. WHAT DOES IT ALL MEAN?

Don't worry, we've nearly reached the end of the overly technical stuff. One more concept that is helpful to understand, and may influence which camera you choose to buy/rent, is that of interlaced or progressive video. Interlaced refers to a method of scanning, in which each frame of the picture (of which you'll now know there are 25 frames per second in PAL and 30 frames per second in NTSC) is made up of lots of horizontal lines, and the picture is achieved by all the even-numbered lines being scanned onto your screen first followed by all the odd-numbered lines. This scanning happens very, very quickly and makes up a complete picture. Progressive scanning, by comparison, doesn't scan all the even lines first followed by the odd lines; rather the entire frame is scanned all in one go, from top to bottom.

What this really means is that there is a different look to the two methods, and each has its own strengths and weaknesses. On the whole, progressive scanning allegedly looks a little bit more like film than video and can handle motion better, but there is sometimes the risk of a 'flicker' in your image. Interlaced has a slightly higher resolution, having more horizontal pixels per line. Until recently, most prosumer cameras used interlaced scanning only, but there are more and more 'progressive' cameras on the market, and even some that allow you to switch between the two. The best thing to do is play with both systems, and see which one you prefer. You might also want to think about where your film is ending up (i.e. on television or in the cinema) as this might dictate which format you, and your broadcaster or distributor, want you to film on.

Now, if all this seems a little overwhelming then don't panic, and don't give up. It takes a while to get used to all these technical terms and differing formats, and even simply shooting a picture can seem, at first, overly complicated. Use this section as a reference guide; keep coming back to it, and it will slowly make more and more sense. What's important is to understand the main principles – rather than just pointing and shooting, you need to understand the basic principles of cinematography. As I mentioned above, if you learn nothing else at this point, make sure you understand the concepts of EXPOSURE, FOCUS and WHITE BALANCE. If that's all you take away with you after reading this it's enough to shoot with. Now all you need to do is understand the grammar of screencraft, and the language of the shoot. This is all detailed in Chapter 11, and then you are truly, once and for all, well on your way to being able to shoot a film that won't be riddled with mistakes, and won't make you want to smash your camera up when you come to the edit. Remember: all the great camerapersons, and camera/directors started knowing nothing.

10. THE BEGINNER'S GUIDE TO CINEMATOGRAPHY: PART THREE – LIGHTING AND SOUND

When filming, so much energy is expended on how to operate the camera and how to conduct the interview, amongst the scores of other things you have to remember, that it's easy to forget to light your shots properly, and get good recorded sound. These are important concepts in cinematography for different reasons. Lighting a shot well will not only ensure that your rushes aren't underlit and ruined, it can also add mood, and hence depth, to your finished film. Sound, as I have mentioned before, is one of those elements of filmmaking that you only really notice if it's bad. And, if you do have bad recorded sound, then, despite great shot composition and a great story, your film is ruined. Period. This chapter therefore looks at a variety of techniques to make sure you get good lighting and sound, ranging from a simple set up using natural light and a shotgun microphone attached to your camera, to more complicated set ups, using three-point lighting and a variety of microphones and using a sound recordist.

LIGHTING

As mentioned before, a lot of documentary films are made using only natural available light, rather than bringing in lights. It's good practice to be able to use natural light effectively (and by natural light I mean sunlight); it helps cut down on the amount you have to think about, and most importantly it keeps costs down. Often, especially if you are filming overseas, you really don't want to be lugging lights around with you.

Using Natural Light

- If filming an interview inside, it's important that you don't sit your interviewee in front of a bright window, unless of course you really want him or her to be a silhouette.
- Don't sit your interviewee too close to a wall, as this could create too much shadow. Make sure you keep them at least one metre from the background.
- If filming outside, pay close attention to how exposed your shot is. Natural sunlight is very powerful and there's always the danger your shots will be over-exposed. Make sure you use a neutral density filter here (remember, good cameras come with good built-in ND filters).
- Also remember that the sun moves, and that if you are doing a lengthy fixed shot outside, the sun will change the lighting situation, creating continuity problems in the edit. Make sure you either shoot very wide shots, or compensate using reflectors and changes to exposure settings when doing close shots.

Using Artificial Light

As discussed in the last chapter, there are situations which may warrant the use of artificial light – either because there is not adequate sunlight or you are shooting a scene in which you want to create a specific mood – such as a lit interview, a candlelit dinner, or an evening scene. Many of the cameras used by independent filmmakers, such as the Sony Z1, perform poorly in low light. Be careful not to rely on the gain function here on your camera; when you get to the edit you'll see that your footage might look really grainy, too much so for a broadcaster.

Artificial light can refer to the lighting available in someone's house – the tungsten light on the ceiling, or a table lamp. Often, though, this won't be enough to light your scene – especially if there is no natural light available. For the rest of this section, when we talk about artificial light, we are going to be discussing dedicated lights for filmmaking.

The Physics of Lighting

A brief digression here on the main functions of light will help you understand some important concepts.

There is no such thing as white light. All visible light is made up of tiny particles called photons, and each of these photons has different wavelengths depending on their colour. There are all the colours of the spectrum from the sun's light, but when all the colours are combined together, this is what gives the illusion of 'white' light. Blue light is comprised of photons with shorter wavelengths whereas red light is comprised of photons with longer wavelengths. So, when you see a blue sky, it's because the photons with shorter wavelengths (i.e. blue ones) are more easily scattered by the various gasses and particles in the earth's atmosphere. Another important characteristic of light is that, when it hits a surface, it either bounces or is absorbed by that surface – all this depends on what colour the surface is. So, a white object will reflect all the wavelengths of light equally, whereas a black object will absorb them all. Colours in between will reflect some wavelengths and absorb others.

'So what does this have to do with lighting my shot?' you may well ask. Well, first of all, since light is made of different colours, you should realise that using different sources of light in the same shot can be problematic, as they all emit different colours. Therefore, a redhead, table lamp and natural daylight when all combined together can make your subject look more like a Martian than a human: even if you don't notice this (your brain often corrects colour discrepancies without you being aware of this) your camera definitely will. Secondly, the fact that objects absorb and reflect light means that certain objects may bounce back specific, sometimes undesired, colour, onto your subject. This also has an impact on the clothes your subject wears and the objects in the room you are shooting. It also helps inform the use of reflectors and they can be a valuable aid in reflecting light onto your subject, or deflecting it away.

Three-Point Lighting

Three-point lighting is the basic way to light a shot, and a term you will hear quite a lot if your film needs the use of formal lighting set ups. As the name suggests, you use three lights (usually redheads, although they can be any high-wattage lights) of equal power. The first light is called the *key light* and, as the name suggests, is the main light, shining directly onto the subject. This light is the principal source of illumination and will dictate the overall hue and intensity of the lit shot. The second light is the *fill light*, which also shines on the subject but from the opposite angle to the *key light*. Its function is mainly to fill the shadows created by the *key*. It will often be softer than the key light – and one way to achieve this is to move it further away from the subject. The third light is the *back light*, which, as the name suggests, is placed behind the subject, lighting him or her from the rear. Its function is to provide definition to the subject, creating a clear outline which distinguishes him or her from surrounding objects. The brightness of the back light can be adjusted from the level of the fill light to that of the key light, depending on the reflectivity of your subject; a darker-skinned person will need more fill light than a Caucasian. The diagram on the opposite page illustrates a typical three-point lighting set up.

If you are doing your own lighting, then it's good to follow a few quick tips regarding caring for the equipment, which will help you to keep the bulbs lasting for longer, and keep you safe from electrical shocks, burns, and other accidents.

- Make sure that you don't touch the bulbs with your hands. Firstly, the bulbs might be hot if you have just used them, but also the oil from your skin can cause the bulb to discolour or even explode next time it is turned on. Always use some kind of clean cloth to handle bulbs.
- Following on from this, make sure lamps have completely cooled before handling them in any way. They are really hot, and can burn you really easily.
- If the bulbs are going to explode, the most common time for this to happen is when they are first turned on. Make sure no one is standing directly in front of them and avoid turning them on within direct eyeline of someone else – if they don't explode they can dazzle and potentially damage a person's eyes.
- Lighting stands and cables: lights often come attached to stands, and you need to make sure that both the stand and its surrounding cables

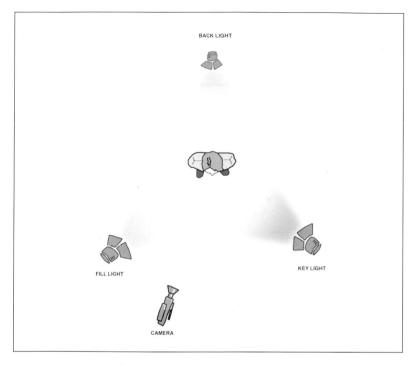

Figure 10. Basic three-point lighting set up

are securely attached to the floor. Weigh the stands down with weights or heavy objects, and make sure that all cables are firmly attached to the floor with gaffer tape.

SOUND

Broadly speaking, there are three ways to record sound when making a documentary film. You can record sound directly into the camera, doing it by yourself using either a shotgun microphone, radio mics or both. You can record sound into camera, going via an SQN mixer, which means you need a sound recordist with you. And you can record sound via a mixer straight into some other recording device, such as minidisc or a DAT recorder. We'll deal with each of these in turn, and then talk more specifically about some important considerations when recording sound.

Doing it All by Yourself

These days, there is an emphasis on the multi-skiller or self-shooter, i.e. a single director/cameraperson who can record their own sound and go it alone. Many budgets, especially for news features and overseas documentaries, are too small to justify bringing a crew with you. As such you need to be quite competent at doing it alone. The best set up for this, I find, is having a decent shotgun mic attached to your camera – something like the Sennheiser 416 shotgun is a great unidirectional microphone – and a set of radio tie mics. This prepares you for all types of filming, from filming a group of people interacting to a formally set up interview. The use of radio mics is invaluable if you are doing an observational documentary, which involves one principal character, as you can follow him or her around whilst still getting good sound. If you are using the shotgun mic by itself, then make sure you put the mic through both channels on your camera, so that you are getting stereo sound.

When doing everything by yourself, you need to be wearing a good set of headphones, and you also need to be keeping your eye on the audio meter on the LCD display. What you are watching out for here is 'peaking' – when the audio levels start to go into the red bit. This means that there is a danger that your sound source is distorting, and you need to lower your levels if this is happening. Conversely, if the audio levels are too low – as shown by the mic levels being too far left in the LCD display – you need to increase the signal slightly. On cameras such as the Sony Z1, this is made easy by the dials on the exterior of the camera. A useful tip here if using a shotgun mic going through both channels is to have the levels in channel one slightly lower and the levels in channel two slightly higher. This means that, should the audio suddenly peak (for example, from someone shouting), then the other channel will not have peaked. Also, if the audio source is suddenly very low, then your 'higher' channel will pick this up. Such a strategy will also prevent you having to continually change the audio levels, although it's not a substitute for keeping a vigilant eye on your LCD monitor.

With a Sound Recordist

If budgets permit, then I would always recommend trying to have a sound recordist with you. You've got enough to worry about, and a person dedicated to sound is nothing short of a blessing. As mentioned above, a sound recordist will put the sound source through an SQN mixer and then has the option of recording straight into the camera or going through an external recording device. I would suggest they just go into camera, unless you want the cleanest possible sound and are anxious about having a back up, in which case I would get them to record into both camera and a DAT recorder. Your sound recordist will usually come with an arsenal of equipment including cables, microphones and a mixer. The things to make sure of here is that he or she knows the camera that you are using in advance, so that they can know the right settings. There are some fundamental differences between recording into camera yourself, and going through a mixer. For example, the input settings would be changed from 'mic' input to 'line' input. You don't need to worry about the nuances of all this, but just make sure that your sound recordist does.

Recording 'Atmos' or Wild Track

Whenever you are in a different location, and recording sound, make sure that you get at least 30 seconds of 'wild track' or 'atmos'. This is simply the ambient sound in the location, without anyone talking. The resulting 'silence' is in fact a whole cluster of sounds, ranging from the hum of the fridge, to the sound of the wind outside. You need this sound, as, when it comes to the edit, you will find it extremely useful for filling some of the gaps in the sound between clips.

Sync Sound, Voiceover, Commentary and Pieces to Camera

When recording a sound source, you need to have a good idea of how it will be used in the edit and hence your final film. Sync sound refers to picture and sound matching each other. So, for example, if you are filming someone talking to you in a restaurant and you know you are going to be using both the image and sound together, then this is known as *sync sound*. However, there may be occasions where you want to use what someone says, but not necessarily have their image there too. For example, they might be describing the local historical sights, and you want to use a lot of cutaways here, or they might be discussing their childhood, and you want to use their audio as something to lay over photographs, Super 8 footage and videos of their childhood. This is known as voiceover, and you need to be careful here. If you are using our example of someone talking in a restaurant then there will be background noise. This is fine, if we get to see the *context* in which they are speaking (i.e. sync sound), but if we don't then it will sound strange if we are hearing voiceover with the noise of a restaurant in the background. Put simply, if you are going to use voiceover then it's a really good idea to get clean sound, which means you need to film somewhere quiet with as little ambient sound as possible.

Commentary refers to someone narrating audio, which helps establish certain information that could not be said succinctly and easily with just the material you have filmed. Often it sets up background information, which might help give a context to your film. Television is rife with commentary these days; sometimes it's used subtly and effectively, but often it comes across as patronising and is used too freely. So, notwithstanding the battles you may have with a commissioning editor, if you are going to record commentary, then it needs to be high-quality, clean audio, which usually means that you will do this in a proper audio suite, rather than on location.

Pieces to camera (or PTC as they are sometimes known) are usually reserved for news pieces, or presenter-led documentaries whereby the presenter or journalist (which could be yourself) will talk directly to camera. There's no special technique required here. As with most sync sound, just make sure you have minimum background noise, unless of course this is part of the film – for example, a presenter in the middle of a war zone.

Good lighting and good audio are essential skills in order to elevate the production value of your film and steer it away from the look of a bad home video. Practise as much as you can. You'll learn more from your mistakes than you ever will just reading a book. Hopefully, over time, a lot of the information here will become second nature, and when it does, it's one less thing to worry about, giving you time to focus on the actual story and narrative of your film – something which we will come to in the next few chapters.

11. THE BEGINNER'S GUIDE TO CINEMATOGRAPHY: PART FOUR – THE GRAMMAR OF DIRECTING

THE MOST IMPORTANT THINGS YOU WILL EVER LEARN ABOUT CAMERA AND SOUND

Both camerawork and sound recording are technical processes. Cameras do not see as we do, and microphones do not hear as we do. This may seem obvious, but it is the most common mistake that filmmakers make. They imagine that because they see an image in a certain way, by just pointing the camera at that object or scene it will capture the same image. What they are forgetting is that what we see, and the simultaneous emotions we feel, are often inextricably linked. The way we visualise and process images is linked with our own perceptual biases and our own subjectivities. In addition, the way we move our eyes, and the way we visualise is generally unique to animals, and particularly unique to humans. There are some similarities in the way a camera lens and a human eye process light, but the comparison really stops there. Only by understanding the principles of cinematography (even at the most elementary level) can you begin to understand how to get the images you want, and not the images you see.

Secondly, the same goes for sound. What we hear and don't hear is often selective. We have learnt to tune things out, and be very discerning in what we listen to. If we are engrossed in conversation with someone in a café, then we can focus on them and block out the sounds around us: the chatter, the coffee machine, the noises of knives and forks on plates. Even if we are in a quiet room with someone else, we can tune out the sound of the air-conditioning unit, the door that slammed down the corridor, or the aeroplane that flies past, miles above our head. Microphones aren't that intelligent. They pick up everything they hear and this can often have disastrous effects on our final film, unless recorded properly and sensitively. Bad sound can not only create countless problems when it comes to editing your film; it can also ruin it.

This chapter, therefore, looks at the grammar of filmmaking – how to understand the language of documentary, and how to use the various tools at your disposal to this end. This is often known as 'screen grammar' and, as with all languages, has its own rules and conventions so that you can communicate effectively. If we extend the metaphor to a written and spoken language for a second, first of all you need to learn the basic structure of a language. Over time, you'll increase your vocabulary, explore more complicated grammatical considerations, and be able to construct reasonably complex sentences and appreciate different styles of the written and spoken form, including classical use of the language, historical uses, and present-day colloquial uses. If you then decided to write a book in this new language you would understand the basic rules and conventions of storytelling, and, once you've understood these, you might feel you want to experiment slightly with structure and form. It's the same with documentary filmmaking. Only once you have understood the grammar and how concepts such as camera angles, frame sizes, composition, shot sequences, the use of the 'cutaway', continuity issues and crossing the line work, can you then really have the skills to tell a story. Then, and only then, should you have the confidence to experiment a little bit. This chapter examines some of the main elements of screen grammar, and Chapter 13 goes on to discuss how to use these techniques to tell an involved and rich story, examining different conventions that attempt to achieve this aim in different ways.

Shot size and framing

As we have already discussed, one of the biggest mistakes made by beginners is to point the camera at the unfolding action, and hope that by simply recording it, they have the material to make a great film. Even if you under-

Figure 11. The six basic shot sizes

stand the various functions of the camera as described in Chapter 9, you still need to know where to actually point the camera. The first thing to consider is how much of your subject you want to fill the screen. If, for example, you are filming an interview with someone who is talking about their experience of divorce, and they become visibly upset, you need to make a choice of whether you want to use a 'long shot', in which the subject might appear quite far away, or whether you want to zoom in on the action, and have a 'close-up shot'. If you experiment with this, you will probably come to realise that a close-up shot of someone who is disclosing something emotional feels much more appropriate than filming them at a distance.

There's no secret formula for your choice of shot – often it's a logical decision to make. If we take the previous example, and imagine that there was no camera involved and you were just having a conversation with them, where would your eyes focus if they were becoming visibly upset? You would no doubt choose to focus quite closely on their face, maybe even focusing in on their eyes. Conversely, if you were talking to someone who was giving you a guided tour of a house they have recently designed, it would make sense for you to focus widely, so that you got to see both them, and the features of the house; if you focused in on their eyes or face, you would miss a lot of the context.

The same goes for screen grammar – the type of shot size you choose helps define emotional context. There are many different types of shot sizes, and it's a good idea to familiarise yourself with terminology here, as they will not only help you make a decision as to which shot to use, but it's also useful to have a common language when communicating with your crew, if for example you are working with a cameraperson.

There is another thing to consider in the composition of your shot, and this relates to the framing of the action in front of the lens. There is a concept

Figure 12.
The Rule of Thirds

known as 'The Rule of Thirds' (see figure 12) which comes from still photography (and other visual arts) and states that images are more aesthetically pleasing if the object you are filming is at one third distance from the edges of the frame.

As you can see from the diagram on the opposite page, The Rule of Thirds states that an image can be divided into nine equal parts by two equally-spaced horizontal lines and two equally-spaced vertical lines. The four points formed by the intersection of these lines can be used to align features in your shot. If you frame your subject around these intersection points it can be much more aesthetically pleasing, as opposed to framing your subject directly in the middle (something many amateur photographers and videographers tend to do). A real example of this can be seen in the framing below.

Figure 13.

The Rule of Thirds should also be used when filming landscapes, as the picture overleaf demonstrates. If the horizon were placed in the horizontal middle of the frame, it would not look as pleasing as when it is placed on the 'thirds' axis. Keep this rule in your head as much as possible and, after practice, it will become more or less automatic.

Figure 14.

There is one final thing to consider when determining the size and framing of your shot. Up to ten per cent of what you can see through the viewfinder, or in the LCD, may not appear in the final image that an audience sees on a television screen. This is due to numerous technical considerations concerning translating a video image onto our television screens, so it's important that you make sure that any important information (especially signs, phone

Figure 15.
Diagram illustrating
14:9 safe mode

numbers or other important written information, as well as people's faces, heads and hats) is not in the outer ten per cent of the LCD. This is known as filming in 'Caption Safe' mode, or '14:9 safe mode', as it's referred to when shooting in 16:9 aspect ratio.

Crossing the line

This is an error that is unique to filmmaking. It does take a while to get your head round it, but, once you do, it will save you from making big mistakes in your shooting which are difficult to rectify in the edit. It usually crops up when you are filming more than one person, and using handheld camera, following the action as it takes place.

Imagine you are filming two people – Jane is sitting on the left, and John on the right. You are standing in front of them. They are talking to each other and you are filming them with your camera, alternating your angle and shot size as the action dictates. If you were to move around to film them from the 'other side' – moving 180 degrees – then Jane will appear to be sitting on the right, and John on the left. When you are editing a sequence together, it will

Figure 16. Diagram illustrating Crossing the Line – also known as the 180 degree rule

suddenly appear confusing. Jane was, for one segment, sitting on the left, and suddenly appears to be sitting on the right. This is confusing for an audience, as perceptually it is difficult to reconcile this change in camera angle. This is known as 'crossing the line' and needs to be avoided[4].

Camera Angles

The camera angle itself can influence the story and add another dimension to your narrative. As with many elements of filmmaking, you only notice the camera angle if it goes against convention and somehow stands out (in the same way you don't notice the audio mixing, unless it's poor quality or mixed in a way to specifically stand out and make a point). On the whole, the angle of the camera will be on the same plane as the subject's eye level (known as a straight angle). If it isn't, then it could be looking down at the subject (known as a high angle), which can often have the effect of making the subject seem somehow vulnerable, small, or weak. The other effect, by looking up at the subject (known as a low angle), can have the opposite effect, making the subject seem somehow powerful or special. You can experiment with different angles when filming your subject, but be careful if you are going with a high or low angle, as, once you have made the choice, there is no going back.

Shooting in Sequences

Let's imagine for a second that you are filming someone change a tyre on their car. Sounds simple, doesn't it? You have thought of the framing, the shot size and you've got the various core skills of using camera, sound and lights. But now you need to think about how to shoot a sequence that allows the viewer to understand the process of someone changing a tyre. First of all, you need to think about an establishing shot, perhaps a wide shot of the car with a flat tyre. Then you might want a wide shot of the person who is about to do the changing of the tyre, perhaps cutting to a close up, so that we can see the frustration or despair on his face. Then you might want to have a close-up shot of the keys in the trunk of the car, followed by a mid shot of the man taking out the spare tyre. And so on. The point here is that you need to think about the various shots needed to tell the story, rather than just think you can film the action from one camera angle with one single shot size. You also need to think about the mood of the sequence. Is it humorous, onerous, or mundane? The shots you pick, and the way in which they will be edited together, will help create the mood and tone of the piece. Shooting in sequences therefore alludes to thinking carefully about the types of shots and the order in which they may appear.

Cutaways

Imagine you have filmed an interview in which a woman, Jennifer, is talking about her experience of post-traumatic stress, following a recent assault in a nearby park. The interview lasted an hour, but you have envisaged using about 15 minutes of the material. This means that, when you come to edit, you may have cut bits together, perhaps in a different order than they were recorded, or you have cut two clips together because you wanted to omit some coughing or irrelevant information between the two sentences. In this situation, you need to fill the cut with some other image, otherwise it's going to look really strange. This other image that you cut into the sequence is known as a cutaway, as one is, in effect, cutting away from the main action. It's also known by the name of 'B Roll' or 'GV' (General View)[5]. You may have seen it, in its crudest form, in news pieces when you suddenly see a shot of the interviewee's hands, or an extreme close up on the eyes. This is usually done in order to cover up two clips that have been cut together. And it really does look pretty awful and unimaginative.

In documentaries, we like to think we are a bit more thoughtful about cutaways. Although they can be used to cover two clips that have been edited together, they can also be used generally to add meaning and depth to the narrative. Rather than see an interviewee talk solidly, uninterrupted for five minutes, it's often helpful to have visual sequences that help add another layer to the film, and take the attention away from just 'talking heads'. In the above example, you may want a dramatised re-enactment of the assault that took place, which would help build tension. Alternatively, you may want cutaways to what Jennifer is doing now with her life: has she become scared to leave the house, or is she resolved to still walk in the park where the assault happened? You may want to use more abstract images to convey Jennifer's internal mental state, or to invoke the assault without being gratuitous or sensationalist. Such images can add an incredible amount of meaning and depth to your film, and can often be far more effective than a person talking on screen. It also means that, when you finally cut back to the interview of Jennifer, it is much more powerful to see her face again, and you listen more acutely to what she is saying.

It takes time to get used to thinking in this uniquely visual way, and it comes easier to some than others. Often, when talking to novice documentary filmmakers, they think that filming action itself, as it is happening, is enough to make a film. And although the observational style of filming can work, it's not always appropriate to the subject you are filming, or, more importantly, to the funder you are filming for. Television these days does not like long interviews, or long cuts; it likes action that continually changes, engages and involves. There have been many films which have used cutaways of visual images over interviews in a brilliant way. Jerome Berkvens' *A Skin Too Few: The Days of Nick Drake* is a visually stunning documentary, which is made up of about ten interviews with friends and family of the late musician Nick Drake. The film uses nature – and more specifically the change in seasons – as a metaphor for Drake's declining mental health. So many of the cutaways involve shots of nature, of English landscapes, snow on windows, and wide shots of village countryside. The way these shots are composed and the way in which they are interspersed throughout the interviews adds much depth and exposition, creating a rich and involving film. In addition, the clever and novel treatment of still photographs also helps add more meaning to the interviews that we hear. Another film, *The Corporation*, by Mark Achbar, Jennifer Abbott and Joel Bakan, is a feature-length documentary that looks at the role of the multi-national corporation and the inherent psychopathy and anti-social nature of such organisations. The film itself contains around 40 interviews with CEOs, social commentators and critics, and makes heavy use of archive – often humorous and at first incongruent – during the interviews, which helps add another layer of meaning to the film (see 'The Layers of Storytelling' diagram.)

Shooting for the Edit

Documentaries are about visual storytelling, and you must never forget to think in visual terms; which shots to choose, what to fill the action with, and how visual sequences will help tell the story in the way that you want. This means that you need, at all times during the filming process, to be able to answer the question: 'What is my film about?' Each shot you make, each question you ask your subject, and where you do and don't point the camera will be informed by the answer to this question. You also need to 'shoot for the edit' which, at its simplest, means that you need to make sure that you shoot in sequences as discussed above, making sure that you have shot from different angles, and with different shot sizes. You also need to have shot enough material to be used when it comes to editing. A fatal but common flaw with many novice filmmakers is to overshoot lots and lots of footage, but actually chronically undershoot *meaningful* footage. For example, you may shoot hours of interviews – far more than you in fact need – but fail to shoot enough cutaways or 'B roll' footage. I cannot begin to tell you how many times I have seen filmmakers come into an edit, confident with the hours of rushes that 'there must be a film here – I've shot 50 hours' worth', only to find that there isn't the necessary visual material to actually tell the story.

As a rule you don't want to be shooting more than a 20:1 ratio. This means for every twenty minutes you have filmed, one minute will end up in the edit. Perhaps you might go further, with a 40:1, ratio if you are doing a long-format observational film, but any more than this and you are getting yourself in trouble. When it comes to editing, you will be truly overwhelmed with the sheer amount of useless material that you have to wade through. Your shooting ratio will decrease as your skills increase, as you learn to be more discerning with what you do and don't shoot.

Another common mistake is in not holding a shot for long enough. This is particularly noteworthy when it comes to cutaways. A director may film the passing of traffic, or a tree or a sunset, for only a few seconds. When they arrive in the edit they realise the material is too short and can't quite fill the spaces. As a general rule, try to film each cutaway shot for *at least* ten seconds, preferably more. And rather than counting in your head (unless you make absolutely sure you count 'one, elephant, two, elephant...') look at the time code on the LCD monitor, so you don't underestimate how long you have been filming. When filming static shots, it will always seem longer than it actually is, so make sure you over-compensate – see Editor's Pet Hates, below:

AN EDITOR'S PET HATES – BY RUSSELL CROCKETT

- Hold your shots! A difficult one this, as the editor will often end up wanting to use your carefully planned shot completely differently to the way you intended. Because you only held it for five seconds, your life will now be made a misery, as the editor has to use the hated slo-mo to make it last 15 seconds.
- Editors of a certain age can often be found huddled in pubs bemoaning the way location sound has been relegated to an afterthought. So, whether shooting with a crew or self-shooting, there is *no* excuse not to shoot 30 seconds of clean atmos during or after interviews/key scenes. Also, always listen as well as look (try closing your eyes) and record any wild tracks, even ones that would appear not to have any use. A good editor will revel in lifting your film into another dimension with a rich, interesting soundtrack.
- Think hard before using in-camera FX – shutter speeds, filters etc. If you do and they work, great. If they don't, you're well and truly stuck. The FX available in the edit/grade are now amazingly sophisticated and you can play to your heart's content.
- Another sound tip: if shooting GVs etc and there is good, usable atmos, don't make it unusable by chatting about the football/boyfriend/how little you're being paid etc.
- All editors like more material rather than less – but within reason. If you turn up at the edit with 300 DV tapes for a 30-minute film you can be sure the enthusiasm level will drop dramatically.
- Music: Although you can now download five million tracks of every possible genre direct into the edit, if you're filming somewhere exotic do and try to record any natural music or get hold of local CDs, cas-

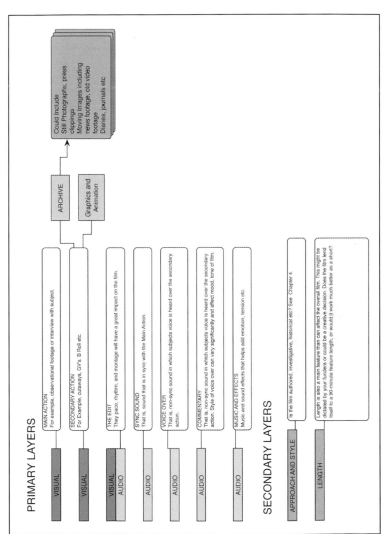

Figure 17. Layers of storytelling

settes etc. (Remember that your production manager will also want any information that will make their life easier in trying to clear it for use.)

- Pans and zooms go in and out of documentary fashion but if (after twelve takes) you are still determined to get that beautiful 30-second pan across a city skyline, bear in mind: that's a 20th of the running time of a ten-minute film. You may find it never makes the final cut.
- Make sure you know what the deliverable format is. Don't wait until the edit to discover you need to crop your beautifully framed pictures.
- Most of all, try to remember to think from an audience's perspective. How would we, as an audience, interpret a particular shot, not only in relation to what looks nice, but how does it inform what we feel, and how does it help carry along the narrative?

Layers of a Documentary Film

Inherent in a documentary film is a narrative or story. As you will have gathered by now, there are numerous elements which are used to create your final documentary film. It's not simply a matter of pointing, shooting and then editing various shots together; as a filmmaker you need to think more holistically and consider how these elements (such as voice over, commentary, animation, rhythm, length and style) all mix together to result in a finished film. This diagram is intended to get you to think about what these elements are. Primary Layers refer to those elements of video and audio footage which we would assemble together in a edited sequence. Secondary Layers refer to more abstract concepts such as the approach and style of the film.

Storyboards

Probably one of the best ways to plan for your shoot, even if it's a little old-fashioned, is to get a pen and paper out and make a storyboard of your planned shots (there are software programmes that help you with storyboarding, such as FrameForge 3D, but pen and paper should really suffice, even if you are really, really bad at drawing, as I am).

Figure 18. A typical storyboard

A storyboard is effectively a visual way of seeing what your film will look like before you've even picked up a camera. It's also a useful tool in communicating what you want to your crew so they can see the shots you have in mind before you start filming. Make sure that each frame shows the type of shot, including camera angles and shot sizes. Also include the potential cutaways you might want to film, and the pans, tilts, zooms and so on. Because it's documentary, rather than fiction, you cannot always predict the action that will unfold, and there might be times when your storyboard is effectively thrown out the window when you're in the middle of filming. But it's important to have a structure in place in the first instance; you're going to have so much to think about when you are making your film that, without some kind of reference to how you wanted the film to look, you're seriously likely to forget everything.

12. INTERVIEW TECHNIQUE

Interview technique is one of the most overlooked skills in documentary film-making. Often we assume that, because we are interested in a particular subject, we can just pick up our camera (or get a cameraperson), meet our subject, have a chat, then somehow piece it together in the edit, and – voilà – we have made a great film. The truth is much more complicated. To interview well, and to interview well for documentary filmmaking, is an often difficult and specifically acquired skill. A good interview can make or break your documentary film, as it often forms the backbone of your story. Some of you will have a natural head start in that you find it easy to engage and build rapport with your subject. Some of you may have come from professions or experiences in which you have been practising interviewing in one way or another. But regardless of your experience, there are some fundamental pointers that can help make your interviews better.

I have been helping documentary filmmakers for some years now, and more often than not it is the interview that lets them down. I have therefore tried to summarise a list of important RULES for directing the documentary interview.

RULE ONE – KNOW WHAT YOUR FILM IS ABOUT

Know what your film is about… I've mentioned this point already throughout this book, and its inclusion here again is because it's really, really important! If you don't know what your film is about, then you really won't know what to cover in the interview. So many times I have known filmmakers who have a general sense of what their film is about, shoot the interview, and then, when it comes to looking at the rushes, feel horribly disappointed that they did not really get the right information, said in the right way, or pitched at the right level. Knowing what your film is about is not simply knowing the subject matter – it's knowing what your approach is, what your style is, and what the narrative is.

For example, saying 'I want to make a documentary about young people in prison' is interesting, but it tells you little about what the film is about. Is it an observational documentary about a group of young offenders shot over the course of a year? Is it an investigative documentary about how young people feel in prison? Is it a film focusing on drug use/misuse and self-harm in prisons? Or is it a musical documentary with young offenders as the stars (as in the BAFTA award-winning documentary *Feltham Sings*)? These are all fine possibilities, and will each make a unique film. But if you don't know this at the outset, then how will you construct an interview that has relevance to the particular film you are making?

RULE TWO – PREPARE, PREPARE, PREPARE

This rule follows on from knowing what your film is about. Before you do an interview, you need to be as prepared as possible. This means not only knowing as much as you can about your subject, but also knowing as much as possible about the subject matter. There's nothing more disconcerting than being interviewed by someone who knows nothing about you or the subject under discussion. Moreover, if you don't know the subject, then how do you know that you will actually ask the right questions? Imagine that you are interviewing someone about his or her experience of being held hostage in Iraq. At the level of general interest you will know to ask questions about what it was like being in captivity, whether they missed their loved ones, whether they thought they were going to get out alive etc. But if you did your research properly, you'd know to extend this line of questioning. Did she or he suffer from depression, get panic attacks, and give up hope? In kidnapping situations, there are often long periods of boredom, punctuated by ghastly bursts of violence, fear and threat. Is this what your subject felt? For many hostages, the lack of hygiene is one of the hardest things to bear, especially if the captivity is long. And then there is the well-known Stockholm Syndrome in which hostages often, over time, become sympathetic towards their captors. Is this something your subject experienced?

If you don't know this information, then you may fail to get the level of richness that such an interview deserves. And it isn't enough to merely assume that your interviewee will be forthcoming with all this information; often people don't have any idea what you want to know, and won't have thought about some of the questions you are asking.

RULE THREE – RAPPORT BUILDING IS PARAMOUNT

Psychological research suggests that people reach very quick judgements as to whether they like you or not, often within the first few minutes, particularly if they know they are only going to spend a limited time with you. This means that either in the early research stages, or in the actual interview, you need to make sure that you do everything possible to engage with your interviewee. An obvious general approach to this is to be prepared, have a polite demeanour, be empathic to their worldview, and sympathetic to their cause (if they have one). But more specifically, you need to make sure that you don't make mistakes that could unintentionally sabotage rapport and prevent you from building engagement. Often with interviewees, especially those who have not been in front of a camera before, it can be an extremely vulnerable situation. Some filmmakers have likened being in a documentary to being in a Catholic confession box. There is often a feeling that interviewees have to bare all, and tell their life story, so it's important that they feel they can trust the person who is interviewing them – i.e. you.

RULE FOUR – DON'T SLOUCH, FIDGET, OR FIDDLE WITH YOUR GOATEE!

Here's an experiment for you to do. Go into a library and watch people who are studying or reading, and you will notice that they invariably have a pet fidget. It might be tapping their feet, twiddling with their hair, rolling a pen in their hand, chewing their lip, or playing with their goatee. All this, despite the fact that they are concentrating on what they are doing. Now, imagine that you are being interviewed by a filmmaker who is furiously tapping her leg.

She might be in the throes of absolute concentration, but to you it looks like she might be impatient and bored. So, be aware – most of you do have a pet fidget, and it's time to give it up – at least during a documentary interview.

RULE FIVE – ACTIVE LISTENING IS THE ONLY WAY TO LISTEN

Here's another gem of psychological insight. If I were reading this chapter to you aloud, then most of you would tune out every few minutes. It doesn't mean that you're bored, it's because listening requires a lot of effort, and such effort is often hard to sustain. There is a fundamental distinction between passive listening and active listening. *Active listening is a way of listening that focuses entirely on what the other person is saying and confirms understanding of both the content of the message and the emotions and feelings underlying the message, to ensure that understanding is accurate.* There are numerous ways to convey that you are actively listening to your subject. Nod your head, show you are interested, and make sure you show the speaker that you truly understand what she or he is saying. Part of this can be achieved by the arts of summarising and paraphrasing: i.e. – repeating back phrases to clarify what the person is saying and to convey that you have understood. Avoid interruptions, and try not to furiously write down everything that is said to you – there's no need, and if you're prepared sufficiently you should not need to look down at a notepad to remind you of questions to ask. Try not to think of the next question when you are interviewing someone – it shows.

Active listening also means looking at the subtext of what is being said. Don't just listen to the words, but look for the meaning behind them. Is someone talking about being fine and relaxed, while seeming visibly nervous and agitated? Do their words have conviction, or is there another layer to their narrative? Look for these subtexts as they can often be extremely revealing.

RULE SIX – THE POWER OF SILENCE

You may find this odd, but silence is one of the most powerful skills you have at your disposal as a documentary filmmaker, and it's also one of the least utilised. Sometimes when we are interviewing people, we become afraid of silence, and quickly try to fill it with another question, or signs of impatience that the interviewee is taking so long to answer a question. But it is through silence that we often get the hidden gems of an interview: the poignant afterthoughts, the revelations and the catharsis as someone slowly unravels and reveals their own inner world. Getting silence right is an acquired skill, which will como with practice. Often you can sense the difference between comfortable and uncomfortable silence; if the former, then be patient and let the interview breathe – you'll often be surprised what your subject may reveal.

RULE SEVEN – INTERVIEWING FOR THE EDIT

If you go to any bar and listen to people having conversations, you'll notice that we are all constantly giving verbal feedback to our partners in conversation. Whether this be a 'Hmm' or 'Uh-Huh', or a groan or chuckle, we are effectively facilitating the conversation. These little sounds are often known as 'minimal encouragers' because they do just that: encourage the conversation to continue. However, in many documentary films the interviewer is neither seen nor heard. The viewer almost forgets that there is a filmmaker, a sound recordist, and cameraperson in front of the subject. In these situations, the interviewer cannot use the encouragers that are part of normal conversation, and instead needs to remain silent. This is because a microphone, even if it's a small lapel mic on the subject, will pick up the tiniest sound from anyone in the room. When it comes to editing the film, unless the interviewer remains silent, there will be all these annoying grunts, groans, chuckles, affirmations and sighs in the background. It's important, therefore, to develop skills that convey the same sentiments, but silently.

This is called *Interviewing for the Edit*, and refers to those techniques required to make sure that the interviewer remains invisible in the edit. Another example of this is the issue of putting the question in the answer. If I (as an interviewer) were to ask you (as an interviewee) what you had for breakfast, you may simply answer 'scrambled eggs on toast.' However, if my voice, and hence my questions, are going to be removed from the film, then your response is more or less meaningless. Instead, we need to make sure that you somehow answer differently. What we need you to say is: 'For breakfast this morning, I had scrambled eggs on toast.' The easiest way for this to happen is to ask you, at the beginning of the interview, to put my questions into your answers, and give you the above example to illustrate my point. The truth is that not all interviewees understand this, and if they do, they invariably forget it at some points throughout the interview. If this is the case, then you need to develop your skills here so that somehow the interviewee is giving a full answer. In the above example, you may ask him or her to describe their morning routine from the point at which they wake up, hoping that at some point in this description you'll get the sentence: 'And then, for breakfast I have....'

You also need to avoid asking closed questions if you are going to edit yourself out of the film. So, questions like, 'Did it hurt?' or 'Did that make you upset?' simply warrant a 'Yes' or 'No' answer, and are therefore meaningless when it comes to the edit. Try, therefore, to ask open questions instead, such as: 'Can you tell me in what ways was that painful?' and 'How did that make you feel?' Such questions lend themselves to much more descriptive answers.

RULE EIGHT – NEVER UNDERESTIMATE THE IMPORTANCE OF LOCAL KNOWLEDGE

It's really important that you understand the cultural background of the persons you are interviewing. This is especially important when filming overseas, but it can also be relevant when interviewing people in our own country who have different ethnic or cultural backgrounds to ourselves. The way we position ourselves, the tone of voice we use, and the way in which we address people can vary from culture to culture and you may unwittingly cause offence, and thus potentially rupture the relationship you are trying to build. For example, when interviewing somebody, regular eye contact is important. However, what seems a reasonable amount of eye contact for Westerners would be extremely difficult for other cultures. In Japan, for example, listeners are taught to focus on a speaker's neck in order to avoid eye contact, and may therefore feel threatened by your attempts to engage in (what they perceive to be) threatening staring. Make sure that you do your background research properly.

RULE NINE – GOOD QUESTIONING VS. BAD QUESTIONING

One of the most important skills as an interviewer is knowing when to ask the right questions and how to ask them. In Rule Seven, we discussed some of the ways to ask questions so that they work in the edit, but you also need to consider the nature of the questions you ask. Try to avoid *leading questions*, which are full of hidden assumptions. These might include asking things such as, 'I guess that you felt really horrible after that?', or 'Ohhh! That must have been really exciting?' There's a difference between empathic statements and leading questions; the latter have the potential to steer the interviewee to answer something that they do not really feel to be true, and that would make for an unreliable piece of filmmaking. Try to make your questions specific, and pitch them at the right level. Don't use complex language that the interviewee might not understand, as they will feel intimidated. A final point: avoid asking multiple questions in the same sentence. We all have a tendency to do this, for example: 'Can you tell me how it felt when you fell in love with Michael? Was it really special? What kinds of things went through your mind?' There are three distinct questions here, and it's very unlikely that your subject will answer all three.

RULE TEN – DEVELOP YOUR PERSONAL STYLE

Are you a Morgan Spurlock, a Michael Moore or a Nick Broomfield? You may choose not to interview for the edit, and decide to keep yourself in the film. This is fine, but make sure you know *why* it is that you have decided to do this, and whether it's the best device for the type of film you are trying to make. Also, consider what kinds of interviews you are comfortable with; some people feel very wary of building rapport with a serial killer, and couldn't be in the same room, let alone make an intimate film about them. Some people feel uncomfortable asking extremely personal questions; others are more than fine doing investigative and confrontational interviews like those seen on

BBC's *HardTalk*. Do you feel it's okay to self-disclose to your subject, increasing rapport and telling him or her how you have had similar experiences, or do you feel documentary filmmakers should be impartial at all times? There are no right or wrong answers to these questions. The important thing is that you need to get to know what you're comfortable with and also what your limits are. You might not know your personal style yet, but it's important to realise that you will have one – and this will influence the kinds of interviews you conduct, and the kinds of films you will make.

13. THE ART OF STORYTELLING

This chapter offers a little respite from the barrage of technical skills that you have just read about, and hopefully allows you to pause for a bit and think about storytelling and the overall narrative of your film. All documentary films tell a story and no matter how good your technical skills, or characters, or storyboards, or research, your film is nothing but a collection of these elements unless they are underpinned by good storytelling. And you must not make the fatal mistake of thinking that somehow the story will 'come together in the edit'. You need to know what the narrative is, and film it. A good editor will make a good story even better, but cannot magic a story into existence if it's not there in the first place.

In Section One we discussed the origin of good ideas, and probed you to start thinking about certain choices regarding the overall approach and style of your film. Having hopefully some of these ideas at least in the back of your mind, it's now time to think about narrative.

Storytelling is not only the domain of documentary films; in fact few people think that documentaries actually tell stories – but they do, and they need to if you are going to capture the attention of an audience. And just because you are documenting reality (or interpreting reality, to quote Grierson), this doesn't mean that there isn't a narrative to your film. Fiction films, short stories and novels all tell stories, and like documentaries they share some common characteristics.

A BEGINNING, MIDDLE AND END

Perhaps this is obvious, but your film will do better if it has some kind of structure. Although there is a place for unstructured, non-narrative films, they are niche, and not the focus of this book.

A beginning, middle and end are often incorporated into what is called a three-act structure, which is a common device used in storytelling and which dates back to ancient times (in fact it was Aristotle who came up with the concept of a beginning, middle and end).

In essence, Act One sets up the story. The characters are introduced, as is the conflict. Let's spend a minute or so thinking about this. Werner Herzog's *Grizzly Man* immediately introduces us to the main character of the film, Timothy Treadwell, a man who spent 13 summers living (often alone) with the grizzly bears in Alaska. Within the first few minutes of watching the film, we learn that Timothy died one summer whilst living with the bears. Rather than spoil the film, this information helps set up and inform the action for the rest of the film: we know who the main character is and that he died, and it's this information which compels us to watch the rest of the film. The main conflict has been established, and we begin to wonder how it happened; how someone who claimed to understand and communicate with these bears ended up being killed by them.

Conflict is important for two reasons. Firstly, it's interesting. Not all intentions and motivations are inherently so; for example, if I were to make a film about someone who is taking his family from Pennsylvania to California for a vacation, there may be some fun moments (if the characters themselves are interesting) but it doesn't automatically make for compelling viewing. But now if I told you that the same family were about to meet their estranged son in California for the first time in 20 years, and that the mother thought he was dead, the film becomes a bit more interesting. And if I were then to tell you that the son doesn't know they are arriving, and that, being Amish, they refuse to drive and are making the journey in a horse and cart, the film can become almost compelling. Conflict keeps us engaged and allows us to ask questions, which we hope will be answered in the rest of the film. Will they make it? What will people think of them travelling in a horse and cart? What will be the reaction of the estranged son? Why is he estranged? And so on.

Most documentaries you have seen are based, to a lesser or greater extent, on conflict. Kevin Macdonald's *Touching the Void* starts off with some climbers on an expedition. Before the end of the first act, we know something terrible has happened in which one of the climbers, Joe Simpson, nearly dies. For the rest of the film, we are wondering how he will make it back home, and how he will deal with facing his friend who cut the rope which caused his terrible accident. Morgan Spurlock's *Super Size Me* introduces him and the main premise of the film in the first act. He's going to do nothing but eat McDonald's food for a month. We see him get his health checked, and set up the rules that he has to live by for the next 30 days. And so the conflict is established. Will his health deteriorate? What will happen to him? These are questions that keep us engaged throughout the film. Of course it's dependent on how Act Two and Act Three are dealt with, but at least the exposition and main thrust of the film have been established. I could go on, but next time you are watching a documentary, look for the structure, the introduction of character, and the conflict and you will notice that most of the time this all happens in the first act, usually the first third of the film.

In Act Two, which is usually the longest part of the film, the conflict that has been established deepens, and further obstacles to achieving the end goal are often introduced. In *Touching the Void*, Joe not only falls and breaks his leg, but now is also trapped in a glacial crevice. Morgan Spurlock becomes increasingly ill, to the point that his doctors are pleading with him to stop his crazy McDonald's-only diet immediately.

Act Three, which is usually the shortest, focuses on resolution of the conflict. So Joe Simpson finds his way back to the base camp, barely alive, but okay. Morgan lives through his ordeal and we are left seeing the negative effect of McDonald's. And so on...

The three-act structure is just one of the ways to think about the narrative of your film. If this seems too complicated, then take a step back and think about the films you have seen and the books you have read and ask yourself, 'What makes them interesting?' and 'Why don't I get bored and stop watching/reading them?' The answer always lies in the structure and the employment of storytelling devices. Therefore, the most important thing – beyond anything else – is to sustain the attention of the audience. You should know, by now, the various layers and tools you have at your disposal and when we come on to editing in the next section of this book you will see how clever and skilful editing can bring the story alive.

Style and approach are important elements of good storytelling. You will notice over the years that documentaries have changed. Many of the documentaries that were on television, say, ten years ago, simply would not get made these days. The methods and tools to engage and/or entertain have shifted, and you need to bear this in mind when thinking about your narrative. For example, two American films were made recently about multinational corporations. One is *The Corporation*, and the other is *WalMart: The High Cost of Low Price* by Robert Greenwald. In my opinion (and you may disagree), *The Corporation* is a thoroughly engaging and absorbing film, whereas *WalMart* falls flat, not quite living up to what it could be. Although it does have great access to some insiders of the WalMart corporation, the narrative doesn't flow, the camera work is at times terrible, but most of all it lacks authorship or a style that could make it an inherently interesting documentary. As it is it's another one of those films that could be lumped into the whole 'liberal anti-globalisation' category. *The Corporation*, on the other hand, is heavily stylised. Although it's essentially a number of uniformly lit interviews with '40 corporate insiders and critics', it's the way it's edited, and the juxtaposition of archive, cartoon and specific images that create a compelling narrative. Its uniqueness lies in its approach – rather than just get sound bites from people about how bad multinationals are, the film puts forward the question that if a corporation were a person, then what kind of person would it be? The answer: a psychopath. And the rest of the film explores this metaphor – to great effect.

Marc Singer's *Dark Days* also treats its subject matter with a unique and engaging style. It's a film about the scores of people that live in New York's disused subways. But its grainy, black-and-white, 16mm shots and soundtrack by DJ Shadow give the film a particular aesthetic and movement. Rather than distort the actuality in front of the camera, it lends a specific aesthetic to the film; whether you like it or not, it defines the film and sets up the context in which we, as an audience, experience it.

Michael Moore has also found interesting ways of telling a story that has mass appeal, rather than being too niche or overly dry in presentation. *Bowling for Columbine* and *Fahrenheit 9/11* mix humour with harsh realities of American society; the films manage to be both didactic and entertaining, and therefore feel inclusive rather than exclusive. How does he do this? First of all, he puts himself in the film. His Socratic method of interviewing, his use of irony in his interviews, his 'everyman' persona on film, and his clear narration make it very easy for an audience to engage with the subject matter. Furthermore, he uses archive, news clips, motion graphics and humorous animation in order to make a serious point.

Style, approach and a good narrative that engages and continues to engage an audience are some of the key components of a good documentary film. At this point in the book you may have one or several ideas about films that you want to make and, if this is the case, think how you would like to see this film as an audience. What would keep you interested? What would make a fascinating story, and what style and approach should you use? Half of this work needs to be done now – the main ingredients of the film need to be in place. The other half will be done in the edit, which you can read more about in Section Three.

14. MANAGING YOUR PRODUCTION

For some, this is the least interesting aspect of making a documentary. For others, it's the exciting nuts and bolts that bring a production to life. Regardless of how you feel about it, the rules, legal issues, processes, budgets and paperwork are absolutely essential components for your film. Whether you are shooting your film all by yourself in your home on a single-chip camera, or using an extensive crew and multiple locations, good production management will help you think about your film – and how feasible it really is – in more detail, and it should also give you answers to a number of important questions, including:

- How do I make sure I am running my film to budget, and how much does my film actually cost to make?
- How do I make sure I am legally covering myself, both in terms of insurance, health and safety, and content of my film?
- How do I ensure that all releases are covered, including my contributors, the use of music, and archive?
- What is the schedule of the film? That is, how long will pre-production, production and post-production go on for? When can I expect to deliver the film, and am I giving myself long enough?
- How to deal with the issues of rights? That is, how do I keep as much control and ownership of my film as I can?

Production management is quite heavy on contracts and forms and various templates. I have included some of the main ones on the DVD that comes with this book, and have highlighted them in **_bold italics_** when referring to them.

HOW MUCH DOES MY FILM REALLY COST?

Your film can cost anywhere between a few pounds and a few hundred thousand, depending on the kit, crew and overheads you have, and whether you want to pay yourself. Let's imagine for a second, though, that you want to get paid for your film, possibly as a television commission or an independent feature documentary. And let's also imagine that you want to clear all the rights for international distribution (I'll explain what this means shortly). So, with this in mind, we're going to give a breakdown of the kinds of things you need to budget for, and how much they might cost.

The low(ish)-budget film

In order to give this budget some kind of context, let's imagine you are making a film about a specific character who lives in London. Her name is Geraldine and she's 26 years old. She works in a local café in Islington, but in her spare time she trains in all-female boxing – a growing niche sport in the UK. You're going to follow her during the few months before the trial for the national championships.

The Crew

By crew, this means all the people who will be involved in the actual making of your film. This could be just one person – yourself – as the director, producer, cameraperson, sound recordist and editor. But for most professional work – and for the sake of this budget we are creating here – let's imagine that you are going to be the producer/director, and that you are going to shoot your own material. You are going to have a sound recordist with you, so it's really only a crew of two. Since it's a small production, with only one principal character, we're going to assume that as the producer you are also going to undertake the role of production manager. Let's also say, for argument's sake, you're doing your own research. That should bring the costs down a little bit. In addition, you're going to need an executive producer. In this context, his/her involvement might not be substantial, but they will be the main interface between you and your broadcaster. They'll give you advice on your production period, act as a mentor, and most definitely come into the edit on a few occasions to see how your film is progressing.

To get an idea of union rates, you should look at the union for the country you are living in – in the UK, it's BECTU (Broadcasting Entertainment Cinematograph and Theatre Union) and Pact (Producers Alliance for Cinema and Television) that set out the going rates. If you are budgeting for television, then these are the rates for production crew which you are entitled to ask for when submitting your budget to a broadcaster. In reality, however – especially on small films – many of you end up working far beyond what you're paid for, a horrible reality but true.

But back to our film... As a producer/director you are entitled to at least £1,000 a week. A sound recordist can be expected to be paid between £200 and £300 a day, and more towards the higher end if it's a long day. A cameraperson can expect to be paid between £250 and £400 per day, depending on their skill level and what you expect them to shoot on – so you're saving money here. An executive producer will cost around £300 per day. With all crew fees, if it's more than a day's work, then try to negotiate a deal.

A quick word about support here: you've got an awful lot to be thinking of whilst making this film. Not only do you have to do the two roles of producer and director, but you have the stress of making one of your first films, dealing with finance, paying people, and filling out lots and lots of forms. Now, you can do this all by yourself, but if your budget allows, it's a good idea to get a production manager (PM) on board, as it will make life a lot easier. So, let's put the PM in for a week during pre-production to help with all the contracts, a week during production to help organise your shoots, and a week in post-production to help with all the paperwork and deliverables.

What you need to do now is calculate how many weeks you will be working on this film. For this particular project, some of the decisions have been made for you. There are only 11 weeks until the championship heats, so you know you have an 11-week production schedule. You've already met her a couple of times, so the 'research phase' has already been completed. You should be aware that not all films are this simple. Sometimes, there is a lot of research that needs to be done in order to get the project ready to the point that it can be filmed and, as such, this should be put into the budget. In terms of a sound recordist, you need to work out how many days you will be filming. This can be quite difficult – and the important thing is not to overestimate this. It's unfeasible and unrealistic to film Geraldine every single day for 11 weeks; not only will it be extremely expensive, but you'll end up with several hundred hours of rushes – mostly of boring and uninspiring footage – when you arrive in the edit suite. Try to think about some of the key things you want to film, and remember you are aiming for a film that is no longer than 30 minutes. You might want to film her in her work environment; with her family at home; out with friends; at her training sessions; at the championship heats etc. You might also want to film other people associated with Geraldine, including her partner, her coach, her parents and maybe some of the other competitors.

Let's assume, therefore, that, with all these events and people to cover, you're going to do ten days of filming in total. For the purposes of this example, all your filming takes place in your home town or city. This is not always the case, and if you are filming around the country then you need to take into account the various transport – and possibly accommodation – costs.

So far, therefore, our budget looks like this (a full, **blank budget template** can be found on the DVD):

Staff/Crew					
	Fee/Rate £*	Pre-Production (Wks/Dys)	Production (Wks/Dys)	Post-Production (Wks/Dys)	Total £
Executive Producer	300	2 days	2 days	2 days	1,800
Producer/ Director	1,000	2 weeks	2 weeks	4 weeks	8,000
Production Manager	800	1 week	1 week	1 week	2,400
Sound Recordist	250		10 days		2,500
TOTAL					14,700

Note that other, larger productions will normally consist of a variety of roles (see Chapter 7) including researchers, production assistants and assistant producers. For those of you who think that the producer/director fee is high, trust me – it's not. For the amount of work you will end up doing, the hours you work, and the amount of time throughout the year that you may find yourself out of work, you need every penny you can get!

Interviewees and Contributors

It's important to discuss the issue of paying contributors, as the issue will come up time and time again. On the whole, it's not recommended to pay contributors. There's no law specifically against it, and broadcasters wouldn't insist on it, per se, but you need to think seriously about what to do if someone demands payment. Documentaries are meant to be representing reality, and the moment money changes hands it becomes something different; you'll never quite know what the agenda of your protagonist is – whether, for example, they are playing a role because you have paid them. And they can always argue, once the film has finished, that you paid them to do or say specific things. To pay expenses is fair enough, as is paying 'experts' such as professors, scientists etc. If you really have to pay a 'normal' contributor, then check with your (executive) producer and/or commissioning editor.

Equipment

Let's imagine you are shooting this by yourself on a Sony Z1 camera. Irrespective of whether you own it or not, you put it in the budget as an expense. Documentary budgets work on the expectation that you hire kit – it's not usually allowed to officially use production money to buy kit – unless of course the amount of spend on a hire would exceed the purchase cost of the kit. For the camera, you'd probably hire it for around £80 per day. Sound equipment, including mics and an SQN mixer, is anywhere between £80 and £120 per day, depending on what microphones you need, and how many. You can either hire this from an equipment rental service, or sometimes the sound recordist will have his/her own kit.

Your kit may vary considerably depending what kind of film you are making. In this scenario we're just using a Sony Z1 camera, and a shotgun mic, a pair of radio mics and a mixer. However, some shoots may require much more expensive equipment such as DigiBeta cameras, a lighting rig, secret/covert filming cameras, filming from helicopter or aircraft, or even underwater cameras.

You also need to budget for tape stock, not only for your camera but for your own viewing copies of the offline edit, and final masters to be submitted to the broadcaster. You could expect to use no more than 30 x 40-minute DV tapes for this production.

Post-Production

You need an editor, and you need the equipment for your editor to edit on. A good editor doesn't come cheap, charging anywhere between £1,100 and £1,500 a week. Don't try to do this cheaply; a good editor is worth their weight in gold. Editing equipment can vary from your desktop in your bedroom to a sophisticated edit suite. The next section of the book will give you more idea of what kind of kit you need, but let's say we're just using a standard offline edit kit which would hire out at around £500 per week. For a half-hour documentary, with no big post-production effects needed, you're looking at around four weeks, including time to digitise all your rushes into the editing system.

Once your offline edit is finished, you'll need to go to an online edit suite and have your sound mixed in an audio facility. As this is explained in the next section of the book, I won't discuss it in too much detail here, other than to say it's essential (because your final film needs to be graded and made broadcast-ready) and it's expensive – around £1,000 per day for each. Allow one day for the online and two days for a decent audio mix. You also need to allow for commentary to be recorded (if needed), along with the hire of a voiceover booth, and the money to pay a decent voiceover artist if you are not going to do it yourself. A voiceover artist can be reasonable (£100 per hour) or really expensive – especially if they are a celebrity. I once got a well-known celebrity to do the narration for a short (three minute) film and it cost

Equipment and Post-Production						
	Name	Fee/Rate £*	Pre-Production (Wks/Dys)	Production (Wks/Dys)	Post-Production (Wks/Dys)	Total £
Editor		1,250			4 weeks	5,000
Editing Suite		500			4 weeks	2,000
Camera (Sony Z1)		85		10 days		850
Mics and Mixer		100		10 days		1,000
Online Edit		1,000			1 day	1,000
Audio Dub		1,000			1 day	1,000
Composer		1,000				1,000
TOTAL						11,850

me over £600 for one hour! Let's assume here that you're doing your own commentary, and it's included within your audio dub fee.

You also need to think about music. Again, this is discussed more in the next section of this book. You have three choices for music for your film. Firstly, you can use popular music that other artists have recorded: this may be one of the latest chart-topping bands, a piece of classical music or a well-known tune. Often, broadcasters have a 'blanket agreement' meaning that you can use this kind of music either for free or for a greatly reduced cost. If your finance is not coming from a broadcaster, or they don't have such a 'blanket agreement', then this can be very expensive. Secondly, you can use 'library music', which is produced by companies who produce literally hundreds of different compositions covering every single mood and theme, along with many effects and ambient sounds ranging from thunderstorms to the sound of birds singing and crowds laughing. This can range from tacky, synthesised music, which sounds like it has been composed on a £200 synthesiser, to beautifully composed orchestral sounds. Prices vary considerably, but, in the UK at least, one of the best and most affordable sources of library music is Audio Networks (www.audiolicense.com). It's an extensive library that can be researched either on the Internet, or via the pack of CDs that they send you.

Thirdly, and often the best solution, is to get the music composed specifically for your film. This allows you to get the music just right, and often you can work closely with a composer to fine tune the composition until it's just what you're looking for. The cost for this can vary considerably, and it depends on who the composer is, how much music is involved, what rights you want for this music (see below), and what kind of deal you can make here. For the purpose of this film, we have put composition in at £1,000. It's a bit on the low end for a professional composer, but it should be very easy to find some talented person who wants to break into doing this kind of tv/film score, and will make a deal with you.

Overheads and Profit, and Insurance

Remember, we are working on a low-budget film here, and as such there's a tendency to forget about paying yourself properly (it's low budget, and not no-budget). Now, you might be working from home, or you might have an office somewhere. There are costs involved here, and you need to pay them somehow. So you have to put some money aside in your budget to cover telephone bill, Internet usage, rent, any other general overheads you have. For this production, we're putting about £1,000 to cover this, assuming you have office rent to pay.

You need to pay for production insurance. This differs from the normal insurance that you might have for your office or for your home contents. It effectively insures you against something going wrong with your production, from damaging equipment, to the main subject of your film dying, or you becoming too ill to film. So, if everything suddenly goes wrong and your film can't go ahead, or gets delayed, then this insurance covers you from having a broadcaster demanding repayment. For this production, let's imagine it's going to cost around £500 for insurance.

When you have finished a budget, all the various items are direct costs, so there is little room for profit as such. Without profit, we'd all have to go back to working in bars, sublet our houses, and pawn our possessions during the gaps between productions. So, we basically need to put a 'production fee' into our budget. This is usually 10% (although sometimes it can be a little bit more) of the budget. For this production, we have costs so far of £28,050, so the production fee would be around £2,800. This is the money that's left at the end of production for you to spend at will, and it's a legitimate way of making profit (there are more illegitimate ones that you may well learn as you gain more experience). Another way to earn profit from your film is by exploiting the secondary rights (see the section on rights and contracts below).

So, your final budget for this film will look something like this:

Full Budget					
	Fee/Rate £*	Pre-Production (Wks/Dys)	Production (Wks/Dys)	Post-Production (Wks/Dys)	Total £
Executive Producer	300	2 days	2 days	2 days	1,800
Producer/ Director	1,000	2 weeks	2 weeks	4 weeks	8,000
Production Manager	800	1 week	1 week	1 week	2,400
Sound Recordist	250		10 days		2,500
Editor	1,250			4 weeks	5,000
Editing Suite	500			4 weeks	2,000
Camera	85		10 days		850
Mics and Mixer	100		10 days		1,000
Online Edit	1,000			1 day	1,000
Audio Dub	1,000			1 day	1,000
Composer	1,000				1,000
Overheads	1,000				1,000
Insurance and Bank Costs	500				500
SUBTOTAL					28,050
Production Fee					2,805
TOTAL					30,855

Most of you will look at this total figure and think that it's really, really expensive to make a documentary – even a short one based in your home town. And the truth is that it can be very expensive (some budgets would exceed the one I have presented you with here for the same film), but you can also make the same film for much less money than this. In fact, if you just made the film, by yourself, doing camera and sound too, and perhaps even the edit, then it would cost you little more than the equipment you use, and you could even borrow this if you really wanted to keep your costs down. There are plenty of opportunities for low- and no-budget filmmakers to make great films, and if you are a hobbyist, or have the luxury of being able to fund your own films, or beg favours from friends and family, then you don't need to worry too much about money. But, if you want to (ultimately) make a living as a documentary maker and work within an industry such as television or feature film, then you need to pay yourself properly, pay others properly and understand what things really cost. This is a really important point, as too many documentary filmmakers, especially at the start of their career, undersell themselves – and this eventually leads to disillusionment. So, aim high, and anything less than that will still be more than you originally expected.

PERMISSIONS, RELEASES AND THE HEADACHE OF FORM FILLING

When I first started making documentary films, I was shocked at the amount of paperwork that was needed, especially if you want anyone to see your film, other than your close friends and family.

Imagine the following scenario related to our film with Geraldine. On your first shooting day, you film her doing a workout in the gym with the radio playing in the background. You film her with some other women doing training, and every now and then you focus the camera on them, asking them some questions about boxing and training. That evening, you film Geraldine at home with her six-year-old niece and ten-year-old nephew. After dinner, she goes out to the local pub with some of her (non-boxing) mates, watching some boxing on television and talking about how crazy Geraldine is to want to do this sport.

This all sounds relatively straightforward. However, if your film is going to be seen in the public domain (and this includes sites like YouTube on the Internet, as well as on the BBC or in cinemas) you have to make sure that you have legally covered yourself for everything that you have filmed.

Here's an idea of the kinds of things you need to cover yourself for from the example above:

- Filming Geraldine in the gym: you need to make sure that you have got the permission to film there (known as a **Location Agreement**). Without this, the owners of the premises could theoretically say you did not have permission to film there, and as such, you would not be able to use any of the footage.

- You need to get Geraldine to sign a **Release Form**. This is a form that gives the production company the right to use the footage for any purpose, including the film you are making, both in this country and throughout the world (see The Overwhelmingly Frightening Release Form).

- You also need to get all the people you film in the gym to sign a release. There are different ways to do this when filming a lot of people but the general rule is, where possible, try to get everyone who speaks or appears on camera to sign a release form. There are occasions where this simply is not possible and you can get away with having a blanket release. For example, this might have involved putting a sign on the door of the gym, saying that you are filming there, and that anyone who walks in is tacitly agreeing to be filmed, unless they make it clear that they don't want to be filmed. But, if they are going to say anything on camera, it's best to get an individual release form signed.

- Note that the radio is playing in the background. In principle, if you can hear the music, then you need to identify and log each piece of music that is playing, and then you or your production manager has to seek individual permission for each piece and most probably pay for it. This is a nightmare to do, and I have sat there in an edit suite till the wee hours of the morning, after filming in a nightclub, trying to identify the thumps and thuds of the music that I am too old to know and too tired to care about. That's why my first reaction, when filming in a situation where there is background music, is to turn it off! Background music also makes editing really difficult, so that's another reason to get rid of it.

- Geraldine is spending time with her niece and nephew. It's not good enough getting them to sign a release form, as they are minors. So, you need to get the legal parents or guardian to sign a form on their behalf.
- She then goes to the pub (location agreement needed), talks to her friends (release form needed for each one of these), and watches the television (you need to source this archive, and pay for the right to use it in your film).

As you can see, it's not an easy task. And that's why having a production manager or an assistant to help you with all this is really important. Let's just quickly deal with each of the main types of permission you will need to secure for your film. Many of the templates for these forms can be found on the DVD that comes with this book.

The Overwhelmingly Frightening Release Form

Release forms vary in how long, how wordy, how complicated and how intimidating they can be but, in essence, they are all about getting someone to legally agree to be in your film. However, in order to protect you as a filmmaker (and whoever is employing you), the contract has to say that you have the right to use the footage of them to do whatever you want with, whenever you want to, and wherever you decide. Phrases like, 'You agree to hereby sign over all rights and allow us to edit in any manner we may think fit, the recording of your contribution', don't necessarily warm the average participant to signing such a form. When they go on to say, 'You may use my contribution throughout the world and the universe, in perpetuity', it becomes even scarier.

It's difficult to gauge who will sign a release form easily and who won't. Sometimes I have presented a subject with the form, terrified that they simply won't agree, and lo and behold, they sign it without any fuss; at other times, the most obliging participant will suddenly panic, and express serious reservations about signing. What do you do in this situation?

First of all, you should try to think when is the best time to give the subject the release form – before, or after filming? If you do it after, then there is always the risk that they may not sign, and then you have potentially wasted a day (or longer) of filming. I try to get it done, and out of the way, at the beginning, although you have to be prepared for a lengthy conversation and potential rapport-busting interaction before the filming starts; nothing is worse than putting a subject ill-at-ease before you start filming and interviewing them. I also find it difficult to be the person who gives the form – for me, it conflicts with my role as a director who is trying to build a relationship with my subject. In an ideal scenario, I would get an assistant to go through the paperwork, thus keeping myself out of unnecessary causes of conflict. Doing this also makes the whole process seem so much more straightforward and 'administrative' and if done correctly will be pitched as essential protocol which needs to be got out of the way.

On this last note, you need to be prepared to answer some of the questions that might be asked by a (justifiably) nervous subject who is about to sign away an awful lot. They may ask to be involved in the edit, to have a final say on what goes in the film, to have control over where the film gets transmitted, even if it's on Mars, and how often. The bottom line is that you cannot give a subject these kinds of controls over your film, and it may not be your choice anyway, if there is a broadcaster or other funding body involved. If your film is being made as part of a broadcast commission, the television company will demand a full release form. And if you give them any kind of editorial power, then you are asking for trouble, as they will think that they can be involved in every step of the production. I try to convey to the subject that we are on the same side and working to a common goal.

People

Every person who appears in your film for long enough to be identified needs to have signed a release form. There are, however, a few limited exceptions to this. People who are deemed 'in the greater public interest' such as politicians or civil servants do not need to sign a release; in their professional capacity, they are answerable to the public. That's why, when film crews doorstep politicians, they don't have to get them to sign a piece of paper, and when Tony Blair and George Bush are filmed chatting to each other unaware they are being recorded, no one has to seek their permission. Another exception to this, for similar reasons, is the filming of a criminal or criminal activity (although with the latter, it opens up a whole other legal can of worms). If you are filming people breaking the law or conspiring to do so, you do not need to seek their permission – that's how some investigative documentaries can get away with filming people without their consent.

Archive

A music recording, a news item on television, a clip from a 1970s film, photographs from a book, or an article from a magazine – all these have their own copyright and as such you need to seek permission to use them. Often, especially with music, photos and film clips, you will have to pay the relevant people to use this. And usually, it's the distributor or agent who needs to be approached. The rate can range from a few pounds through to thousands dependent on what it is, how much you want to include in your film, and where your film is going to be shown. With regard to this last point, you often pay less if your film is confined to one medium, one use and one territory (for example, on a DVD, for educational use, in the UK only). If your film is for television in the US, with the possibility of selling it around the world, and maybe one day a DVD release, then it's probably best to secure worldwide rights in the first instance; it's more expensive, but it will save you having to go back and pay more in the long run. A good example of this is the film *Tarnation*, which was lauded as being the quintessential low-budget documentary. It was allegedly made for $218 and ended up in cinemas around the world. It tells the story of Jonathan Caouette's life, and specifically his relationship with his mother who had a long history of psychiatric problems. The film is edited using old VHS and Super 8 footage that Jonathan had shot throughout his childhood, along with still photographs and answer-machine messages. It was edited using the editing software *iMovie* that comes free with Apple Mac computers. However, the real costs of the film, in order to prepare it for public release, were more around the $400,000 mark, as money had to be paid for the release of music that was in the film, as well as some other archive that was used in order to add mood and narrative to the film. This just gives some idea of the excessive amount that archive can cost.

Fair Dealing

There are specific instances when you can get away with not paying for archive, even though 'officially' you should pay for it. This is known as Fair Use (a term mainly used in the UK) or Fair Dealing (a term used in the US). It's a complicated area, so you need to make sure you consult either a lawyer or a very good production manager before attempting to use archive without securing the rights to do so. The concept refers to the idea of using archive without securing the rights (and paying the high cost) because you are somehow making a comment on that particular archive, rather than just using it to make some other point. Documentary filmmakers may not be able to afford the high cost of using archive, but also may be prohibited from accessing it. The concept of fair use, in principle, provides an avenue for using archive without permission or payment.

An example of fair dealing comes from the documentary *Outfoxed* by Robert Greenwald. The film focuses on the alleged right-wing and conservative bias inherent in the way news is portrayed by the Fox News channel. Not only would the amount of archive used far exceed the budget of the film (around $300,000) but, had attempts been made to legally access the archive, much of it may have been refused. Instead, Greenwald applied the principles of 'fair dealing' here, since he was using material in order to directly comment on it.

The laws underlying copyright and fair dealing are different from country to country and, as you are reading this, are also undergoing changes. Documentary producers in both Europe and North America are making active attempts to make the laws more liberal here. If you are using archive, and think that you may be able to state the case for using it under the principles of fair dealing, then check with your national/regional producers' organisation, union or, if you can afford it, a lawyer.

CONTRACTS AND RIGHTS

Many of you may think that this will be a really, really boring part of this book. But it's important to understand a little about rights and how they work, so that you don't sign away the rights to your film, and can maximise its potential for financial return.

Historically, in the UK at least, a broadcaster used to buy your film. They'd pay you a certain amount of money, you'd go off and make it, and then they would own all the rights, and if they felt like it (and they often didn't), they would go and sell it in other countries and make lots of money. In the 1990s, much of this changed, and the changes were negotiated by an organisation called Pact (Producers Alliance for Cinema and Television). The result was that broadcasters agreed to assign a portion of the rights to the production company. This means that the broadcasters kept a portion of the rights (known as Primary Rights) for themselves (usually this would be the right to broadcast the film a couple of times on their channel, and prevent the production company from selling the film in that country for a period of time – say, five years). But all the other international rights – for example, the right to sell the film to other countries (known as Secondary Rights) – now resided with the production companies, allowing them to earn money from selling the film elsewhere. This was a big breakthrough for independent production companies and with the many possibilities of exploitation of new media rights (Internet and mobile phones) these terms of trade are continually being renegotiated. For an update on the current state of play, see the Pact website (www.pact.co.uk) or corresponding organisation in your country.

HEALTH AND SAFETY

Whether you are working by yourself as a multi-skilling filmmaker, or working in a large crew, you need to be aware of important issues of health and safety in order to ensure the safety of yourself, your crew, the subject in your film, and the general public. If an accident happens whilst on a shoot, and anybody gets injured, then ultimately it's your responsibility (or the company you work for) and unless you have adequately assessed and managed the various risks then there is a danger not only that your insurance company might not pay up, but that you might be legally liable for injury or even loss of life on set. It sounds dramatic, but accidents do happen, and it's your job to minimise the chances of this as much as possible. This means no climbing up the side of a building with a camera in one hand, a mic held in your teeth, just to get that brilliant camera angle!

You need to really fill in a **Risk Assessment Form** in order to determine what the various risks are on each location. This involves assessing the obvious risks such as cables, filming in the street or filming in a car, and the less obvious ones such as filming in extreme weather conditions, or underwater, or from the top of a building, on scaffolding, or using special effects. What's important is that for every risk you identify, you have an action point for dealing with each one. For example, if you're filming underwater, you need to have someone with first aid skills available.

CALL SHEETS

The key to managing your production safely, on schedule and with as few mishaps as possible is to ensure that everybody involved knows what their role is, where they are meant to be on a certain day at a certain time, what equipment they are responsible for, and who to contact should anything go wrong. In professional teams, it's expected that each member of the production team will receive a call sheet, which summarises this information. Even if you are working solo, it's still a good idea to have a call sheet, as you never know when, 300 miles from home, you might need some all-important bit of information which you left pinned to your fridge in your kitchen.

There is a full **Call Sheet** to be found on the DVD with this book. This was one that was used for an actual production, but you can delete and insert your own details as appropriate. If you look at it, you will notice that all contact details of all relevant crew are given, along with other important contacts such as the local film office (who granted permissions for outdoor filming), the hire company (should anything go wrong with the kit during filming), the contact details of the local hospital (just in case) and the police station (you never know). And, of course, there are those all-important maps to help you get where you should be going.

FINALLY, DON'T BE AFRAID TO ASK!

No one expects you to understand everything about managing a production – not even the best producers know all of the important nuances, and that's why they hire people who do. But, if you are working solo, or in a really small team, then make sure you're not afraid to ring round and ask for help. Ring another local production company for advice (they might not give it, but there's no harm in trying), or your local film agency, or union. There are various organisations that might offer you this kind of specific help. The Documentary Filmmakers Group (www.dfgdocs.com), for example, offers some support in answering general production management (and other) issues.

SECTION THREE
POST-PRODUCTION

15. PREPARING FOR THE EDIT

If you've been reading this book sequentially, we're now moving on to the final part of the production process. Having shot your film, you're almost ready to start editing it (either by yourself, or with an editor). I say 'almost' because there is actually a fair bit of work to do before you embark on the journey that will find you sitting in a darkened room for the next few weeks/months, trying to make sense of your rushes and carve them into a great narrative. Many documentary filmmakers I know find this final part of the filmmaking process the most rewarding, and also the most terrifying. In some ways, it's the moment of judgement, when you find out whether you've actually got a film, or just a collection of images that don't hang together.

Before you start editing, you need to know your material. So this means watching all your rushes. But you should avoid spooling back and forth on your master tapes. It's always a good idea to dub them (transfer them from the original source to another secondary source) onto VHS tape or DVD, then lock the masters away for safe keeping until it's time to digitise them into your computer. When you are dubbing them, make sure that you lay down (or 'burn in' as it's sometimes known) the time code onto your DVD or VHS tape, so that you can accurately log your rushes.

LOGGING

Make sure you set ample time aside for this. Usually, if I've shot 30 tapes or so, I want a good two weeks to get to grips with my material before I go into the edit. With a longer film, you should perhaps take longer. The process of logging is at some points painstakingly boring, but really important. Don't let someone else do this for you, as it's you who needs to get to know your material as well as you possibly can. And don't think just because you've been around during the shoot (or even shot the thing yourself) that you know the material. You don't; and when it comes to looking through your material you'll see how what you thought you had is sometimes vastly different from what you've really got.

Logging is effectively a process of seeing what images and sound you actually have on your tape. As you go through your rushes, you need to fill out a logging sheet in which you record the time code, the visual action, the sound, as well as other notes on whether it was a good shot etc. By looking through all the rushes you are familiarising yourself with the material but also getting a sense of what shots are worth keeping (and therefore digitising) and what shots you should just not bother with. Therefore, using the quick checklist below – devised by a colleague of mine, Anton Califano – is a good idea:

Viewing & Logging your rushes: Checklist

For each short shot that you capture, look at what you have shot and ask the following questions. If you have any ticks in the right-hand column (i.e. a 'no' answer regarding the picture or a 'yes' answer regarding audio) then your shot doesn't meet the minimum technical requirements and you should NOT capture the clip unless you really don't have anything else!!

ANALYSING THE PICTURE	Yes	No
Is the shot in SHARP focus throughout?		
Have you correctly white balanced? Are the skin colours correct?		
Is the shot correctly exposed?		
Does the exposure remain fixed during the shot? (i.e. was it set to 'manual'?)		
Framing		
Does the framing look nice?		

Is the 'looking room' on the correct side? Is your character looking into space?		
Is the camera angle appropriate?		
Have you followed the rule of thirds in your shot composition?		
Does the eyeline feel right?		
Is the boom/mic completely out of the shot?		
Operating		
Is the shot steady (enough)?		
Is the tripod level?		
Does the camera feel at the correct height?		
Lighting		
Does the lighting look nice?		
Technical issues		
Is the shot completely clear of digital dropout?		
If the shot is a cutaway, have you recorded a minimum of 15 seconds?		
Have you recorded an *extra* 5-10 seconds at the start and end of the shot?		
Shots with camera movement		
Does the camera movement have a definite start point?		
Does the camera movement have a definite end point?		
Is the panning/tilting/tracking smooth enough?		
Is the panning/tilting/tracking at the appropriate speed?		

ANALYSING THE AUDIO	Yes	No
Are the audio levels peaking?		
Are the audio levels so low that they hardly register?		
Is there any dropout or distortion in the sound?		
Can I hear every word clearly?		
Is there any distracting echo/reverb?		
Is the background noise (in an interview) distracting or too loud?		

THE PAPER EDIT

A Paper Edit, as the name suggests, is a way of mapping out what your film will look like by writing it down on paper. It involves really thinking about the structure of the film before you go into the actual edit. This is an important stage of preparation for the edit; it's all very well walking into the edit knowing your rushes back to front, but it's another thing to actually have some idea of the structure of your film. When you were logging your rushes, you should have been asking, 'What's my film about?' and 'What's the beginning, middle and end?'

There are two kinds of 'Paper Edit' you can do. The first literally involves cutting up little bits of paper, and arranging them in some kind of sequence. The second is a more formal written edit, which can, if necessary and detailed enough, be used to convey to an editor EXACTLY how your final film should look. I'll deal with each of these in turn.

The 'Little Bits of Paper' Paper Edit

When you come to finally edit your film, you will have, in its simplest form, an audio track and a video track for each clip. Sometimes, these tracks will be in sync; that is, we will see the visual footage of someone talking, and we will hear the corresponding audio. At other times you will choose not to sync image and sound. Bearing this in mind, what you need to do for a 'little bits of paper' Paper Edit is first of all select, from your logs, the main clips you think you might want to put in your film. Cut a little piece of paper, fold it horizontally in half, and write the name of the clip twice – once on the top half, and once on the bottom half. Next to the name on the top half write 'VIDEO' and next to the name on the bottom half write 'AUDIO'. Now tear the paper in two along the horizontal divide and you now have an 'audio' and 'video' representation of your clip. Do this with all your clips and then it's merely a matter of playing around with these little bits of paper, putting them in different orders, and visually seeing whether or not certain sequences of clips work or not. It's a crude yet effective mimicry of editing software, and allows you to start building sequences and constructing the backbone of your film.

Figure 19. A typical Paper Edit

The Tabular Paper Edit

This is a more formal Paper Edit, whereby you actually describe the edit in detail, using a table format, on pieces of paper. It works in a similar way to the example above, but can be much more precise; so precise in fact, that you can even describe, frame by frame, exactly how the final film will look. This is not necessarily the way to edit, and one would only use it in this way by necessity. For example, the popular *Race Around the World* series on the Australian ABC network involved numerous filmmakers going to different countries around the world to make a short documentary. They were only allowed to spend ten days in each country, and then had to send their rushes and a very detailed Paper Edit back to Australia, where they could be edited *exactly* as the director intended. In order to accomplish this each filmmaker really needed to give very detailed instructions in terms of the time code for the edit, the voiceover, narration, music and so on. A Paper Edit can be constructed using a simple table with columns for time code, visual images, audio, and commentary.

With your film, you will most probably be working alongside an editor, and the level of detail need not be as precise as that in the above example; the film will develop and evolve during the edit. However, it's a good idea to have some sense of the narrative structure, and consider – at least in skeletal form – what your film will look like.

BRING ALL THE INGREDIENTS TOGETHER

If you recall our 'Layers of a Documentary Film' diagram (figure 17) then you will remember that there are many components which all contribute to your final film. Now is the time you need to really think about these different ingredients and do as much preparation as possible, so that when it comes to working with an editor (or even editing the film yourself) you have all the different ingredients needed to construct a well-made film. I have briefly broken this down into sections to talk about the different types of things you need to consider:

Archive

This alludes to still photographs, video archive and audio (for example from a radio broadcast). You need to make sure you have all these materials, but more importantly that you have them in the right format. Photographs should be high resolution, and you need to ensure you have a digital version of them. This means, for example, that if you receive an actual photograph, then you need to scan it into a computer and convert it into the right format, and this in turn can be imported into the editing software. This means a minimum of 300 dpi (if you don't know what this means then talk to the people you are getting the stills from, or make sure that someone who is scanning the photograph using Photoshop or a similar programme knows what they are doing). You also need to make sure that the photograph is big enough. Most of the time you will be editing in 16:9 aspect ratio, which means that your photographs are ideally 1024 x 576 pixels, although you need to check with your editor for precise sizes.

If you are dealing with video archive, you also need to check what format the original source is on. Archive may come from specialist online video archive libraries and they often offer them in Quicktime formats, with varying types of resolution. Again, you need to check with your editor what format you are editing in (e.g. DVCam, HD, HDV) and make sure that you have this downloaded onto an external hard drive or CD/DVD prior to the commencement of editing. If your video archive comes on tape, you need to check what format (Beta SP, DigiBeta, HD, DVCam), and if it's on a format that you don't have a deck for, then you will have difficulties getting it into your editing system. For example, if I have shot a film on DVCam, and want to use some archive that only comes on DigiBeta, then it means I either have to pay for the DigiBeta to be transferred onto DVCam (this can be quite costly) OR I have to make sure I have access to a DigiBeta deck – and if you don't have one it can be quite costly to hire one in.

The same really goes for audio. Make sure you have all music, sound effects, and archive put together on a CD before editing commences. Composed music or a score for your film is often done towards the end of the edit (or even afterwards), but you can at least prepare as much as is available at this time.

Animation and Motion Graphics

You may want to put motion graphics or animation into the film. Although this is something that you don't need to decide right now, if you have an inkling that they might be used, then you need to at least think about where in the film they will appear, what kind of animation, how long it will last, and who is going to do it. It's a good idea to start talking to animators now, and perhaps get some rough tasters to start playing with in the edit.

Commentary

You may want to put commentary in your film. Although commentary is usually something you add once the film is finished, you still may want to think about what kind of commentary you want, and how it will guide the narrative of your film. There may be specific instances where there is a definite need for commentary, and it's a good idea to devote some time to thinking about this before the formal editing phase starts proper.

16. EDITING YOUR DOCUMENTARY

This chapter is not a 'how to' guide on editing documentary; there are plenty of books (and indeed practical courses) which will guide you through the skills needed to develop the craft of editing. Rather, this chapter outlines the functions similar to all non-linear editing systems, and discusses the important grammatical aspects of editing for documentary.

As mentioned earlier, non-linear editing has led to a breakthrough in the way documentaries are made. It's non-destructive, which means that everything you do with your footage in the editing system is reversible. If something is cut a particular way, or a transition doesn't quite work, then you can simply go back and start again. It allows for limitless experimentation and infinite possibility. Moreover, editing systems which were previously the domain of expensive post-production facilities are now so affordable that you can install them on your home computer, and edit professional-looking films yourself.

THE KIT

As with the production phase of your film, you need to be properly kitted out. You can either do this on a shoestring budget, or you can spend thousands of pounds, but the principles are much the same. The main difference will be the degree of flexibility you have with your footage; a very cheap system will have software with limited functionality, and hardware which might make the whole process a bit too slow; spending more money will give you better software, a system which runs much faster, extra storage space and a much more robust system, less prone to crashing. Regardless of the money you spend, there are some fundamental pieces of computer hardware and software that you need in order to be able to edit your footage into a documentary film. Remember though: editing systems, irrespective of how much they cost, are only as good as the person using them; so make sure you use a competent editor, or acquire some really decent skills if you are editing yourself (see figure 20).

A Computer

You need a computer in order to edit, and this can either be a PC or Apple Mac, the only difference between the two being the type of editing software you can run. All modern computers are probably more than capable of running editing software, but you need to make sure that they have a 'firewire' port on the back or side, as this is the main mechanism by which you get your raw footage into your computer. You also need to make sure that it's a fast enough computer (in terms of a fast processor), has adequate hard disk space (see below about storage), and lots of RAM (Random Access Memory) as this will be one of the main things that determines whether your computer runs sluggishly slow, or furiously fast. Rather than give details of specific technical requirements (as they change all the time), the best advice you can take is to get as much RAM as possible, and the highest specs you can for your computer. Check that you have, at the very least, the minimum technical requirements to run the editing software, and then try to aim higher.

Figure 20. Illustration of a typical hardware set up

Hard Disk Space – Most computers these days come with large hard disks (storing 80GB and over). If you don't have much hard drive space on your desktop or laptop, you can always buy an external hard drive to store your rushes. Make sure you get a fast one that is geared up to handle video footage – manufacturers like 'Lacie' or 'G-Technology'. In fact, I always prefer to capture my video footage on external drives as they are often more robust and, of course, more portable than desktop computers.

One tip about your computer – if possible, try to have a dedicated computer for editing, rather than using your laptop or home computer. Of course, finances don't always allow for this, but once you start having lots of applications on your hard drive, and regularly connecting to the Internet, then you open your computer to lots of potential viruses, glitches, and other problems.

A Deck

You need somehow to get your rushes into your computer. This means that you need some kind of player, or deck to play your tapes. Most of the time, people will use their video cameras for this purpose, and this is fine, but can cause unnecessary wear and tear. If possible, try to buy a dedicated deck or 'VTR' for this purpose. They're not cheap, but they are much more robust for cameras. Having said that, within a few years, tapes per se might not be used much, as people will record directly onto hard disk. But for now, it's a good idea – if you can afford it – to get one.

Monitors

You can edit on a single monitor without any difficulty. However, it's good to have two, side by side, so that your viewing area is bigger. Check that your computer can be configured to have two displays, and if so, it's worth investing. However, you should be aware that, when editing on your computer displays, you aren't seeing how the image will really look; for a true representation of the quality of your finished film, you need a dedicated external monitor which receives a signal from your editing software, via a deck or camera. Fully professional calibrated monitors cost a lot of money, but you can always use your standard television to view your film.

Speakers

A good set of speakers connected to your computer will allow you to get a sense of what the recorded audio actually sounds like. Avoid using the internal speakers on your computer – an investment of £100 or so is all you need here.

Editing Software

There are lots of different software packages on the market. They start with the free ones that come with your computer – I-Movie on Apple Macs and Windows Movie Maker on PCs. There are also a number of other cheap or free packages that you can find on the Internet. On the whole, these packages are extremely limited in functionality and flexibility. They allow for very simple edits to be made, but lack any of the features that most professional editors require. If you are a complete novice at editing, they are a good introduction, but you will soon discover their limitations and become frustrated. In terms of more professional software, the three most common editing pack-

Figure 21. Final Cut Pro

ages are Adobe's Premiere, Apple's Final Cut Pro, and the Avid series of editing packages. Premiere runs on PCs only, Avid runs on both PCs and Macs and Final Cut Pro runs on Macs only. Although Premiere has, in recent years, become much more professional, it's Avid and Final Cut that have become industry standards and offer the greatest flexibility and reliability. Which one you choose is really up to personal preference; Final Cut Pro is often the system of choice for independent filmmakers – its ease of use and logical interface give it an inherently quick learning curve. Avid has many different versions ranging from the prosumer *Avid Xpress* for a few hundred pounds to the much more expensive integrated hardware and software systems like Avid 'Nitris' or Avid 'Media Composer'.

THE PRINCIPLES OF EDITING

Whichever editing system you use, they all share some fundamental similarities, and a similar workflow. First of all you need to digitise (sometimes known as 'capturing') the footage on your tapes (mini-DV, DVCam, HDV etc). Next, you edit your footage into one sequence. Finally, you export your sequence into a delivery format, whether this is DVCam, DVD, or to an online suite for mastering onto DigiBeta or film (we'll discuss this in the next chapter in more detail). Now, of course this is a simplified version of the edit workflow, and I'll go into a little bit more detail now about how to actually edit your footage. I'll be using Final Cut Pro as an example, although the main principles apply to most editing software packages.

Organising Your Rushes

The key to editing is to organise all your raw material (rushes) in a way that makes sense to both you and/or your editor. When digitising your rushes onto a hard drive (either in your computer or an external hard drive) you need to put them in various folders (known as bins) in a way that makes sense to you for easy access. So, for example, let's say you are making a film in a local school about an after-hours study class; you might have filmed some interviews with the students and with the teachers, and some observational footage of the study group. In addition you may have some GVs of the exterior of the school. You need to put these clips in relevant bins so that you can find them easily. You may, for example, have an 'I/V with students' bin for all the interviews, with clips inside of each student interview, along with bins for 'I/V with teachers', 'GVs of study group', 'GVs of ext. school' etc. This helps you quickly identify which clips are where within your editing software.

From Assembly Edit to Picture Lock

Once you have logged your rushes, digitised them into your editing system and arranged them in relevant bins, it's then a matter of forming a sequence on your timeline. This simply means that you create one long collection of clips on your timeline, without necessarily focusing on precise editing. For example, you might just have all the wide shots of specific actions, rather than focusing on fine cutting of different shot sizes and framing of the same action. The idea here is that you get a sense of the narrative of your film, seeing if you have all the necessary footage you need to make your film, and getting some idea if the order of the clips makes sense in terms of story structure. This 'assembly edit' may include bits of your rushes, any archive you might want to use, and 'slugs' or blank spaces for where you may be putting bits of animation or graphics. The assembly edit is usually far longer than your final film will be.

The next stage is to edit your film into a 'rough cut' stage, in which you look much more carefully at the shots you have and concentrate more on story structure, exploring different narratives within the film, and focusing on specific sequences. Don't bother with music, effects or even commentary at this stage. The key to this phase of editing is to be able to look at your footage and ask, 'Does it work? Does it make sense?' Your editor (if you are using one) will help you here, but I always find that it is helpful to bring in a third person – one who isn't familiar with either your rushes, or your film – to see whether they can see a story here, and perhaps point out some of the gaps or weaknesses that neither of you have noticed because you are simply too close to the footage.

You will then be aiming towards a 'fine cut' for the rest of the edit, which is a point at which your film is almost finished, and each scene is almost 'frame accurate'. You will have put any commentary in, added music and effects.

During this phase of editing, you may hit certain stumbling blocks. Certain sequences may simply not work; the moods and motivations of characters that you witnessed during filming may simply not come across in your edit. Sequences may have to be dropped, and other elements from your rushes might need to be introduced that you had not considered before. At times, it can be overwhelming, and there are instances when the film simply doesn't work. All the elements are there, but somehow when put together something seems to be missing. Of course, this doesn't always happen, but do be prepared for some frustrating days in the cutting room.

At several stages throughout the editing period, various people might want to see your film. Your producer or executive producer, if you have one, will want to see the film and maybe make suggestions as to how the film can be improved. It's sometimes difficult to stay clear-headed and dispassionate when, after you have slaved away in the edit suite for week after week, someone walks in for an hour and starts saying that specific sequences don't work. If they are skilled at what they do, then you need to take a step back and listen to them, and at least consider what they are asking. It's precisely because they have not been immersed in the film that they have a degree of objectivity that you simply don't have, and their advice is meant to help and not invalidate you. After all, when you show your film to an audience, they will only watch it once, and make a judgement from this single viewing. A producer or commissioning editor is imagining what an audience will think and their relative impartiality is useful, and their advice, usually (though not always, admittedly), is worth listening to at the very least.

The final process of editing is one which takes you from a fine cut to 'picture lock' which, as the name suggests, simply means that you will now make no more changes to the picture – so it has, in effect, been 'locked'. The next stage is to do an online edit of your film and an audio mix, both of which are discussed later in this chapter.

The Grammar of Editing

The process of editing is often the most exciting part of production. It's the time at which you bring all the elements of your film together. It's also easy, during the edit, to lose sight of what your film is about; try to keep in mind your treatment when editing and remind yourself of what it is you are actually trying to say. Documentary editing can often be very different from fiction films. The former is like a blank canvas, and the possibilities in terms of approach and narrative can be infinite. Fiction films, by contrast, owe much of their structure to the earlier, scriptwriting and storyboarding phase of production. So, depending on your viewpoint, the documentary edit can either be an exciting and creative endeavour in which you watch something come together which is greater than the sum of its parts, or it can be overwhelmingly stressful as the blank canvas in front of you refuses to yield any clues as to what your film will eventually look like. Either way, a good editor will help give some shape to your film, but it's useful to think about what the main ingredients are that make for a successful, or disastrous, edit.

Editing is not simply putting your rushes in a certain order and ending up with a film. Certain shots work only with others and the decision, for example, to cut from one shot cannot be a random choice, but needs to be informed by some key principles. You need to make sure each new shot contains new information and that there is continuity between one shot and the next. This is just one rule of *screen grammar*, a concept that refers to some of the visual rules that need to be adhered to in order to make your collection of shots combine to form a narrative. Much has been written about the grammar of editing (see the 'Recommended Reading' section for some suggested books). Just as written and spoken language has a 'grammar' – rules which make it easier to construct sentences and be understood by someone else – the editing of a film has rules which enable an audience to see a collection of shots as an unfolding and compelling story. The rules have evolved over the years. As Walter Murch, the award-winning editor of films such as *Apocalypse Now* and *Cold Mountain* states:

> There are underlying mathematical influences that determine how a film gets put together, which are amazingly consistent, seemingly independent of the films themselves. Over the years, I've come to rely on these influences – navigation points – as I work on each film. For instance: 2.5 – an audience can process only two and a half thematic elements at any moment; 14 – a sustained action scene averages out to 14 new camera positions a minute; 30 – an assembly should be no more than 30 percent over the ideal running length of the film.

But these are perhaps just islands above a larger submerged continent of theory that we have yet to discover

Actually, when you stop to think about it, it is amazing that film editing works at all. One moment we're at the top of Mauna Kea and – cut! – the next we're at the bottom of the Mariana Trench. The instantaneous transition of the cut is nothing like what we experience as normal life, which seems to be one continuous shot from the moment we wake until we close our eyes at night. It wouldn't have been surprising if film editing had been tried and then abandoned when it was found to induce a kind of seasickness. But it doesn't: we happily endure, in fact even enjoy, these sudden transitions for which nothing in our evolutionary history seems to have prepared us.

(excerpt taken from *The Conversations: Walter Murch and the Art of Editing Film* by Michael Ondaatje. 2002 Bloomsbury Publishing PLC)

These rules (or mathematical influences, as Murch calls them) include when to cut from one shot to another, when (and how) to use dissolves, when to use close-up shots, as opposed to wide shots, when to use fades, and so on. However, as you can probably gather, an editor can only work with the material that has been shot, and – unfortunately – cannot perform miracles with shots that are badly framed, lack continuity and have poor sound. It's essential, therefore, to make sure that you shoot for the edit, i.e. make sure that your filming takes into account how the shots will be put together. It's common (especially for new filmmakers) to sit in the edit, and lament that they didn't get enough different shot sizes for a particular sequence, didn't shoot enough cutaways, forgot to record wild track and didn't hold shots long enough.

As we mentioned in the last chapter, good preparation of your rushes is essential for a smooth editing period. As you enter the cutting room (or as you sit by your home computer) for the first time, you need to know your material well. A good knowledge of your rushes, a Paper Edit, and a strong sense of structure are the building blocks of a good edit. Make sure you prepare as best you can.

The 'Online' and the 'Audio Mix'

Once your edit is 'picture locked' you now need to finish the film off with the online and the audio mix. The phrase 'online edit' is actually a bit misleading. It traditionally referred to re-digitising the rushes (after you had finished an 'offline edit') on a superior editing system at a higher resolution (or lower compression) than your own editing system could handle. So, for example, you may have recorded in DV, digitised at a much lower resolution, and then, when you had 'picture locked', exported an EDL (Edit Decision List) and taken this, with your master tapes, to a production facility, where they would have re-digitised the rushes at full resolution. However, with today's powerful computers and large storage facilities, we can often edit 'online' on our own edit systems, without the need to re-digitise. An exception to this may be if you are filming in High Definition (a format which requires a great deal of storage and computer processing power); you may choose to capture in DV and then do an online in true HD.

So, most of the time these days, an 'online edit' refers not only to finishing off the film in the lowest compression but also to numerous other processes which are better handled in expensive and state-of-the-art post-production facilities. This includes *colour grading*, in which your film is effectively 'touched up' either to make poor filming techniques look better (e.g. shots which were too dark, or over-saturated) or to stylistically give your film (or certain sequences within your film) a certain colour and mood. The 'online' also involves making sure your film is in the right format for final delivery (broadcast, theatrical release, DVD etc), so that it conforms to the extensive technical specifications that need to be met.

An audio mix (often referred to as an 'audio dub') is a process whereby your final audio is mixed properly by a sound engineer using dedicated software and hardware such as 'Pro Tools'. All the music and effects are mixed properly with your sync sound and this is the stage at which you might add professionally recorded commentary too.

Both the online edit and the audio mix are completed on professional monitors and speakers, leading to a high-quality, broadcast-standard finished product, so it's a really important stage of the production process. It can be expensive, and you may need to devote a couple of days to the process, but it's something that is invaluable if you want your finished film to have a decent opportunity for distribution.

17. DISTRIBUTING YOUR DOCUMENTARY

At last! You have a finished film! First of all, congratulations for getting to this stage. It's a major feat to have made a documentary, and now is the time to let all this hard work start paying for itself by making sure that as many people as possible get to see your film, and hopefully getting an income for it too.

This is one of the most exciting times ever for documentary distribution. The explosion of television channels, broadband channels, new media opportunities and feature film distribution is greater than it has ever been before and it's a rapidly growing area. This chapter deals with some of the opportunities available, and gives some advice on how to navigate this ever-growing, ever-complex world.

WORKING WITH DISTRIBUTORS

If you have made your film independently (with no funding from broadcasters or other film agencies), then this would usually mean that you, or your company, own the rights to the film. This puts you in a strong position, as you don't have to deal with the issue of rights at all. Assuming you have made a film that broadcasters are interested in (see Chapter 6 for more details on this) then you now have a great product to sell. On the whole, filmmakers usually employ the services of a distributor here, as it can cut out a lot of the groundwork. A good distributor serves three functions that make your life a little bit easier. Firstly, they are often well connected with various broadcasters across the world, and stand more chance of getting your film noticed than you, who will have to do loads of research and send unsolicited DVDs to various broadcasters. Secondly, they attend the various markets around the world such as MipDoc (www.mipdoc.com) and Sunnyside of the Doc (www.sunnysideofthedoc.com). And thirdly, they will undertake a great deal of the laborious paperwork and contracts on your behalf. They want, naturally, in return for this, a slice of the action. This usually amounts to about 30% of the net profit from your film, leaving you with 70%.

There are many distributors to choose from and you need to look at their track record when it comes to distributing the kind of film that you have made (in order to get a sense of where to begin, the Documentary Filmmakers Group in the UK has a comprehensive list of distributors available for its members – www.dfgdocs.com). If possible, meet with prospective distributors, or at least have a decent phone conversation with them. Send them your film, and see what they think, and what plans they would have in terms of distributing it. On the whole, distributors want to try and sell your film to as many outlets as possible – this will mean broadcasters, but also might include DVD sales, online distribution, in-flight entertainment on aeroplanes, cruise ships, and sometimes, theatrical distribution. They'll also want worldwide rights so that they can distribute in any country. You can negotiate with them here as to what rights you want to give them; sometimes you might want to hold back certain rights such as online rights, in case you can give these to another distributor who has more experience in this area, or else attempt to distribute yourself.

SELF-DISTRIBUTION

Sometimes you might consider distributing your film on your own. Bear in mind that with broadcasters, it's probably a good idea for you to have developed some kind of relationship with them in the first place, or at least for your film to have done well at a film festival (see below); otherwise you are making work quite difficult for yourself. However, there is a whole world of distribution that you may be adequately equipped to deal with yourself if you want to cut out the 'middle man'. This is really the area of online and DVD distribution.

With DVDs you can produce a DVD by yourself and then market it. You might want to set up your own website with a shopping cart that allows people to purchase directly from you. However, you are going to have to do considerable marketing in order to attract a substantial customer base. You can also attempt to get in touch with individual organisations to promote your DVD such as other film organisations, networking sites, and perhaps even individual retailers to see if they want to sell the DVD too. Be prepared, however, as this can be very time-consuming. You need some capital in place to produce DVDs, make all the marketing material and then face the arduous task of ringing around trying to sell your film wholesale to various outlets. It might pay off, and indeed there are various success stories, but be prepared for a long haul. You need to ask yourself whether your time wouldn't be better spent moving on to your next film, and leaving the hard slog to distributors. Of course, there might be a situation in which no distributor is interested in your film; if this is the case, then seriously ask yourself, 'Why?' before launching on your own path of self-distribution – after all, if the distributors don't think they can sell your film, then why would you be able to?

Online distribution is a rapidly expanding area, and even within a few months from the publication of this book, the landscape will have evolved considerably. There are many companies that are starting online distribution of films. Apple's ITunes Music Store now sells films and television programmes online. Many other companies have started doing similar things, either allowing the user to purchase a film to download, or rent (either through a digital-rights-managed download or streaming online) for a limited period of time. Some of these companies will focus on blockbuster movies, whilst others will offer more niche titles, including independent documentaries. The model by which you can earn money for these vary; some of these services, like Babelgum (www.babelgum.com), may offer you a one-off fee to acquire your film; others may offer you a revenue share for every time someone downloads your film. The best part about these services is that you can often submit your film as an individual, and directly reap the financial rewards. Since this is a rapidly developing area, it's difficult to give a comprehensive list of those services that offer this, but Babelgum, Joost and Jalipo are good places to start.

THE IMPORTANCE OF FILM FESTIVALS

Film festivals offer a unique opportunity to attract as much possible interest for your film, either directly from sales agents and distributors who attend the festival, or by maximising its marketability due to its inclusion (and perhaps the awards it will win) at one of the major film festivals. In addition, by attending festivals you get a rare opportunity to network and meet a whole host of people, and often (though not always) you get an all-expenses-paid trip to different places across the globe. Also, you get to show your work to an interested audience and talk about your film. But where do you begin? There are literally hundreds, if not thousands, of festivals around the world, and to navigate which ones to enter your film into is no easy matter. You have to plan carefully, and also make sure that you don't spend half your salary entering your film into small festivals which really aren't going to help much at all.

Which Festivals?

Two of the most important festivals to get your film into are the International Documentary Festival Amsterdam (known as IDFA – www.idfa.nl) and the Hot Docs International Documentary Festival in Toronto, Canada (www.hotdocs.ca). IDFA takes place in November each year, and HotDocs takes place at the end of April. Both are high-profile events and extremely important. They are well attended by 'the industry' – producers, commissioning editors, press, sales agents and distributors. The opportunities to network, talk about your film, and generate interest are invaluable. As with all big festivals, they prefer your film to have some kind of 'premiere' status – if not a world premiere, then at least a national or European (or North American in the case of Hot-Docs) premiere is helpful. So, try to get your timing right and put your film into either of these festivals, and avoid submitting to other smaller festivals beforehand. The good news with HotDocs is that, even if your film is not accepted, it is still held in a videotheque there, and it's listed in a big handbook which is made available to buyers, other festival programmers, and distributors. These people may choose to sit down and watch your film, even if it's not selected. So it's definitely worth submitting. In addition there is also a Shadow Festival run alongside IDFA (www.shadowfestival.nl), so it's also worth submitting your film there.

In the UK, there is the Sheffield DocFest, which currently takes place in November, although this may change. This again is an important industry event, with seminars, workshops, talks, discussions, a videotheque, numerous screenings, and of course that all-important bar to meet others and 'network' (a word which I personally hate, but it's impossible to deny the importance of meeting people, talking to them, exchanging business cards, and promoting yourself and your film).

There are numerous other festivals worth considering. A full listing of worldwide documentary festivals can be found at Documentary Filmmakers Group website (www.dfgdocs.com). Research these lists and look for those festivals that have 'industry' events alongside screenings, as these are usually the best to publicise your work. Look at previous festival programmes, and see if the kinds of films screened are the kinds of films you like (and ones you may have heard of) – if they are, the odds are it's full of like-minded people, and a good audience to appreciate your film. Many of these festivals are extremely hospitable, looking after you, arranging special 'directors' events and dinners, so make sure, if you do go, that you make the most of these opportunities. If you've made a short then it's also worth submitting your film to the British Council. They offer a unique service, in which they act as a central clearing house for short films seeking international festival screenings. See www.britishcouncil.org/arts for more info.

How to submit your film

This is easier than it sounds. Film festival applications are often complicated, lengthy, time-consuming and sometimes expensive. There are services that help with this, offering a centralised clearing house (see www.withoutabox.com). These can cost some money, and they don't necessarily cover all relevant festivals, but they can be handy if you want to submit to quite a few festivals. If you are going to do it on your own, then give yourself plenty of time before the deadline to get the necessary materials together. These can include:

- VHS or DVDs of your film. Make sure, if using VHS, you have NTSC copies for American festivals as well as PAL. A word of advice here: don't just send a black cassette/DVD with plain sleeve – label them properly with title, director, contact details, aspect ratio, length etc.
- Full production credits, biographies of filmmaker(s) (including filmography) and transcripts (some festivals demand this).
- Stills. Festivals often want hi-res digital stills (minimum of 300 dpi) from your film. These are sometimes requested on a CD, although some festivals will accept them by Email, ISDN, or by File Transfer Protocol (ftp).

If your film is accepted, then you need to send them a master tape. The most common format here is DigiBeta, or Beta SP, or sometimes 35mm or 16mm film. (Some festivals can only handle Beta SP.) You may have your film on 35mm or you may only have a mini-DV copy. Check with the festival regulations to see if they can accept your format, and pay attention to the aspect ratio here (16:9, 4:3, Full Height Anamorphic etc). Note that you may need to have more than one master in circulation at a time, as they do the rounds at various festivals. This, again, can be costly, so be prudent in how many festivals you send your film to.

What to take with you

Having been selected, sent your master tape, and bought your plane ticket, it's time to go to your festival. But you need to make sure you are prepared. It's helpful to consider taking the following with you:

- Business Cards. No matter how much you might hate them, they are an invaluable way to quickly give someone your details. Get some printed, and take a good supply with you.
- Posters and Flyers. Festivals often allow you to put up posters of your film, so take a couple of large quad-size posters with you. Also print flyers of your film (remember to put contact details on) and distribute them around. Major festivals often have pigeon holes for all delegates,

so you can leave promotional material in them.

- DVD copies of your film. Take a good supply with you, so that you can give them out to people. Again, make sure they are properly labelled and have contact details on them.

Festivals often put themselves out to make you welcome, and it's expected, at the very least, that you attend every screening of your film, to introduce it, and to stay around afterwards for a Q&A. Then, having traumatised yourself discussing your film with an audience of 300 people, you can go for that long-earned drink in the delegates' bar.

SECTION FOUR

18. SOME FINAL WORDS AND SOME UNANSWERED QUESTIONS

This book has looked at the process of making a documentary from the initial concept through to delivery of the final film. An attempt has been made to contextualise the making of documentaries within the real world so that hopefully your film will be seen by as large an audience as possible, which means you need to consider both funding and distribution opportunities. The making of documentaries is a rich, rewarding, and at times frustrating experience. On the whole, it doesn't pay well, but this is balanced by a unique opportunity, which is often unparalleled in other careers, to become immersed in the fascinating worlds of other people and places. What are often overlooked, however, are the many moral and ethical issues which the whole process evokes, and I want to spend some time here examining some of these in detail.

WORKING WITH SUBJECTS

As a documentary filmmaker you may sometimes find yourself caught between two worlds; there might be a conflict between the wishes of the contributor you are filming and the demands of your commissioning editor. Or the conflict might be between what you know your film to be, and what your contributor thinks it is. It doesn't always happen like this, but when it does, it can put you in a difficult position. Take, for example, the following two scenarios:

1. You are making a film in which your contributor ends up, in a particular instance, very angry and emotional. He's recovering from a drug addic-

tion and you are making a film following him through the process. On this particular day he feels he's about to relapse and ends up taking it all out on you, shouting and telling you it's all your fault. Regardless of his regret afterwards, his outburst makes compelling television and reveals – to you as a filmmaker – an important aspect of the 'recovery' process, that of blame and projection. The following day he's very apologetic and asks, emphatically, that you don't include this outburst in the final film. You say nothing but, in the edit, both you and your producer feel that it is important that it's included. What do you do?

2. You are filming political dissidents in Tibet: a group of people, who despite Chinese wishes are actively involved in the Free Tibet campaign, and are receiving secret communications from the Dalai Lama. You feel strongly that this film shows the voices of local Tibetans and how they feel living under Chinese rule. However, you know that if this film gets seen by a wide audience, there's a possibility that the Chinese authorities may identify the people in the film, search them out, and arrest them. What do you do?

Both the above scenarios are real examples of documentary films, which involve a moral dilemma. In such situations, there are no absolute right or absolute wrong answers. They both rest on a conflict between the needs of the film as a product, and the needs of the people in the film. Is it always necessarily the right thing to let a contributor decide what should (and should not) go into a final film? And is it always the right thing to put people at risk, if there is some 'higher purpose' or social objective to the film you are making? It's these kinds of dilemmas that have often been the subject of extensive debate, and it's worth realising that these are important questions that, as a filmmaker, you need to ask yourself.

Perhaps the yardstick by which you decide what is right and what is wrong rests on your own integrity as a filmmaker, and the integrity of your relationship with your contributors. The assumption here is that you don't want to needlessly offend, upset, misrepresent or vilify your subject. Some filmmakers make a contract with their subject, and will not put anything in the film that the subject doesn't want in there; other filmmakers are less liberal, but will build a trusting relationship with the contributor(s) and use their own judgement as to whether or not the final edit is betraying, or honouring, that trust.

DECEPTION

Is it okay to deceive the subjects in your film? Are there some situations when deception is warranted? What about deceiving the audience? Can this ever be justified? There are obviously investigative films in which the filmmaker knowingly deceives his subject in order to either infiltrate a group of people, or to expose a criminal act, and, as a society, we deem such intrusions as justifiable. However, what if it's not such a clear-cut 'black or white' situation? Robert Flaherty's *Nanook of the North*, an infamous documentary (if there is such a thing), contains scenes that are deliberately staged, and characters that are not who they purport to be (the 'family' in the film was not, in fact, a family at all). The audience are led to believe that they are seeing ethnographic footage of life amongst the Inuit people. Flaherty's defence rested on the assumption that a filmmaker must often distort the truth in order to catch the true spirit of a subject, and many filmmakers have followed in this vein; indeed Grierson's definition of documentary as the 'creative interpretation of actuality' sets the stage for justifiable 'deceptions' throughout one's film. Can we justify deception in the name of a 'greater good', and can we say that somehow, if we maintain 'integrity' with regard to both our subjects and our audience, then it's okay, paradoxically, to deceive both?

INFORMED CONSENT AND THE EFFECTS OF BEING IN A DOCUMENTARY

Documentary filmmakers often state that the integrity of the relationship between filmmaker and subject is based on the notion of informed consent, meaning that as long as the subject knows what the film is about, and knows how he will be represented, then our duty, as filmmakers, is done. But this isn't really true, as it really depends to what extent we 'inform' our subject. A similar defence of 'informed consent' is used in reality television, without acknowledging that most people who sign up to being in a reality TV show have little idea what the impact of the programme will be, both during filming and afterwards. The whole genre of reality TV is littered with enough suicides, mental breakdowns and psychological damage to contributors to serve as a warning to even the most conscientious of documentary filmmakers, who should seriously challenge the assumption that informed consent means a full understanding of what being in a documentary is all about.

Then there is the other side of the argument, when we perhaps give too much to the contributors. Nicholas Philibert's award-winning observational documentary *Être et Avoir* depicted a group of schoolchildren and a charming teacher in a small village in rural France. Both the teacher and the children (via their parents or guardians) gave consent to being in the film. However, when the film was a commercial and financial success, the 'cast' somewhat changed their stance. George Lopez, the teacher, made a charge against Philibert of counterfeit (claiming to be co-author of the film because fragments of his courses are depicted in the film) and of infringement of his 'image rights' (which derives from the right to respect for private life). The parents of the schoolchildren made a claim of 20,000 euros each, saying that they should be paid as actors because they sometimes had to repeat certain scenes. Again, is this taking things a step too far, or do the subjects of the film have some kind of legitimate claim to its authorship?

PAYING SUBJECTS

This leads us on to the greater issue of whether we pay subjects who appear in our films. One would assume the answer to this question to be a resounding 'no', and yet there are literally countless examples of filmmakers paying out – either in cash, or 'in kind', to the people who appear in their film. What does this say about the nature of truth, and can we, as an audience, really be expected to believe that the action we see unfolding on the screen is genuine if the people in the film are the recipients of money?

I have hinted at some of the moral, ethical, and professional issues which arise in the process of making a documentary. The discussion is by no means exhausted and there are no doubt countless other examples of such dilemmas which can be found in documentary films. However, hopefully you get the idea that there are no right or wrong answers, no black and white, but merely a whole host of situations in which we find ourselves, and have to ask whether what we are doing is the best thing to do, in any given circumstance. If we accept that documentary is NOT a record of objective reality, but rather an interpretation of it, then we have to accept some responsibility for this interpretation and for any important considerations or decisions that may arise as a result of it.

I'll leave it on that hopefully not too grave note, but there is a weight of responsibility in making a film about real people and real events and the very least we can do, as filmmakers, is try to consider, as thoroughly as possible, the implications of the decisions we make.

SECTION FIVE
RESOURCES

19. SOURCES FOR RESEARCH

There are hundreds of small and specialist archives and footage libraries, and if you're looking for something historically, geographically or stylistically specific then you should certainly explore those options. You can find listings either via Focal (see below) or a facilities search service such as Kemps (www.ktftv.com). The following is a list of the larger libraries offering a range of material.

FOCAL International (Federation of Commercial Audiovisual Libraries)
Pentax House, South Hill Avenue, South Harrow, Middlesex HA2 0DU
T: +44 (0)20 8423 5853
F: +44 (0)20 8933 4826
E: info@focalint.org
www.focalint.org

FOCAL is a membership-based, not-for-profit trade association pairing film researchers with archives and vice versa. It runs a free footage-finder service via its website, and is a great place to start if you're looking for something niche or specific.

BAPLA (British Association of Picture Libraries and Agencies)
18 Vine Hill, London EC1R 5DZ
T: +44 (0)20 7713 1780
F: +44 (0)20 7713 1211
E: enquiries@bapla.org.uk
www.bapla.org.uk

The UK trade association for libraries and archives, the BAPLA represents over 440 companies, and you can search their database by category online.

THE BIG GUYS

View any archive-based doc, and you're likely to see one of these in the credits. The footage that they hold will cover a wide range of topics, and they tend to have offices throughout the world:

ITN Source
200 Gray's Inn Road, London WC1X 8XZ
T: +44 (0)20 7430 4480
F: +44 (0)20 7430 4453
E: uksales@itnsource.com
www.itnsource.com
Represents: ITN; Reuters Television Archive; Granada, Channel 4; British Pathe and Images of War
Categories: News and Current Affairs, History, Arts, Science, Sport

BBC Motion Gallery
BBC Worldwide Ltd
Room E251, Woodlands, 80 Wood Lane, London W12 0TT
T: +44 (0)20 8433 2861/2862
F: +44 (0)20 8433 2939
E: motiongallery.uk@bbc.co.uk
www.bbcmotiongallery.com
Categories: News and Current Affairs, History, Arts, Science, Sport

Getty Images
101 Bayham Street, London NW1 0AG
T: 0800 279 9255 (or +44 (0)20 7544 3445)
F: film.sales@gettyimages.com
www.gettyimages.com
Categories: News and Current Affairs, Arts, Sport

AP Archive

The Interchange, Oval Road, Camden Lock, London NW1 7DZ

I: +44 (0)20 7482 7482

F: +44 (0)20 7413 8327

www.aparchive.com

info@aparchive.com

Represents: ABC America; ABC Australia; Calyx Television; CCTV China; CTV Canada; KRT North Korea; RTR Russia; Sky News UK; Sports News TV; 20th Century Archive; Universal Newsreel; UN and UN Agencies; Vatican TV; WWF

Categories: News and Current Affairs, History, Sport

THE REST

BDFL British Defence Film Library

Chalfont Grove, Narcot Lane, Gerrards Cross, Buckinghamshire SL9 8TN

T: +44 (0)1494 878 278

F: +44 (0)1494 878 007

E: BDFL.Customerservices@ssvc.com

www.bdfl.co.uk

Categories: History

Clips and Footage

Studio 112, Spitfire Studios, London N1 9BE

T: +44 (0)20 7287 7287

F: +44 (0)20 7439 4886

www.clipsandfootage.com

Categories: History, Arts

CNN Imagesource

Turner House, 16 Great Marlborough Street, London W1F 7HS

T: +44 (0)20 7693 1540

F: +44 (0)20 7693 1541

www.cnnimagesource.com

Categories: News and Current Affairs

Corbis

111 Salusbury Road, London NW6 6RG
T: +44 (0)20 7644 7644
F: +44 (0)20 7644 7646
www.corbismotion.com
Categories: News and Current Affairs, Sport

Huntley Film Archives

22 Islington Green, London N1 8DU
T: +44 (0)20 7226 9260
F: +44 (0)20 7359 9337
E: films@huntleyarchives.com
www.huntleyarchives.com
Categories: History

Imperial War Museum Film and Video Archive

All Saints Annexe, Austral Street, London SE11 4SJ
T: +44 (0)20 7416 5291
F: +44 (0)20 7416 5299
www.iwmcollections.org.uk
Categories: History

National Geographic Digital Motion

77 Oxford Street, London W1D 2ES
T: +44 (0)877 730 2022
F: +44 (0)20 7287 1043
www.ngdigitalmotion.com
Categories: History, Science

Oxford Scientific (OSF)

Ground Floor, Network House, Thame, Oxfordshire OX9 3UH
T: +44 (0)1844 262 370
F: +44 (0)1844 262 380
www.osf.co.uk
Categories: Science

Press Association
292 Vauxhall Bridge Road, London SW1V 1AE
I: +44 (0)20 7963 7474
F: +44 (0)20 7963 7476
www.pressassociation.co.uk
Categories: News and Current Affairs, History, Sport

TWI Archive
McCormack House, Burlington Lane, London W4 2TH
Tel: +44 (0)20 8233 5500
Fax: +44 (0)20 8233 6476
E: twiarchive@imgworld.com
www.twiarchive.com
Categories: Sport

Wellcome Library for the History of Medicine
210 Euston Road, London NW1 2BE
T: +44 (0)20 7611 8722
F: +44 (0)20 7611 8369
E: library@wellcome.ac.uk
www.library.wellcome.ac.uk
Categories: History, Science

World Images
8 Fitzroy Square, London W1T 5HN
T: +44 (0)20 7388 8555
www.world-images.org
E: info@world-images.org
Represents: Amnesty International; Greenpeace UK; International Fund for
    Animal Welfare; WWF; In Depth Solutions; Farm Animal Welfare Network
Categories: News and Current Affairs, Science

ZDF Enterprises GmbH
Fred Burcksen
Vice President, Distribution, Merchandising and Investments

T: +49 (0)6131/991-280
F: +49 (0)6131/991-259
burcksen.f@zdf.de
Categories: News and Current Affairs, History and Science

PICTURE LIBRARIES

AKG Images
Berlin, London, Paris
T: +44 (0)20 7610 6103
F: +44 (0)20 7610 6125
enquiries@akg-images.co.uk
www.akg-images.com
Categories: Arts, History, Science

Bridgeman Art Library
T: +44 (0)20 7727 4065
london@bridgeman.co.uk
www.bridgeman.co.uk
Categories: Arts

Mary Evans Picture Library
59 Tranquil Vale, Blackheath, London SE3 0BS
T:+44 (0)20 8318 0034
Toll-free (USA only): 1-866-437-9381
F: +44 (0)20 8852 7211
E: pictures@maryevans.com
www.maryevans.com
Categories: History

Mirrorpix
T: +44 (0)20 7293 3700
desk@mirrorpix.com
www.mirrorpix.com
Represents: The Daily Mirror; The Daily Herald; Sunday Mirror; The People;

Daily Record and Sunday Mail
Categories: News and Current Affairs, History, Sport

The National Archives
Kew, Richmond, Surrey TW9 4DU
T: +44 (0)20 8392 5225
F: +44 (0)20 8487 1974
E: image-library@nationalarchives.gov.uk
www.nationalarchives.gov.uk/imagelibrary
Categories: History

Natural History Museum Picture Library
NHM Image Resources (Photography/Picture Library/Filming)
Cromwell Road, London SW7 5BD
T: +44 (0)20 7942 5401/5324
F: +44 (0)20 7942 5212
E: nhmpl@nhm.ac.uk
www.piclib.nhm.ac.uk/piclib/www/index.php
Categories: History, Science

Nature Picture Library
c/o BBC Broadcasting House
Whiteladies Road, Bristol BS8 2LR
T: (0)117 974 6720
F: (0)117 923 8166
(USA only) Toll-free: 1-866-350-6744
www.naturepl.com
Categories: Science

Press Association
292 Vauxhall Bridge Road, London SW1V 1AE
T: 020 7963 7474
F: 020 7963 7476
www.pressassociation.co.uk
Categories: News and Current Affairs, History, Sport

Wellcome Library for the History of Medicine

210 Euston Road, London NW1 2BE
T: +44 (0)20 7611 8722
F: +44 (0)20 7611 8369
E: library@wellcome.ac.uk
www.library.wellcome.ac.uk
Categories: History, Science

LIBRARIES

British Library

St Pancras, 96 Euston Road, London NW1 2DB

Boston Spa
Wetherby, West Yorkshire LS23 7BQ

British Library Newspapers
Colindale Avenue, London NW9 5HE
T: +44 (0)870 444 1500
www.bl.uk

The British Library receives a copy of every item published in the UK and Ireland and has Reading Rooms in St Pancras and Colindale (the Newspaper Reading Rooms).

British Library of Political and Economic Science

London School of Economics and Political Science
10 Portugal Street, London WC2A 2HD
T: +44 (0)20 7955 7455
F: +44 (0)20 7955 6923
E: ibss@lse.ac.uk
www.lse.ac.uk/collections/IBSS/

Institute of Historical Research

University of London

Senate House, Malet Street, London WC1E 7HU
T: +44 (0)20 7862 8740
F: +44 (0)20 7862 8745
E: ihr.reception@sas.ac.uk
www.history.ac.uk

The National Archives
Kew, Richmond, Surrey TW9 4DU
T: +44 (0)20 8876 3444
www.nationalarchives.gov.uk

National Library for Health
www.library.nhs.uk

A complete library service for medical and research professionals; still in development.

Wellcome Library for the History of Medicine
210 Euston Road, London NW1 2BE
T: +44 (0)20 7611 8722
F: +44 (0)20 7611 8369
E: library@wellcome.ac.uk
www.library.wellcome.ac.uk
Categories: History, Science

NORTH AMERICA

ABC News VideoSource
125 West End Avenue, New York, NY 10023, USA
T: +1 212 456 5421
F: +1 212 456 5428
E: abcvideosource@abc.com
www.abcnewsvsource.com
Categories: News and Current Affairs, History

BBC Motion Gallery

BBC Worldwide Americas

747 Third Avenue, 29th Floor, New York, NY 10017, USA

T: +1 212 705 9399

F: +1 212 705 9342

E: motiongallery.ny@bbc.co.uk

BBC Worldwide Americas

4144 Lankershim Blvd., Suite 200, North Hollywood, CA 91602, USA

T: +1 818 299 9720

F: +1 818 299 9763

E: motiongallery.la@bbc.co.uk

BBC Worldwide Canada

130 Spadina Avenue, Suite 401, Toronto, Ontario M5V 2L4, Canada

T: +1 416 362 3223

F: +1 416 362 3553

E: motiongallery.toronto@bbc.co.uk

Categories: News and Current Affairs, History, Arts, Science, Sport

CBC TV Archive Sales

Box 500, Station A, Toronto, Ontario M5W 1E6, Canada

T: +1 416 205 7608

F: +1 416 205 6257

E: archives@cbc.ca

www.cbc.ca/archives

Categories: History, Arts, Science, Sport

CBS News Archives

524 West 57th Street, New York, NY 10019-2985, USA

T: +1 212 975 2834

F: +1 212 975 5442

www.bbcmotiongallery.com

Categories: News and Current Affairs, History

Canamedia Productions Ltd
381 Richmond St. East, Ste 200, Toronto, Ontario M5A 1P6, Canada
T: +1 416 483 7446
F: +1 416 483 7529
E: itn@canamedia.com

CNN ImageSource, USA
One CNN Center, Atlanta, GA 30303, USA
T: +1 404 827 3326
F: +1 404 827 1840
E: cnn.imagesource@turner.com
www.cnnimagesource.com
Categories: News and Current Affairs

Corbis Motion, US & Worldwide
710 2nd Avenue, Suite 200, Seattle, WA 98014, USA
T: +1 866 473 5264
E: info@corbismotion.com
www.corbismotion.com
Categories: History, Arts, Science, Sport

CTV Archive Sales
9 Channel Nine Court, Toronto, Ontario MIS 3K6, Canada
T: +1 416 332 7389
F: +1 416 332 7384
www.archivesales.ctv.ca
Categories: News and Current Affairs, History, Sport

F.I.L.M. Archives
432 Park Avenue South, Suite 1007, New York, NY 10016, USA
T: +1 212 696 0417
F: +1 212 696 0021
E: info@filmarchivesonline.com
www.filmarchivesonline.com
Categories: News and Current Affairs, Arts, History

Global ImageWorks
65 Beacon Street, Haworth, NJ 07641, USA
T: +1 201 384 7715
F: +1 201 501 8971
E: info@globalimageworks.com
www.globalimageworks.com
Categories: News and Current Affairs, Arts, Science

HBO Archives
1100 Sixth Avenue, New York, NY 10036, USA
T: +1 866 825 3317
F: +1 212 512 5225
E: researchrequest@hboarchives.com
www.hboarchives.com
Categories: History, Science, Sport

Internet Archive
Creative Commons project and online library
www.archive.org
Categories: History

ITN Source
The Empire State Building, 350 Fifth Avenue, Suite 7304, New York,
NY 10118-7304, USA
T: +1 646 723 9540
F: +1 646 792 4668
E: nysales@itnsource.com

3500 West Olive Ave, Suite 990, Burbank, Los Angeles, CA 91505, USA
T: +1 818 953 4115
F: +1 818 953 4137
E: lasales@itnsource.com
www.itnsource.com
Categories: News and Current Affairs, History, Arts, Science, Sport

MacDonald and Associates
5660 N. Jersey Avenue, Chicago, IL 60659-3694, USA
T: +1 773 267 9899
F: +1 773 267 7796
E: macfilms@worldnet.att.net
www.macfilms.com
Categories: History, Arts

National Film Board of Canada
3315 Cote de Liesse Road, Saint-Laurent, Quebec N4N 2N4, Canada
T: +1 514 496 9470
F: +1 514 283 5729
E: stockshots@nfb.ca
www.nfb.ca/stockshots
Categories: History, Science

National Geographic Digital Motion
1145 17th Street NW, Washington, DC 20036-4688, USA
T: +1 877 730 2022
F: +1 202 429 5755

9100 Wilshire Blvd, Suite 401E, Beverly Hills, CA 90212, USA
T: +1 310 734 5300
F: +1 310 858 5801
www.ngdigitalmotion.com
Categories: History, Science

NBC News Archive, Library Sales
30 Rockefeller Plaza, New York, NY 10112, USA
T: +1 212 664 3797
F: +1 212 703 8558
E: footage@nbc.com
www.nbcnewsarchives.com
Categories: News and Current Affairs, History, Arts, Science

Reelin' in the Years Productions LLC

T: +1 619 281 6725
F: +1 858 578 6337
www.reelinintheyears.com
Categories: Arts (Music)

Sherman Grinberg Film Library

T: +1 818 717 9200
E: kacinla@aol.com
Categories: History, Arts, Sport

WGBH Stock Sales

125 Western Avenue, Boston, MA 02134, USA
T: +1 617 300 3939
F: +1 617 300 1056
E: stock_sales@wghb.org
www.wghbstocksales.org
Categories: History, Arts, Science

WPA Film Library

16101 South 108th Avenue, Orland Park, IL 60467, USA
T: +1 708 460 0555
F: +1 708 460 0187
E: sales@wpafilmlibrary.com
www.wpafilmlibrary.com
Categories: History, Arts

Picture Libraries

Christie's Images Inc

13-06 43rd Avenue, Long Island City, NY 11101, USA
T: +1 718 472 5030
F: +1 718 472 9005
E: thepicturelibrary@christies.com

www.christiesimages.com
Categories: Arts

Custom Medical Stock Photo
3660 West Irving Park Road, Chicago, IL 60618-4132, USA
T: +1 773 267 3100
F: +1 773 267 6071
E: sales@cmsp.com
www.cmsp.com
Categories: Science

Corbis
Rights Managed & Royalty-Free
Corbis Canada
T: +1 450 466 6600
F: +1 450 466 9739
E: canada@corbis.com
www.corbis.com
Categories: News and Current Affairs, History, Arts, Science, Sport

Daily News Pix
E: photosales@dailynewspix.com
www.dailynewspix.com
Categories: News and Current Affairs, Sports

Getty Images
122 South Michigan Avenue, Suite 900, Chicago, IL 60603, USA
T: +1 312 344 4500

6300 Wilshire Blvd, 16th Floor, Los Angeles, CA 90048, USA
T: +1 323 202 4200

75 Varick Street, New York, NY 10013, USA
T: +1 646 613 4000

601 N. 34th Street, Seattle, WA 98103, USA
T: +1 206 925 5000

T: 800 IMAGERY
E: sales@gettyimages.com
www.gettyimages.com
Categories: News and Current Affairs, Arts, History, Science, Sport

Stock Montage
1817 N. Mulligan Ave, Chicago, IL 60639, USA
T: +1 773 637 9790
F: +1 773 637 9794
E: images@stockmontage.com
www.stockmontage.com
Categories: History

National Oceanic and Atmospheric Administration
Skip Theberge
NOAA Central Library
T: +1 301 713 2600 x115
E: albert.e.theberge.jr@noaa.gov
www.photolib.noaa.gov/index.html
Categories: Science

New York Public Library Picture Collection
Photographic Services & Permissions
T: +1 212 930 0091
E: permissions@nypl.org
www.digital.nypl.org/mmpco
Categories: History

The Library of Congress, Prints and Photographs Division
101 Independence Ave SE, Washington, DC 20540, USA
T: +1 202 707 8000
E: photoduplication@loc.gov

www.loc.gov
Categories: History

Images from the History of Medicine
Light, Inc.
12160-A Tech Road, Silver Spring, MD 20904-1914, USA
T: +1 301 680 9700
F: +1 301 680 0575
E: nlm.requests@yahoo.com
wwwihm.nlm.nih.gov

Libraries

The Library of Congress
101 Independence Ave SE, Washington, DC 20540, USA
T: +1 202 707 6394
www.loc.gov

U.S. National Library of Medicine
Reference and Web Services
8600 Rockville Pike, Bethesda, MD 20894, USA
T: +1 301 594 5983
F: +1 301 496 2809
E: custserv@nlm.nih.gov
www.nlm.nih.gov
Categories: History, Science

20. RECOMMENDED FILMS

The best way to learn about documentary filmmaking, apart from practising and reading books, is to watch films. This is a selection of films that I would recommend you try to watch. It is by no means exhaustive and represents only a handful of films that will help inform you as a filmmaker and further your knowledge of the documentary genre. It's listed chronologically to give you some idea of the evolution of the documentary genre over time. If a film is available on DVD, then it's indicated. If not, it's worth contacting your local film institute or library, or the production company that made the film, to see how you can get hold of a copy to watch.

1920s

Nanook of the North
Dir. Robert Flaherty, US/France, 1922
Nanook of the North is considered to be the first significant non-fiction feature film, and should be watched for this reason alone. Robert Flaherty spent several years living in Canada and observing Eskimos before deciding to document their lives in detail. Specifically, the film documents the daily life of Nanook, an Inuit Eskimo, and his family, revealing the rituals of trading, fishing, hunting and the migration of a group of people far removed from our industrial civilisation. *(Available on DVD)*

Man with a Movie Camera
Dir. Dziga Vertov, Soviet Union, 1929
This film is truly amazing and, in many ways, was way ahead of its time.

Soviet director Dziga Vertov's experimental film stemmed from his belief that the proper goal of cinema should be to present life just as it is lived. The film, therefore, is a day-in-the-life portrait of a city from dawn until dusk, though they actually shot their footage in several cities, including Moscow, Kiev, and Odessa. The film, originally released in 1929, was silent, and accompanied in theatres with live music. It has since been released a number of times with different soundtracks including one by the composer Michael Nyman. *(Available on DVD)*

1930s

Triumph des Willens (Triumph of the Will)
Dir. Leni Riefenstahl, Germany, 1935
A stunning piece of filmmaking, which shows the art of propaganda filmmaking at its best. The film centres on the Third Reich's 1934 Nuremberg Party Rally, and is an ambitious epic of a film. It was commissioned by Hitler in 1934 and the director, Leni Riefenstahl, faced heavy criticism in the following years for being pro-Nazi and she was tried for, but found not guilty of, war crimes following the end of World War Two. For those who want to learn more about the filmmaker, see the fascinating 1993 documentary *The Wonderful, Horrible Life of Leni Riefenstahl* directed by Ray Müller. *(Both films available on DVD)*

Night Mail
Dir. Basil Wright and Harry Watt, UK, 1936
A film-poem about the Royal Mail express train from London to Edinburgh, with music by Benjamin Britten and the now famous commentary by WH Auden; a poem that mirrors the rhythm of the train, building to a speeding, breathless crescendo. Bearing Cavalcanti's influence, the young director Harry Watt – together with Basil Wright, though authorship has since been disputed by both parties – produced a film with the ostensible intention of showing how the overnight mail service worked. Shots of workers sorting mail are intercut with sweeping night-time landscapes and shapes in shadow, and the excellent sequences demonstrating the mechanical system for collecting

trackside mail bags at high speed. The film has achieved such cult status that it was used as inspiration for a famous British Rail advertisement of the 1980s. *(Available on DVD)*

1940s

Listen to Britain

Dir. Humphrey Jennings and Stewart McAllister, UK, 1942

With no spoken commentary or interviews, this lyrical portrait of Britain in the war years employs a series of tableaux of everyday life, linking them into a coherent whole. The importance of the film's montage is indicated in the co-director's credit given to its editor, Stewart McAllister. Using sound from music performances, radio broadcasts and actuality footage, layered over images of 'ordinary' Britons going about their lives and contributing to the war effort, the film creates a portrait of a Britain united by a common foe. The narrative moves through layered sequences of Britons at work and at leisure; images of rural Britain are accompanied by the sound of RAF squadrons flying overhead, and the film shifts to show uniformed men and women, working and at a dance hall, with the voice of a radio announcer reading the news. It has endured beyond its primary function as propaganda, however, as an early example of the power of documentary. Widely seen as a classic of British documentary, this film has influenced filmmakers from Lindsay Anderson to Mike Grigsby. *(Available on DVD)*

1950s

Nuit et Brouillard (Night and Fog)

Dir. Alain Resnais, France, 1955

This film is an unsettling view and one of the most vivid depictions of life inside the Nazi concentration camps of World War II. Filmed in 1955 at the post-war site of Auschwitz, the film combines colour footage with black-and-white newsreels, and stills found in German, Polish and French archives, to tell the story of the Holocaust and the horror of man's brutal inhumanity. *(Available on DVD)*

O Dreamland

Dir. Lindsay Anderson, UK, 1953

Part of the British 'Free Cinema' movement, *O Dreamland* is a documentary about a famous amusement park, which shows the irony of its manufactured fun. Free Cinema was a movement aimed at breaking away from the entrenched Grierson school of commentary-led industrial documentary, and at making their more impressionistic films accepted as a new direction for documentary. *(Available on DVD)*

1960s

7 Up

Dir. (7 Up) Paul Almond; Michael Apted on all subsequent installments, UK, 1964

Produced as part of Granada's *World in Action* series, the film interviews 14 children from various backgrounds about their views on life and the world around them, and their aspirations for the future. Michael Apted, who was the researcher on the first film, has returned every seven years to catch up on the lives of the original participants, leading to one of the most successful documentary series to come out of the UK. *(Available on DVD)*

Primary

Dir. DA Pennebaker, US, 1960

This is a feature documentary that follows presidential hopefuls John F Kennedy and Hubert Humphrey during the 1960 Wisconsin primary. The film chiefly concentrates on the personality of Kennedy, but is also considered to be one of the most groundbreaking moments in cinema history – not only for leading the revolutionary movement known as cinéma vérité, but also as an intimate portrait of both Kennedy and the American political experience. *(Available on DVD)*

Don't Look Back

Dir. DA Pennebaker, US, 1967

Another Pennebaker film, this time focusing on Bob Dylan, on his triumphant concert tour of England in 1965. Pennebaker's camera follows him from airport to hall, from hotel room to public house, from conversation to concert. Joan Baez and Donovan, among others, are on hand. It charts the period when Dylan shifted from acoustic to electric, a transition that not all fans applauded. Pennebaker catches Dylan on the cusp of a radical career change, a man who seems to be overwhelmed by his boundaries and is in search of some sort of escape route. *(Available on DVD)*

Chronique d'un Été (Chronicle of a Summer)
Dir. Jean Rouch and Edgar Morin, France, 1960
Documentary investigation into the lives of a group of ordinary Parisians, consisting mainly of tape-recorded interviews. 'Tell us, are you happy?' One simple question put forth to Parisians, from a market researcher, stirs and ignites this manipulated cinéma vérité snapshot of France in the 60s. Rouch was one of the first filmmakers to use hand-held 16mm camera with sync sound. Rouch and Morin coined the term 'cinéma vérité' to describe their approach to filmmaking, which is sometimes described as 'fly-on-the-wall filmmaking' because the filmmakers attempt to make their presence as unobtrusive as possible... although their specific practice, in which they often placed people in situations and provoked specific responses, differs from what later came to be called vérité films. *(Available on DVD)*

Titicut Follies
Dir. Frederick Wiseman, USA, 1967
Frederick Wiseman's highly controversial documentary chronicling life inside a Massachusetts psychiatric institution for the 'criminally insane'. The film was subjected to a worldwide ban until 1992 because the Massachusetts Supreme Judicial Court ruled that it was an invasion of inmate privacy. The film goes behind the walls of the asylum to show severe and graphic images revealing the treatment of inmates by guards, social workers, and psychiatrists. The film is seen, by many, as a masterpiece of the Direct Cinema movement, which has often been described as the North American counterpart to the European cinéma vérité movement. It's characterised by using natural light, portable cameras, sync sound and through observational filming

to capture reality (and, as its exponents have claimed, even truth) on screen. *(Available on DVD)*

The War Game
Dir. Peter Watkins, UK, 1965
Using non-professional actors and documentary techniques, the film imagines the effects of a nuclear strike on an unprepared Britain. The scenes of chaos and destruction were so plausible that it was banned by the BBC at the time, and not broadcast for another 20 years.

In the Year of the Pig
Dir. Emile de Antonio, US, 1968
A historical account of Vietnam beginning in the 1840s and showing events leading to the longest war. Made by celebrated and controversial filmmaker Emile de Antonio, it was a criticism of American involvement at the height of the war's intensification.

1970s

Battle of Chile
Dir. Patricio Guzman, Chile, 1975
An extremely frank and incisive view into the minds of the Chilean upper class and atmosphere surrounding the murder of President Allende by General Pinochet. The first of the two films, *The Battle of Chile: The Insurrection of the Bourgeoisie* (1975), inspects the escalation of rightist opposition following the left's unexpected victory in Congressional elections held in March 1973. Finding that parliamentary democracy would not stop Allende's socialist policies, the right wing shifted its tactics from the polls to immediate action on the streets. *The Battle of Chile: The Coup d'Etat* (1976) opens with the attempted military coup of June 1973, which is put down by troops loyal to the government.

Punishment Park
Dir. Peter Watkins, UK, 1970
A little seen but profound film. Like *The War Game*, it is a docudrama, this

time set in the US during the height of the Vietnam War. It follows anti-war protestors who fall foul of a law that criminalises dissent, as they are put through a brutal punishment in the Californian desert. *(Available on DVD)*

The World At War

Dir. Ted Childs, Michael Darlow, David Elstein, John Pett, Hugh Raggett, Martin Smith, UK, 1974

A multi-volumed documentary mini-series, and seen as one of the most definitive television series covering the entire history of World War Two from the causes of the 1920s to the aftermath of the Cold War in the 1950s. *(Available on DVD)*

The Family

Dir. Paul Watson, UK, 1974

Credited as the genesis of 'fly-on-the-wall' documentary on UK television, this 12-part series focused on the working class Wilkins family in Reading. Filming 18 hours a day over three months, the documentary was controversial at the time because of some of the issues it raised about class, race and manners in 70s England.

Grey Gardens

Dir. Albert Maysles, David Maysles, Ellen Hovde, Muffie Meyer, US, 1975

Edith Bouvier Beale, nearing 80, and her daughter Edie are a secluded pair who live together in a run-down mansion in East Hampton, on the Long Island coast. There are hints that Edie came home 24 years earlier to be cared for, rather than to care for her mother. Intimate conversations are interspersed with private celebrations, as the women address the camera, talking over each other and sharing 'public' reminiscences of their past life in New York high society. *(Available on DVD)*

1980s

The Life and Times of Rosie the Riveter

Dir. Connie Field, US, 1980

The manpower shortage of World War Two necessitated the entry into the workplace of millions of women, leaving them to work in areas such as welding, riveting etc. The film reveals the harassment and discrimination that women were often subjected to in the years of the war, and the situation after the war when they were released upon the return of the soldiers.

Sans Soleil
Dir. Chris Marker, France, 1983
Sans Soleil is a non-linear essay film by documentary filmmaker Chris Marker. It consists of a collage of images gathered from Japan, Africa, Iceland, San Francisco, and France, presented without direct sound. The soundtrack consists of occasional spells of electronic music while a woman's voice-over narrates letters written by a possibly fictional traveller in poetic verse. The outwardly miscellaneous footage that makes up this film is randomly assembled, jumping from one country or continent to another in the same breath. It remains one of the director's most masterly accomplishments. *(Available on DVD)*

Handsworth Songs
Dir. John Akomfrah, UK, 1986
Filmed in London and Handsworth during the 1985 riots, this documentary takes a detailed look at the historical, social and political background responsible for racial turmoil, and the reasons for the fury and disenchantment felt by many from the ethnic communities in Britain, specifically pertaining to the Asian and West Indian ethnicities.

Atomic Café
Dir. Kevin Rafferty, Pearce Rafferty and Jayne Loader, US, 1982
Atomic Café is an ironically funny collection of film clips taken from American propaganda films of the 1950s. The propaganda is used to reveal the lies told by the government concerning the atomic bomb. One of these clips is the classic instructional film 'Duck and Cover'. Here, the government assures its citizens that schoolchildren will be safe from a nuclear explosion simply by crouching under their desks, and covering their heads. *(Available on DVD)*

Shoah

Dir. Claude Lanzmann, France, 1985

Claude Lanzmann directed this 570-minute documentary about the Holocaust, which consists only of interviews, including those of survivors, witnesses and ex-Nazis. Lanzmann does an excellent job of asking the most specialised and detailed questions, which effectively make an appalling portrait of the events of Nazi genocide. Through the interviews, Lanzmann calls attention to the belief many of the time had: that what happened was not as 'unthinkable' as it may seem to contemporary viewers, and can happen anywhere and at any time. *(Available on DVD)*

Thin Blue Line

Dir. Errol Morris, US, 1988

Using interviews and re-enactments, the film examines the 1976 murder of a Dallas police officer, Robert Wood, and the wrongful conviction of one of the two men mixed up in the killing. With a score from Philip Glass, the film has the mood of a thriller or detective story, more common to fiction filmmaking. *(Available on DVD)*

1990s

The Leader, His Driver, and the Driver's Wife

Dir. Nick Broomfield, UK, 1991

One of Broomfield's better films. While trying to gain access to far-right South African leader Eugene Terreblanche, Broomfield meets his driver, JP, and JP's wife Anita. As with many of Broomfield's films, he opens the audience up to the process of filmmaking, and much of the film focuses on trying to get an interview with the right-wing leader. With all Broomfield's films, you either love them or hate them – but either way, it's important to see the work of someone who has been pivotal in shaping contemporary British documentary. *(Available on DVD)*

The War Room

Dir. Chris Hegedus and DA Pennebaker, US, 1993

The film takes us inside Bill Clinton's 1992 presidential campaign and the exciting race that proved to be one of the most memorable in US history, and came to define American political discourse for the 1990s. The documentary explores national politics that take place behind the curtain, by examining the day-to-day operations of Bill Clinton's campaign staff. *(Available on DVD)*

Hoop Dreams
Dir. Steve James, US, 1994

This documentary follows two inner-city Chicago high-school boys with a love for basketball. Beginning at the start of high school and following the boys through recruitment, the documentary exposes the hurdles the boys had to jump in order to escape the ghetto, and the immense difficulty of achieving their goals when everything is working against them. The obstacles these young men face include parental drug addiction, family poverty, and inner-city violence, as well as those that arise in competition, such as physical injuries. *(Available on DVD)*

Crumb
Dir. Terry Zwigoff, US, 1994

This documentary chronicles the life and times of Robert Crumb. Robert Crumb is a respected but controversial underground comic-book artist and writer whose creations include the popular 'Keep on Truckin'' and 'Fritz the Cat' (1972). Crumb's adult subject matter includes weird sexual obsessions, social criticism, and personal, confessional observations about abnormal human psychology. Interviews with his mother, two brothers, wife and ex-girl-friends, reveal an upbringing that has crippled Crumb but is also responsible for having fuelled the artist's groundbreaking work. Through these interviews, along with selections from his vast quantity of graphic art, we are treated to a darkly comic ride through one man's subconscious mind. *(Available on DVD)*

The Dying Rooms
Dir. Brian Woods and Kate Blewett, UK, 1995

Producers and directors Brian Woods and Kate Blewett uncover the systematic neglect of abandoned babies in Chinese state-run orphanages. They find rooms where orphaned children are left in appalling conditions, often living little more than a few months. These are known as 'The Dying Rooms'. The film, in the long term, had a positive effect on the one-child policy, and brought worldwide attention to the issues. A good film to watch and realise that maybe documentaries can change the world. *(Available on DVD)*

When We Were Kings
Dir. Leon Gast, US, 1996
In 1974, boxers Muhammad Ali and George Foreman came to the still-developing and politically insecure African nation of Zaire for what Ali called the 'Rumble in the Jungle', a highly publicised world heavyweight championship fight. Promoter Don King wanted to make a name for himself and offered both fighters five million dollars apiece to fight one another. Filmmaker Leon Gast flew to Zaire to film the fight. Gast's footage was shelved for 22 years due to legal and financial problems, but, when it was finally released in 1996, *When We Were Kings* provided a brilliant portrait of the contentious Ali. *(Available on DVD)*

Buena Vista Social Club
Dir. Wim Wenders, US, 1999
A group of legendary Cuban musicians, some in their 90s, were brought together by Ry Cooder to record the Grammy-winning album, *The Buena Vista Social Club*. Excited by these colourful characters and their extraordinary music, Wenders travelled to Havana, Cuba to chronicle the cooperation and camaraderie between Ry Cooder and his veteran musician friends. In this film, we see and hear some of the songs being recorded in Havana. Wenders explains: 'In Cuba the music flows like a river. I want to make a film that'll just float on this river. Not interfere with it, just drift along.' *(Available on DVD)*

2000 – PRESENT

Les Glaneurs et la glaneuse (The Gleaners and I)
Dir. Agnès Varda, France, 2000

A profound, picaresque investigation into French life as lived by the country's poor and the film's own director, Agnès Varda. A documentary capturing the world of French gleaners who collect and make use of what others have discarded. The film is notable for its use of a hand-held camera and for its unusual camera angles and techniques. *(Available on DVD)*

Dark Days
Dir. Marc Singer, US, 2000

Marc Singer goes into New York's underground to live with entire communities of Manhattan's homeless. Singer was a novice filmmaker, and the film is testament to how the 'Credit Card Film' can actually have resounding success (winning at Sundance). Shot on film, in black and white, with an amazing soundtrack by DJ Shadow, the film is incredibly evocative and stylised. It never shies away from the gloomy reality of these subterranean dwellers, most of whom are or were drug addicts. The people themselves have wit, intelligence, and spirit. *(Available on DVD)*

Être et Avoir
Dir. Nicolas Philibert, France, 2002

An intimate portrait of a village school in rural France, which was a surprise hit at cinema box offices. Although a wonderful character piece, director Philibert was also capturing a disappearing way of life in France. *(Available on DVD)*

Bowling for Columbine
Dir. Michael Moore, US, 2002

Filmmaker, author, and political activist (and some would say propagandist) Michael Moore trains his satirical eye on America's obsession with guns and violence. It is a film about the state of the Union, and the violent soul of America. Moore sets out to explore the roots of this bloodshed. One of the biggest-grossing documentaries of all time, it should be watched in order to appreciate Moore's unique style that has made him one of the most successful contemporary documentary filmmakers. *(Available on DVD)*

The Last Peasants

Dir. Angus Macqueen, UK, 2003

Following three families in a remote Romanian village in the Maramures area, where every family has an illegal immigrant abroad. Shot in Romania, London, Paris and Dublin over 18 months, it is a series about the death of an old world and the reality of the new.

Touching the Void

Dir. Kevin Macdonald, UK, 2003

Director Kevin Macdonald reconstructs mountaineers Joe Simpson and Simon Yates's fateful climb in the Peruvian Andes in 1985, combining dramatic re-enactments and interviews. Following a successful ascent, disaster struck when Simpson fell and broke several bones in his leg. Yates unknowingly lowered Simpson over the lip of a crevasse and was no longer able to hold on. Certain they were both about to be pulled to their deaths, Yates cut the rope. But Simpson astoundingly survived the 100-foot fall, and made it back to base camp three days later despite a broken leg and having eaten nothing but ice. We hear the real-life Simpson and Yates painfully detailing their death-defying experiences, whilst non-speaking actors Brendan Mackey and Nicholas Aaron are filmed on location at over 20,000 feet in the Peruvian mountains, cramping around in crampons, abseiling down rock faces, and chipping away with ice axes. *(Available on DVD)*

The Corporation

Dir. Mark Achbar, Jennifer Abbott, Joel Bakan, US, 2003

In the mid-1800s, corporations began to be recognised as individuals by US courts, granting them unprecedented rights. *The Corporation* delves into that legal standard, essentially asking: if corporations were people, what kind of people would they be? This film makes an in-depth psychological examination of the organisation model through various case studies, and cleverly uses archive (much of which was free) to great effect. The frequency of corporate influence on our lives is explored through an assessment of efforts to influence behaviour, including children's behaviour. The filmmakers interview several leftist figures like Michael Moore, Howard Zinn, Naomi Klein and

Noam Chomsky, and give representatives from companies Burson Marsteller, Disney, Pfizer and Initiative Media a chance to relay their own points of view. *(Available on DVD)*

Fog of War: Eleven Lessons from the Life of Robert S McNamara
Dir. Errol Morris, US, 2003
A documentary about Robert McNamara's career as Secretary of Defence under the Kennedy and Johnson Administrations. McNamara reveals the tragedies and glories of the 20th century, and discusses experiences and teachings learned during his tenure. The film primarily focuses on McNamara's 'eleven lessons' learned during this time. Morris used his patented Interretron – a two-way mirror that allows a subject to speak into the camera while seeing Mr Morris's face. The result is part-film, part-confessional, which makes compelling viewing. *(Available on DVD)*

Capturing the Friedmans
Dir. Andrew Jarecki, US, 2003
The Friedmans are a seemingly normal middle-class family living in the affluent New York suburb of Great Neck. In the 80s, Professor Arnold Friedman is arrested for possession of some magazines of child pornography. A further investigation by the police discloses that Arnold and his son Jesse allegedly molested his young students during their private computer class. *Capturing the Friedmans* follows their story from the public's perspective and through home-movie footage of the family in crisis, shot inside the Friedman house, often by Arnold's children. The documentary shows how the family is torn apart in the midst of scandal. *(Available on DVD)*

My Architect
Dir. Nathaniel Kahn, US, 2003
My Architect is filmmaker Nathaniel Kahn's intimate exploration of his father's life. Louis Kahn, the renowned architect, was found dead in Penn Station in 1974. His obituary in the *New York Times* mentioned Kahn's importance to modern architecture, but did not mention that he had a son. Louis Kahn in fact had two illegitimate children with two different women outside of his

marriage. Nathaniel traces his father's past, from childhood through his career, visiting his father's buildings throughout the world, meeting his father's contemporaries, colleagues, students, wives and children.

Super Size Me
Dir. Morgan Spurlock, US, 2004

In 2002, director Morgan Spurlock subjected himself to a diet based only on McDonald's fast food three times a day for thirty days and without working out. Spurlock is out to prove the detrimental physical and mental effects of consuming fast food. While doing this, he also provides a look at the food culture in America through its schools, corporations, and politics as seen through the eyes of regular people and health advocates. *Super Size Me* is a movie that sheds a new light on what has become one of the nation's biggest health problems: obesity. *(Available on DVD)*

Fahrenheit 9/11
Dir. Michael Moore, US, 2004

Another Michael Moore film, in which he reflects on the current state of America, including the powerful role oil and greed may have played after the September 11, 2001 terrorist attacks. He also depicts alleged dealings between two generations of the Bush and bin Laden families, and other Saudi groups. Through facts, footage and interviews, Moore illustrates his contention that Bush and his cronies have landed America in worse trouble than ever before and why Americans should not stand for it. *(Available on DVD)*

Born into Brothels
Dir. Zana Briski, Ross Kauffman, US, 2004

While documenting the experiences of prostitutes in Calcutta's red-light district, photojournalist Zana Briski befriended many of their children and decided to provide them with a chance to record images from their own lives. After several years of learning in workshops with Briski, the kids created their own photographs with point-and-shoot 35mm cameras. Their images capture the intimacy and colour of everyday life in the overpopulated sections of Calcutta. *(Available on DVD)*

A State of Mind

Dir. Dan Gordon, UK/ North Korea, 2004

After the 2002 RTS award-winning documentary *Game of Their Lives*, Very-MuchSo Productions were granted permission from the North Korean film authorities to make a second documentary in what is one of the world's least-known societies. This observational film follows two young gymnasts and their families for over eight months in the lead up to the Mass Games, which involves thousands of participants in a choreographed social realist spectacular, perhaps the biggest and most elaborate human performance worldwide. The film unravels some of the cultural meanings behind this epic celebration and places the country's current political status as a 'rogue nation' in perspective using some of its most important historical moments. *(Available on DVD)*

The Power of Nightmares

Dir. Adam Curtis, UK, 2004

A three-part series broadcast on BBC2, *The Power of Nightmares* explores the ideological basis behind the 'war on terror', linking it to the Cold War and exploring the idea that an organised, global terror network is an illusion. The series consists of three one-hour films, consisting mostly of a montage of archive footage with Curtis's narration. A feature-film version has also been made. *(Available on DVD)*

Control Room

Dir. Jehane Noujaim, US, 2004

Egyptian-American filmmaker Jehane Noujaim directs *Control Room*, a documentary investigating the ethics of media-managed wars. A chronicle which provides a rare window into the international perception of the Iraq War, courtesy of Al Jazeera, the Arab world's most popular news outlet. The station has revealed (and continues to show the world) everything about the Iraq War that the Bush administration did not want us to see. *(Available on DVD)*

The 3 Rooms of Melancholia

Dir. Pirjo Honkasalo, Finland/Germany/Denmark/Sweden, 2004

An award-winning documentary examining how the Chechen War has psychologically affected children in Russia and in Chechnya. The film concludes with profiles of a handful of children who have been traumatised by the war, ranging from a boy gang-raped by Russian troops to another whose own mother was driven mad and tried to kill him.

Darwin's Nightmare
Dir. Hubert Sauper, Austria/Belgium/France/Canada/Finland/Sweden, 2004
In the 1950s or 1960s, the Nile perch was released into Lake Victoria. In just a few decades, the large, voracious predator has all but eliminated the other species of fish, turning the lake into an ecological wasteland. The larger scope of the story explores the gun trade to Africa that takes place under the covers – Russian pilots fly guns into Africa, then fly fish back out to Europe. The hazards and consequences of this trade are explored, including the pan-African violence propagated by the constant flow of weapons into the continent. The Africans are in grave jeopardy, even as they survive in the only ways they know how.

Grizzly Man
Dir. Werner Herzog, US, 2005
Using footage shot firsthand by his subject, Herzog pieces together the story of Timothy Treadwell, an animal-rights activist who for 13 summers lived in the Alaskan wild with grizzly bears as his main companions. Herzog injects his own perspective into the archive, resulting in a film that is part-nature documentary, part-psychological profile into a fascinating individual. *(Available on DVD)*

Sisters in Law
Dir. Kim Longinotto and Florence Ayisi, UK, 2005
Fighting to eradicate corruption from their country's patriarchal legal system, *Sisters in Law* follows the women endeavouring to make an impact in the courtroom. With the number of reported cases of assault, domestic violence and statutory rape on the rise, this film explores the changing role of women in Cameroon's legal system. Beatrice is a judge in the Court of First Instance

in Kumba where she is often confronted with cases highlighting the need for more female legal representation. Juliana is a Court Registrar struggling to become a judge in the local Customary Court.

21. RECOMMENDED READING

This book's main purpose has been to give you a succinct yet comprehensive introduction to the art and craft of documentary filmmaking. However, there are numerous other books which specialise in specific areas of this genre. I've listed a selection below:

Erik Barnouw (1993) *Documentary: A History of the Non-fiction Film*. Second Revised Edition. Oxford University Press. This is a good comprehensive introduction to documentary history, starting from 1895 and going up to 1993.

Sheila Curran Bernard (2003) *Documentary Storytelling for Video and Filmmakers*. Focal Press. This is a great book for looking in-depth at narrative and storytelling within the documentary genre.

Michael Rabiger (1997) *Directing the Documentary*. Third Edition. Focal Press. At over 400 pages long, this is one of the most detailed resources available on this subject matter. It focuses much more on the craft, as opposed to 'industry' skills, but is an invaluable resource.

Michael Tobias (Ed) (1999) *The Search for Reality: The Art of Documentary Filmmaking*. Michael Wise Productions. This book is basically a collection of essays from over 40 documentary filmmakers. Includes some useful insights.

Ilisa Barbash (1997) *Cross-Cultural Filmmaking: A Handbook for Making Documentary and Ethnographic Films and Videos*. University of California Press. An excellent book for those interested in an ethnographic or anthropological approach to documentary filmmaking.

Alan Rosenthal (2002) *Writing, Directing, and Producing Documentary Films and Videos*. Third Edition. Southern Illinois University. A good introductory handbook, with a skew towards North American readers.

Adam P Davies & Nic Wistreich (2005) *UK Film Finance Handbook – How To Fund Your Film*. Netribution (available through their website www.netribution.co.uk). Although it's about film finance in general in the UK, there are some very useful tips to be gained for documentary funding, especially feature documentaries.

Roy Thompson (2004) *Grammar of the Edit*. Focal Press. A succinct and very readable introduction to the grammar of editing, which is invaluable to both filmmakers and editors.

Karel Reisz and Gavin Millar (1989, first published in 1953) *The Technique of Film Editing*. Second Edition. Focal Press. A bible for film editing, this 400-page book is seen as a classic. Despite being first published over 60 years ago, it hasn't particularly aged and is a must-read for those who really want to learn more about this area.

Walter Murch (2001) *In the Blink of an Eye*. Second Revised Edition. Silman-James Press. Murch is one of the foremost contemporary film editors. In this book, he breaks down why and how cuts work, and writes about the all-important grammar of film editing.

22. LIST OF COMMISSIONING EDITORS

Below is a list of most of the UK commissioning editors for documentaries (and factual programming). For a list of European commissioning editors, the most comprehensive resource is the Television Handbook published by the European Documentary Network (www.edn.dk).

Please note that commissioning editors chop and change their jobs, often with little notice, and therefore this list is by no means set in stone, and is meant only as a guide. Check with the broadcaster that the person you have listed is still working for that company and in that job. The contact details listed below should still route you to the new commissioning editor. Where possible, I've also included the website details for producers, which should give up-to-date details of who's who, and what they are looking for in terms of ideas.

BBC

British Broadcasting Corporation
BBC White City
201 Wood Lane, London W12 7TS
www.bbc.co.uk/commissioning

The BBC structure is ever-changing and at the time of going to press it's going through a major upheaval. In the past, all documentary commissioning has been part of the factual department. Now this has been replaced with a new structure called 'BBC Knowledge' which incorporates documentaries, factual features and formats, arts, performance and religion, specialist factual (history, natural history and science), current affairs and daytime factual. The newest changes also mean that there are two sets of commissioning editors – those who commission in-house and those that purely commission from independent production companies. The details given below are from those who largely commission from the independent sector, except for strand editors who commission across the board. At the moment, the BBC has pledged to commission a minimum of 25% of its output within BBC Knowledge from independent companies.

The BBC officially instruct all companies to submit proposals through its on-line e-commissioning system. However, although you ultimately do have to submit your proposal this way, in the first instance I'd advise trying to have some kind of direct dialogue with the commissioning editors, perhaps sending them a paragraph about your idea. If you are going to submit a proposal online, send a hard copy too in the post, as the visual presentation of a good-looking proposal with still photos etc. may grab the much-needed attention of a commissioning editor.

Commissioning in General

Glenwyn Benson
Controller, Knowledge Commissioning
(Encompasses Documentaries; Current Affairs; Specialist Factual; Arts, Music and Religion; and Multi-Platform)
Email: glenwyn.benson@bbc.co.uk

Krishan Arora
Independents Executive
Email: krishan.arora@bbc.co.uk
Krishan doesn't commission projects, but is the liaison between independent producers and the BBC, hopefully making the BBC's commissioning process a little clearer to the rest of us.

Documentaries

Richard Klein
Commissioning Editor, Documentaries
Room 6060, BBC TV Centre, Wood Lane, London W12 7RJ
Email: docs.proposals@bbc.co.uk
Prefers to receive proposals by Email.

Ben Gale
Executive Producer, Factual Features and Documentaries (BBC THREE)
Email: ben.gale@bbc.co.uk

Charlotte Moore
Executive Producer, Documentaries
Email: charlotte.moore@bbc.co.uk

Maxine Watson
Executive Producer, Documentaries
Email: maxine.watson@bbc.co.uk

Current Affairs & Investigations

Karen O'Connor
Commissioning Editor, Current Affairs & Investigations
Room 1172, BBC White City, 201 Wood Lane, London W12 7TS
Email: curraffairs.proposals@bbc.co.uk
Prefers to receive proposals by Email.

Lucy Hetherington
Executive Producer, Current Affairs
Email: lucy.hetherington@bbc.co.uk

Specialist Factual

Emma Swain
Commissioning Editor, Specialist Factual
Responsible for: History, Natural History, Science and Business
Room 6060, BBC TV Centre, Wood Lane, London W12 7RJ
Email: specfact.proposals@bbc.co.uk
Prefers to receive proposals by Email.

Martin Davidson
Executive Producer, Specialist Factual
Email: martin.davidson@bbc.co.uk

Arts, Music and Religion

Adam Kemp
Commissioning Editor, Arts, Music and Religion
Room 6060, BBC TV Centre, Wood Lane, London W12 7RJ
Email: arts.proposals@bbc.co.uk
Prefers to receive proposals by Email.
Jacquie Hughes
Executive Editor for Arts and Religion
Email: jacquie.hughes@bbc.co.uk

Features and Factual Entertainment

To be announced
Commissioning Editor, Features and Factual Entertainment

Mirella Breda
Executive Producer for Factual Features and Factual Entertainment
Email: mirella.breda@bbc.co.uk

Network Contacts in the Nations

Independent producers have the choice of whether to offer ideas to Network via the Genre Controller/Commissioning Editor or via the contact in individual Nations.

Northern Ireland

Mike Edgar
Head of Programme Production
Responsible for: Northern Ireland (Entertainment & Events)
Room 229, BBC Northern Ireland, Broadcasting House, Ormeau Avenue, Belfast BT2 8HQ
Tel: (02890) 338 375
Fax: (02890) 338 175
Email: mike.edgar@bbc.co.uk

Jeremy Adams
Factual and CA Network and Commissions – TVCA NI
BBC Northern Ireland
Broadcasting House, Ormeau Avenue, Belfast BT2 8HQ
Tel: (02890) 338 359
Fax: (02890) 338 591
Email: jeremy.adams@bbc.co.uk

Scotland

Andrea Miller
Head of Factual Programmes, Scotland
Responsible for: Scotland (Factual)
Room 3169, BBC Scotland, Queen Margaret Drive, Glasgow G12 8DG
Tel: (0141) 338 3646
Email: andrea.miller.01@bbc.co.uk

Neil McDonald
Creative Director, Specialist Factual
Responsible for: Scotland (Specialist Factual)
Room 3177, BBC Scotland, Queen Margaret Drive, Glasgow G12 8DG
Tel: (0141) 338 2798
Fax: (0141) 338 2510
Email: neil.mcdonald-factual@bbc.co.uk

Wales

Adrian Davies
Head of Factual Programmes, BBC Wales
Responsible for: Wales (Factual)
Room 4020, BBC Wales, Broadcasting House, Llantrisant Road,
Cardiff CF5 2YQ
Tel: (02920) 322 976
Fax: (02920) 322 418
Email: adrian.davies@bbc.co.uk

David Jackson
Wales Music and Arts
Responsible for: Arts, Classical Music/Performance (all ideas from outside the M25) and Wales Entertainment
Room E4113, BBC Wales, Broadcasting House, Llantrisant Road,
Cardiff CF5 2YQ
Tel: (02920) 322 111
Fax: (02920) 322 544
Email: davidm.jackson@bbc.co.uk
Happy to receive ideas on paper or Email

Strands

Nick Fraser
Commissioning Editor, Storyville
(Co-production, pre-sale and acquisition of single, international, documen-

tary films)
Room 202, 1 Mortimer Street, London W1T 3JA
Tel: 020 7765 5211
Fax: 020 7765 5210
Email: storyville@bbc.co.uk
Will consider any subject – not specifically Arts
For further information about the strand see bbc.co.uk/storyville

Andrew Cohen
Editor, Horizon
Room 5110, BBC White City, 201 Wood Lane, London W12 7TS
Tel: 020 8752 6134
Fax: 020 8752 6155
Email: horizon@bbc.co.uk
Prefers to receive written proposals, ideally one or two pages long.

Clive Edwards
Executive Producer, Money Programme
Room 4116, BBC White City, 201 Wood Lane, London W12 7TS
Tel: 020 8752 7400
Initial contact should be to the central desk at the phone number above or in
writing to the executive producer.

John Farren
Editor, Timewatch
Room 3150, BBC White City, 201 Wood Lane, London W12 7TS
Tel: 020 8752 7079
Fax: 020 8752 6336

Hugh Faupel
Executive Producer, BBC Religion & Ethics
Responsible for: Songs of Praise
Manchester New Broadcasting House, Oxford Road, Manchester M60 1SJ
Tel: (0161) 244 3222
Janet Lee

Series Producer, Imagine
Room 2358, BBC White City, 201 Wood Lane, London W12 7TS
Tel: 020 8752 7338
Fax: 020 8752 6812

Tim Martin
Series Editor – Natural World
BBC Natural History Unit
Broadcasting House, Whiteladies Road, Bristol BS8 2LR
Tel: (0117) 974 2139
Fax: (0117) 974 2187
Email: tim.martin@bbc.co.uk

Vyv Simson
Executive Editor, Wild
BBC Natural History Unit
Broadcasting House, Whiteladies Road, Bristol BS8 2LR
Tel: (0117) 974 6975
Fax: (0117) 923 8867
Happy to receive proposals by Email initially. Have up to 11 half-hour or 40-minute slots in any one WILD season, which runs from October to March with a break for Christmas.

Karen O'Connor
Editor, This World
Room 1362, BBC White City, 201 Wood Lane, London W12 7TS
Tel: 020 8752 7877
Fax: 020 8752 7599
Email: karen.oconnor@bbc.co.uk

Sandy Smith
Editor, Panorama
Room 1118, BBC White City, 201 Wood Lane, London W12 7TS
Tel: 020 8752 7863

Fax: 020 8752 7199
Email: sandy.smith@bbc.co.uk

Anthony Wall
Series Editor, Arena
Room G05, 1 Mortimer St, London W1T 3JA
Tel: 020 7765 0020

Programme Acquisition

George McGhee
Controller, Programme Acquisition
Assistant: Kellie Ashley
Room 6023, BBC White City, Wood Lane, London W12 7RJ
Tel: 020 8743 8000
Email: george.mcghee@bbc.co.uk

Dave Stanford
Executive Editor, Network Current Affairs, Manchester
Responsible for: Real Story (strand)
The Scanner Hall, BBC Manchester, Oxford Road, Manchester M60 1SJ
Tel: (0161) 244 3899
Fax: (0161) 244 3916
Email: dave.stanford@bbc.co.uk

CHANNEL 4

Documentaries

Angus Macqueen
Head of Documentaries
Assistant: Clothilde Redfern
Tel: 020 7306 8010
Email: credfern@channel4.co.uk

Meredith Chambers
Commissioning Editor, Documentaries
Assistant: Daniella Eversby
Tel: 020 7306 5192
Email: deversby@channel4.co.uk

Simon Dickson
Commissioning Editor, Documentaries
Assistant: Clothilde Redfern
Tel: 020 7306 8010
Email: credfern@channel4.co.uk

Sarah Mulvey
Commissioning Editor, Documentaries
Assistant: Daniella Eversby
Tel: 020 7306 5192
Email: deversby@channel4.co.uk

Kate Vogel
Editor, 3 Minute Wonder
Tel: 020 7306 8431
Email: kvogel@channel4.co.uk

History, Arts, Science, Religion

Hamish Mykura
Head of History, Science and Religion
Editorial Administrator: Beth Beamer
Tel: 020 7306 8283
Email: bbeamer@channel4.co.uk

Aaqil Ahmed
Commissioning Editor, Religion
Assistant: Megan Harries

Tel: 020 7306 8447
Email: mharries@channel4.co.uk

Ralph Lee
Commissioning Editor, History
Editorial Assistant: Sagina Shabaya
Tel: 020 7306 6960
Email: sshabaya@channel4.co.uk

David Glover
Deputy Commissioning Editor, History and Science
Editorial Assistant: Sagina Shabaya
Tel: 020 7306 6960
Email: sshabaya@channel4.co.uk

Jan Younghusband
Commissioning Editor, Arts and Performance
Editorial Assistant: Libby Watson
Tel: 020 7306 8303
Email: lwatson@channel4.co.uk

News and Current Affairs

Dorothy Byrne
Head of News and Current Affairs
Editorial Administrator: Jessica Harber
Tel: 020 7306 8664
Email: jharber@channel4.co.uk

Kevin Sutcliffe
Commissioning Editor, News and Current Affairs
Assistant: Fatou Jeng
Tel: 020 7306 5359
Email: fjeng@channel4.co.uk

Mark Roberts
Editor, News and Current Affairs
Assistant: Helen Picridas
Tel: 020 7306 1061
Email: hpicridas@channel4.co.uk

Fiona Campbell
Commissioning Editor, Indy Fund
Tel: 020 7430 4329
Email: fiona.campbell@itn.co.uk

Education

Janey Walker
Head of Education
Assistant: Anita Tunstell
Tel: 020 7306 8282
Email: atunstell@channel4.co.uk

Matt Locke
Commissioning Editor, Education
Editorial Administrator: Becky Macklin
Tel: 020 7306 8305
Email: bmacklin@channel4.co.uk

Adam Gee
Commissioning Editor, Interactive
Tel: 020 7306 8306
Email: agee@channel4.co.uk

More4 and Documentary Events

Peter Dale
Head of More4

Assistant: Sharon Tyler
Tel: 020 7306 8749
Email: styler@channel4.co.uk

Katie Speight
Editor, More4
Assistant: Zinia Scroggs
Tel: 020 7306 8676
Email: zscroggs@channel4.co.uk

E4 and Factual Entertainment

Angela Jain
Commissioning Editor, Factual Entertainment
Assistant: Sandra Christian
Tel: 020 7306 8672
Email: schristian@channel4.co.uk

Andrew Mackenzie
Commissioning Editor, Factual Entertainment
Assistant: Helena Peacock
Tel: 020 7306 6432
Email: hpeacock@channel4.co.uk

Dominique Walker
Commissioning Editor, Factual Entertainment
Assistant: Sandra Christian
Telephone: 020 7306 8672
Email: schristian@channel4.co.uk

Ruby Kuraishe
Editor, Factual Entertainment/E4
Assistant: Sandra Christian
Telephone: 020 7306 8672
Email: schristian@channel4.co.uk

Nations and Regions

Stuart Cosgrove
Director of Nations and Regions
Assistant: Debbie Walker
Assistant Phone: (0141) 568 7105
Email: dwalker@channel4.co.uk
4th Floor, 227 West George Street, Glasgow G2 2ND
Email: scosgrove@channel4.co.uk

ITV

ITV Network Ltd
200 Gray's Inn Road, London W1X 8HF
Tel: 020 782 8000
www.itv.com/commissioning

Factual

Alison Sharman
Director of Factual & Daytime
Tel: 020 7843 8000
Email: alison.sharman@itv.com

Jeff Anderson
Controller, Current Affairs and Documentaries
Assistant: Lucinda George
Tel: 020 7843 8000
Fax: 020 7843 8158
Email: lucinda.george@itv.com

Jane Rogerson
Controller, Features

Assistant: Sian Atkinson
Email: sian.atkinson@itv.com

Liam Keelan
Controller of Daytime
Assistant: Lucinda George
Email: lucinda.george@itv.com

Matthew Angel
Head of Business Affairs, Factual and Daytime
Tel: 020 7843 8125
Email: matthew.angel@itv.com

FIVE

22 Long Acre, London, WC2E 9LY
www.five.tv/aboutfive/producersnotes

News, Current Affairs and Documentaries

Chris Shaw
Senior Programme Controller (News, Current Affairs, and Docs)
Assistant: Rachael Jenkins
Assistant Phone: 020 7421 7123
Assistant Email: rachael.jenkins@five.tv
Tel: 020 7421 7166
Email: chris.shaw@five.tv

Ian Russell
Deputy Controller, News, Current Affairs, and Docs
Email: ian.russell@five.tv

Science

Justine Kershaw
Controller of Science
Assistant: Elaine Weir
Assistant Phone: 020 7550 5653
Tel: 020 7421 7112
Email: justine.kershaw@five.tv

History

Alex Sutherland
Controller of History
Assistant: Elaine Weir
Assistant Phone: 020 7550 5653
Tel: 020 7421 7129
Email: alex.sutherland@five.tv

Acquisitions

Sally Kenchington – Factual Acquisitions Senior Consultant
Finished programmes should be clearly marked and posted to Sally Kenchington at the Five address. Failure to comply will result in a delayed response.
Submit a brief synopsis in writing (Email is acceptable). They aim to respond
within four weeks.

Bethan Corney – Wildlife and Factual Acquisitions
Assistant: Amy Burgess
Assistant Phone: 020 7421 7194

Factual Entertainment

Steve Gowans
Controller, Factual Entertainment

Assistant: Alison Walton
Assistant Phone: 020 7421 7119
Tel: 020 7421 7119
Email: steve.gowans@five.tv

Ian Dunkley
Deputy Commissioning Editor, Factual
Email: ian.dunkley@five.tv

Daytime, Arts and Religion

Kim Peat
Controller, Daytime, Arts, Religion
Assistant: Louisa Carbin
Assistant Phone: 020 7421 7113
Tel: 020 7421 7113
Email: kim.peat@five.tv

SKY ONE

British Sky Broadcasting Group
Grant Way, Isleworth, London TW7 5QD
www.sky.com

Factual

Emma Read
Head of Factual
Tel: 020 7705 3000
Email: emma.read@bskyb.com

Steve Regan
Development Executive, Factual
Assistant: Harpal Uhbie

Tel: 020 7705 3000
Email: steve.regan@bskyb.com

Factual Entertainment

Paul Crompton
Commissioning Editor, Factual Entertainment
Tel: 020 7705 3000
Email: paul.crompton@bskyb.com

Jamie Roberts
Commissioning Editor, Factual Entertainment
Assistant: Helen Devonald
Assistant Phone: 020 7805 8482
Tel: 020 7705 3000
Email: jamie.roberts@bskyb.com

Acquisitions

David Smyth
Head of Acquisitions
Tel: 020 7705 3000
Email: david.smyth@bskyb.com

Discovery Channel UK
Discovery Networks Europe
160 Great Portland Street, London W1W 5QA
www.discoverychannel.co.uk

Jill Offman
Senior Vice President, Discovery Networks UK
Tel: 020 7462 3600
Fax: 020 7462 3700
Email: jill_offman@discovery-europe.com

Marian Williams
Vice President, Programming, Discovery EMEA (Europe, Middle East and Africa)
Tel: 020 7462 3600
Fax: 020 7462 3700
Email: marian_williams@discovery-europe.com

Barbara Bellini
Vice President, Programming, Discovery EMEA
Email: barbara_bellini@discovery-europe.com

23. THE DV SHOOTING GUIDE

This section is aimed at summarising some of the key points raised in Section Two of this book. It also contains quick tips, and checklists for when you are actually on the job.

Having read this book, you will no doubt have realised that there's an awful lot to learn. And during your shoot, it's sometimes hard to remember what it is you need to remember! In addition, the last thing you need is to have to look through a whole book or camera manual in order to make sure you haven't forgotten anything, or if you are confused about a particular button on the camera. This Shooting Guide (also available as a PDF document on the DVD, so you can print it out and take it with you) is essentially a quick reference for when you are on a shoot. The assumption here is that you are doing the filming yourself, but it's equally useful if you are directing and have a cameraperson with you.

This guide is broken down into the following sections:

- Guide to Camera Set Up and Menu Settings
- Shooting Checklist
- Important Shooting Tips
- Kit Lists

THE CAMERA SET UP

Most cameras, both professional and semi-professional, have a whole set of menus, and often menus-within-menus. If you've rented, borrowed or bought a camera, you need to know what the right settings are and, unfortunately, the manuals don't really come with a 'Default' set up for documentary film-making. Below is a quick reference guide to the typical menu set up you will need for a documentary shoot. Although this section refers specifically to the Sony Z1 camera, most of the settings easily translate to other cameras.

Please note: the assumption here is that you are self-shooting and doing your own sound, and recording in PAL. The menus might be slightly different if you are using a sound recordist (with SQN mixer). Also, if you are using a camera-person, they may have their own choice of menu set up. If you are recording in NTSC, then consult your manual to make necessary adjustments.

Manual versus auto

The golden rule here is shoot in manual mode so that as many of your controls as possible are set to manual, including focus, aperture, white balance, gain and shutter speed. There is no substitute for getting to know the camera and adjusting the functions manually. The only exception to this should be when you use the 'PUSH AUTO' button as a guide to focusing, and if you are in an emergency situation and very quickly need to shoot something then – and only then – should you rely on the camera's automatic mode.

Format

The Z1 can record in HDV, DVCam and DV. All formats record onto a mini-DV tape (or DVCam tape, but essentially it's the same thing). The important thing to remember here is that if you are shooting in HDV or DV mode then a 60-minute mini-DV tape will record 60 minutes of footage. If you are in DVCam mode, and using a 60-minute mini-DV tape, then it will only record around 40 minutes. Think carefully before choosing a format to shoot in. HDV is great, but it requires more storage capacity and a high-spec editing system.

LCD screen

Make sure that the brightness of the LCD is set in the middle, otherwise you will think something is too overlit/underlit, when it might not be. Also, make sure the backlight is on (unless you are filming in very bright light), otherwise the screen will make it look as if everything is underlit. The settings for LCD & Viewfinder are in the LCD/VF SET menu.

Status check

A button on the back of the camera, which enables you to quickly see some of your settings at a glance.

Picture profile

It's used to fine-tune specific settings such as colour and contrast. Unless you are very experienced in using this, it's best to leave it off.

Autolock

This button effectively locks all of your settings apart from focus. Use it when you are worried you might knock some of the buttons and dials (especially shutter speed on the Z1, as it's the easiest button to knock). However, remember what you have done. If you're in the middle of filming and nothing seems to work it could be because your AUTOLOCK is on!

Zebras

I don't like them because they lead to an over-reliance on the camera when it comes to judging exposure. I would suggest you keep them off, particularly when you first start using the camera. It's hard enough at this stage to concentrate on all the other things going on on the LCD.

MENU SETTINGS

Once you have adjusted the menu settings, the camera will not change them unless you do – a strong argument for being quite guarded about who you lend your camera to. If I have left any of the menu items off, then this means you just need to ignore that function.

Camera set menu

MENU SETTING	RECOMMENDED DEFAULT	COMMENTS
WB PRESET	(OUTDOOR)	But, try to always use manual white balance.
WB LEVEL	(0)	
SHOT TRANS	(NOT RECOMMENDED)	These are in-camera effects, and should be avoided. (You can do all of this in the edit.)
COLOUR CORRECT	OFF	
STEADYSHOT	ON	Theoretically, you should turn this off when using a tripod, but the world won't end if you forget.
STEADYSHOT TYP	STANDARD	
PEAKING	COLOUR: WHITE LEVEL: HIGH	
AF ASSIST	(OFF)	
AE RESPONSE	FAST	This is the speed of auto-exposure, but try to stay in manual mode.
MARKER	(OFF)	
MARKER SELECT	DON'T USE THIS	
HANDLE ZOOM	H 8; L 2	Sets the speed for using the handle zoom.
BARS TYPE	TYPE 1	
FRAME REC	OFF	Unless you are wanting to use the camera to do stop-frame animation.

In/out record

The setting here depends on whether you are recording in DVCam mode or HDV.

Audio set

MENU SETTING	RECOMMENDED DEFAULT	COMMENTS
AUDIO MONI	**CH1, CH2**	
AUDIO OUTPUT	**2Vrms**	
AUDIO MODE	**FS48k**	
AUDIO LOCK	**LOCK MODE**	This is automatic in DVCam mode.
AUDIO LIMIT	**OFF**	Depends on the situation. Normally keep off unless very loud (e.g. in a factory).
MIC NR	**OFF**	
INT MIC SELECT	**OFF**	
XLR SET	**XLR CH SEL: CH1, CH2**	This will mean that a single input of a microphone will record onto both channels. Obviously, change this if you are using two different microphone sources (e.g. shotgun and radio mics).
XLR ACG SET	**SEPARATE**	
INPUT 1 LEVEL	**MIC (0db)**	
INPUT 1 WIND	**OFF**	
INPUT 2 LEVEL	**MIC**	
INPUT 2 TRIM	**0db**	
INPUT 2 WIND	**OFF**	

LCD/VF set

MENU SETTING	RECOMMENDED DEFAULT	COMMENTS
LCD COLOUR	Way Up	
LCD BL LEVEL	NORMAL	
VF B LIGHT	NORMAL	
VF COLOUR	ON	
VF POWER	AUTO	

TC/UB set

MENU SETTING	RECOMMENDED DEFAULT	COMMENTS
TC PRESET	00:00:00:00	Adjust the first digit for each new tape you put into the camera.
UB PRESET	00:00:00:00	Press reset if it's not on this setting.
TC RUN	REC RUN	This means that the time code advances only while recording.
TC MAKE	REGENERATE	

Other menu settings

Many of these are obvious – such as world time and language – so I have omitted them.

MENU SETTING	RECOMMENDED DEFAULT	COMMENTS
QUICK REC	OFF	
BEEP	OFF	Important, so that the camera does not beep every time you start recording.
REC LAMP	OFF	

MENU SETTING	RECOMMENDED DEFAULT	COMMENTS
IRIS DIAL	**NORMAL**	Otherwise, direction of dial will be inverted.
REMAINING	**ON**	Will display remaining tape on LCD.
ZOOM DISPLAY	**BAR**	To display zoomed position using bar.
EXP FOCUS	**AUTO OFF**	Releases expanded focus after certain time.
DATE REC	**OFF**	Make sure it's off, otherwise the date will be burnt into the picture.
50i/60i SEL	**50i**	For DV PAL.

CHECKLISTS

Before the shoot

Below are just some of the most common issues to keep in mind when preparing for the shoot.

Camera and kit

- Is the lens clean?
- Are the camera batteries powered?
- Do I have spare batteries for the camera?
- Do I have spare batteries for microphones?
- Does my tripod work, and have you definitely got the tripod plate?
- Have I set the right time code?
- Are the lighting conditions right to shoot in?
- Have I checked all my menu settings?
- Am I sure that I am recording in the right format (DVCam, HDV etc)?
- Am I clear on the shot list?
- Have I laid 30 seconds of colour bars down on the tape?
- Finally, have I checked all my equipment is working?

- Health and Safety: Make sure you have done a full risk assessment.
- Releases: Make sure you bring all relevant release forms.

Sound

- Is the sound going into the camera, and are my levels okay?
- Are my headphones working properly?
- Am I using the right microphone(s) and is it the right distance from the subject?
- If using a boom, is it definitely out of shot?
- Have I got at least 30 seconds wild track (or 'atmos') for each location I am shooting in?
- Is the sound clean, avoiding excessive wind/background noise?

Checklist during the shoot

- Am I sure I know what my film is about, and that all shots and interviews reflect this?
- Are my crew (if any) also informed enough about the shoot?
- Have I produced a comprehensive call sheet, so that everyone knows what they should be doing, and when?
- For interviews, do I know all the questions I should be asking? And, when the interview has finished, have I asked them all?
- Have I got at least 30 seconds wild track (or 'atmos) for each location I am shooting in?
- Am I shooting enough cutaways?
- Am I holding my shots for long enough?
- Make sure that if something spontaneous happens, I am free to follow this action.
- Did I really get that right? Or should I do it again as a second take?
- Am I shooting for the edit? Holding pans and tilts, avoiding zooms etc?
- Avoid 'crossing the line'.

Remember, the key to shooting well is making sure you are aware, at all time of the following:

- FOCUS
- APERTURE
- SHUTTER SPEED
- WHITE BALANCE
- SOUND LEVELS

IMPORTANT SHOOTING TIPS

Below is a list of general tips that will help you in your shooting, and also help you to make sure that you 'shoot for the edit'.

- Remember the 'Rule of Thirds' and always try to frame your shots with this in mind. Make sure your subjects have adequate 'head room' at the top of frame.
- Think about location. Not only does it need to be well lit, but it's also helpful if location informs the narrative.
- Try, where possible, to avoid mixing natural and tungsten (artificial) light.
- Make sure you use a variety of shot sizes, as it will make your video much easier to edit.
- Be wary of excessive camera movement, as it can be a problem in the edit.
- Hold shots both before and at the end of tilts and pans.
- Try to avoid using the zoom: often it looks unprofessional and can create problems when it comes to editing. If you are going to use the zoom, try to avoid using it during important action.
- Shoot in sequences. Think carefully as to how the footage will look in the edit (using a storyboard if this helps) and make sure your shots cover all the action.
- Don't be afraid of taking time to get a shot right – even if this sometimes means doing it again.
- Avoid using the automatic functions on the camera, unless you really, really have to.
- Try to avoid a large shooting ratio. Although there is a tendency to just

carry on shooting, it will mean you have far too much material when it comes to the edit. Be conservative.

- Make sure you're in control of the shoot. This means both crew and contributors know what is expected of them, and how long it's going to take.
- Be prepared for problems, and learn to think quickly on your feet. For example, if your headphones stop working, look carefully at your audio levels on the LCD.
- Think ahead. You need to know what you are going to do next.

KIT LISTS

It can sometimes be difficult to make sure you bring everything you need on a shoot, and nothing is more frustrating than travelling hours to your location, only to suddenly find you have left an important piece of kit back at the office or at home. Below is an extensive kit list for a DSR450 camera, including things that you might often forget like lens caps, manuals, cleaning kit, cleaning cassette, filters, top light, camera cases, extra cables and so on. If you are shooting on a small camera (like a Z1) then your list might be a little smaller (e.g. no extra lenses), but this is a useful guide as to EVERYTHING you might need to consider in terms of camera, lighting, sound, tripod and monitor.

DSR450 kit:

1 SONY DSR450WSPL CAMERA
1 SONY ECM-77 PERSONAL CLIP MIC
1 RODE NTG-2 GUN MIC
1 CANON YJ12 X 6.5 B4 IRS W/A LENS
1 VARIOUS 105MM UV CLEAR FILTER
1 SACHTLER DSR500/450 TRIPOD
1 RYCOTE RADIO MIC RX CAMERA MOUNT
1 RYCOTE 21/22 SMALL SOFTIE
1 SONY DSR/PD/A1 ONBOARD MIC FOAM

1 SONY CCD CAP

1 SONY DSR500/450 RUBBER EYECUP

1 DSR500/450 BACK FOCUS CHART

1 CANON ZOOM BAR

1 CANON ZOOM BAR

1 CANON B4 REAR LENS CAP

1 CANON B4 REAR LENS CAP

1 VARIOUS MINI-DV CLEANING CASSETTE

1 CLEANING KIT

1 DV SOLUTIONS CLEANING CLOTH

1 PORTABRACE DSR450/SPX900 SOFT

1 PORTABRACE DSR450/SPX900 CASE

1 82MM CLEAR FILTER

1 SONY DSR450 MANUAL

1 SONY DSR500/450 ONBOARD GUN MIC

1 SONY DSR500/450 SHOULDER STRAP

1 SONY ECM77 WIND SHIELD

1 SONY ECM77 TIE CLIP

1 IEC C-13 MAINS KETTLE LEAD

1 GENERIC DSR500/450 BATTERIES

1 GENERIC DSR500/450 BATTERIES

1 GENERIC DSR500/450 BATTERIES

1 GENERIC DSR500/450 BATTERIES

1 GENERIC DSR500/450 CHARGERS

1 GENERIC LARGE HEADPHONES

2 GENERIC PELI CASE

1 GENERIC PELI CASE

1 GENERIC SOFTIE/COAT

3 GENERIC XLR LEADS

1 CANON J12 LENS CAP

1 CANON J17E X 7.7 LENS

1 CANON J17 LENS CAP

1 SACHTLER LARGE TRIPOD CASE SACH

1 SONY MEMORY STICK FOR THE DSR450

1 RODE NTG-2 GUN MIC FOAM

1 RODE NTG-2 GUN MIC POUCH

1 PORTABRACE WHITE BALANCE CARD

1 PORTABRACE DSR 450 BLUE CAMERA

1 VIDEO 18P TRIPOD KIT TEMPLATE

1 SONY VCT-14 TRIPOD MOUNTING PLATE

1 SACHTLER VIDEO 18P TRIPOD PAN BAR

1 SACHTLER VIDEO 18P TRIPOD

1 RYCOTE Z1E MIC MOUNT (CCA)

1 TOP LIGHT WITH BATTERY

Lighting:

1 DEDO DLH1X150 24V SOFT LAMP

3 DEDO DLH4 24V 150W LIGHT

1 ARRI 300W FRESNEL HEAD

1 ARRI 650W FRESNEL HEAD

1 10M COIL 4 SOCKET MAINS EXT CABLE

1 13 AMP FUSE

2 13 AMP FUSE

3 DEDO 150W 24V BULB (BLACK TIP)

1 DEDO 150W 24V BULB (CLEAR)

1 PHOTON BEARD 2 HEAD ARRI LIGHT

1 2M 4 WAY MAINS SOCKET

1 2M 4 WAY MAINS SOCKET

1 300W 240 VOLT BULB (ARRI)

4 3 AMP FUSE

2 3 AMP FUSE

1 501/PRO5 TRIPOD BAG STRAP

1 501/PRO5 TRIPOD BAG

1 650W 240 VOLT BULB (ARRI)

2 MANFROTTO K-CLAMP

6 LARGE CROCODILE CLIP

6 SMALL CROCODILE CLIP

1 ARRI D700B LAZY ARM

1 DEDO HARD CASE FOR DEDO LIGHTS

1 DEDO SILVERDOME DIFFUSION SHEET

1 DEDO DT24-1E 24V DIMMER (240V)

1 DEDO DT24-1E 24V DIMMER (240V)

1 DEDO DT24-1E 24V DIMMER (240V)

1 DEDO DT24-1E 24V DIMMER (240V)

1 DEDO MEDIUM SILVER DOME IN POUCH

1 DEDO G-CLAMP BRACKET

3 DEDO GEL + GOBO FRAME

1 LARGE STANDARD GEL SET

1 GENERIC REFLECTOR

1 GENERIC SOCKET SAFETY TESTER

1 GENERIC SOCKET SAFETY TESTER

1 DEDO GRID FOR SILVERDOME

3 LARGE LIGHTING STAND

2 MANFROTTO LIGHTING CABLE BOND

2 LIGHTING GLOVE

2 LIGHTING GLOVE

4 DEDO LIGHTING STAND

1 DV SOLUTIONS MINI 1/2 CTB DEDO LIGHT

1 DV SOLUTIONS MINI 1/4 CTB DEDO LIGHT

1 DV SOLUTIONS MINI FULL CTB DEDO LIGHT

1 DEDO MOUNTING PLATE

1 PORTABRACE ZIPPED BLACK POUCH

1 MANFROTTO LAZY ARM KNOB & SPRING

4 RCD PLUG-IN SAFETY ADAPTOR

3 RCD PLUG-IN SAFETY ADAPTOR

1 VARIOUS REFLECTOR POUCH

1 DV SOLUTIONS FULL CTB GEL

1 DV SOLUTIONS 1/2 CTB GEL

1 DV SOLUTIONS 1/4 CTB GEL

1 VARIOUS SMALL DIFFUSION GELS

2 MANFROTTO SPIGGOT

4 DEDO STIFFENING ROD FOR SILVERDOME

Monitor:

1 SONY PVM-6041QM 6"CRT MONITOR
1 SONY MINIJACK TO 3X FEMALE PHONO
1 PORTABRACE SOFT CASE FOR 6" MONITOR
1 BNC FE TO FE BARREL ADAP
1 BNC FE TO PHONO MA ADAP
1 BNC MA TO PHONO FE ADAP
2 BNC TO BNC LEAD
2 IEC C-13 MAINS KETTLE LEAD
1 GENERIC NP1 BATTERY
1 GENERIC NP1 BATTERY
1 GENERIC NP1 BATTERY
1 GENERIC NP1 BATTERY
1 GENERIC NP1 CHARGER
1 GENERIC PELI CASE

1 x MICRON EXPLORER RADIO MIC SET
1 x SONY DUAL RADIO MIC SET
+ MINIDV STOCK
+ BATTERIES

SECTION SIX
INTERVIEWS WITH
FILMMAKERS

This section contains interviews that have been conducted with four filmmakers (three of whose documentaries are included on the DVD that comes with this book) – Esteban Uyarra, Erik Bäfving, Marc Isaacs and Ben Hopkins. All interviews were conducted by Kerry McLeod of the Documentary Filmmakers Group and offer an insight into the filmmaking process, and, more specifically, their unique approach to directing documentaries.

24. INTERVIEW WITH ERIK BÄFVING, DIRECTOR OF *BOOGIE WOOGIE PAPPA*

Biography

Born in Malmö, 1973, Erik studied at the film school in Skurup from 1996–1998. In 1998 he directed *Set designer PA Lundgren*, a 58-minute documentary about the set designer of Ingmar Bergman, followed by in 2000 *Hard to Smile with a Black Tooth in your Mouth*, a 58-minute documentary about the struggle of an alternative rock band. In 2000 he started to work at WGfilm and made *Boogie Woogie Pappa*, a 12-minute short film about his father who died, which won eight international awards. More recent work includes *Get Busy* (2003), a 72-minute documentary about the life of a hiphop group living in the suburbs of Malmö, sharing the tragedy of a friend's suicide. Since 2003, Erik has edited several documentaries and is now working on a documentary and a short fiction film.

About the film

Constructed solely using still photographs taken by the filmmaker's father, this is an intimate story of Erik and the relationship with his father as told through thousands of previously undeveloped negatives. The film reveals a father's private life and the clues that lead towards his tragic fate. The film has won numerous awards, including a Golden Gate Award at the San Francisco International Film Festival, Le Prix Planete at the Marseille Documentary Film Festival, and the Golden Dove and Young Jury Prize at the International Leipzig Film Festival for Documentary and Animated Films, Germany.

Can you explain a little about the film and the story behind it?

As I say at the beginning of the film, I thought of the idea of making a film from my dad's stills when I was looking in one of his folders. I was surprised at how good he was as a photographer, not only capturing the joys of the family but also the moments in between, the sadness, loneliness and fear. I felt a yearning to tell his story, about what went wrong, and try to give form to this big occurrence in my life, and how he slipped away from us. But I never thought I would dare to do it. In Sweden at the time there was a programme on TV named *Ikon*, which showed short documentaries from 1 to 12 minutes long. I sent them a list of ideas of short documentaries. The film about my dad was one of them and I hoped that if they liked any it wouldn´t be *Boogie Woogie Pappa*. But of course that´s the one they picked.

Were you sure from the outset of the style that you wanted for the film, or did it develop later?

I was sure about the form. When I was a child there was a TV programme for kids about an ordinary Swedish boy called Kalle; the story was told only with stills and a speaker and I loved that programme. I wanted my film to be like that one: simple, with the focus on the story and the images.

How did you go about structuring the film and creating a narrative from the archive and the music?

I loaded the stills I liked on to my computer and then started to write down the story. It was a strange process switching between the person who remembered and felt, and the filmmaker, the craftsman who thinks about dramatic structure. Sometimes I let the stills bring out the narrative of the memories, and sometimes I looked for stills that could give form to some specific memories. I wanted to be personal but not private. I wanted the audience to recognise themselves in the feelings and atmosphere of my childhood, and was careful not to exclude them.

You created the film wholly from still photographs. Obviously the subject matter informed this decision, but did it present any limitations or problems working in this way?

At one stage in the process I used a Super 8mm film of my dad, at the end, where he walked on a beach with his camera hanging round his neck, a wonderful shot that finishes with him turning to the film camera and taking a picture of it. But I realised that the Super 8mm shot at the end stole focus and energy from the stills so I had to kill that darling. And then I understood the power of the simple still photographs. But these limitations, only using the stills and keeping it within 12 minutes, were very useful and provided a supporting framework for the exploration of some painful memories.

How and where did you get the funding?

The Swedish Television through the TV programme *Ikon* funded the film along with the Swedish Film Institute, Film i Skåne, and the production company WGfilm.

Were there any compromises between your stylistic choices and those of the funders?

Not more than the 12-minute limit that *Ikon* gave me, but I really enjoyed that limitation. At some stage I was planning to make a longer version but I´m glad I never did. Some people also wanted me to make the film in a slightly different way, using more emotions in the commentary, but I was very certain that this wasn't the way to do it. I knew how important this film was for me so I didn´t compromise.

Many people think short documentaries are easier to make than longer format, but I think the opposite. It's really important to get the pacing and narrative exactly right. Can you tell us a little bit about the narrative? For example, why you chose to reveal the reasons for your father's death only at the end?

I wanted the film to be chronological. When you have been through something scary or confusing you have to tell the story over and over again for yourself so that you can begin to understand. You start with the beginning and work towards the end, trying to find clues. Maybe I also wanted, in quite a sadistic manner, for the audience to experience the shock that I had experienced when I knew my dad had taken his life. I myself still get a high pulse rate at the ending of the film even though I've seen it so many times. But you can´t tell a story about a childhood memory without creating some suspense in the beginning. That´s why I presented the two sides of my dad: the happy, playful dad, and then the other, more mystifying dad. I think this creates curiosity and suspense.

Boogie Woogie Pappa is a very personal film. Was this difficult for you to make? Was it cathartic?

It was painful at some points but it was more exciting and relieving than I thought at the beginning. When my dad died I never spoke to anyone about it. It was taboo and filled with shame, and I felt very lonely. I made the film from the fury I felt against this feeling of shame and those stupid taboos. It was a relief to say 'ouch' and make the film in such a way that people understood what I was talking about. But the first time I saw it on a huge movie screen with 500 people in the audience at a big festival in Sweden it was quite an experience. I felt: 'My God what have I done? Stop the film, I take it all back!'

Why documentaries?

I don't separate fiction and documentary storytelling that much. It´s all about telling a story and making it good. In fiction you make it all up in a script and then produce the images from scratch. In a documentary you work the other way around, you try to find the script in the images. I'm not very fond of shooting a documentary; I like the part where you sit with all the images and scenes trying to create a film from it. So to answer your question, I don´t yet know, it could be fiction in the future.

How did you become involved in documentary filmmaking?

I finished film school and heard about an old man living in my hometown. His name was PA Lundgren and was the set designer for Ingmar Bergman. No one had made a film about him. We visited his small apartment and from a closet he brought out sketches and paintings from _The Seventh Seal_ and other great Swedish films. A friend from school and I saw the great opportunity of doing a portrait of him. I really wanted to make fiction but it felt so complex. A documentary was easier, you could just pick up the camera and look for a good story and images.

What inspires you? What do you think makes a good idea?

When it comes to documentaries, I have always been more interested in the art of filmmaking rather than a specific subject. I can get more inspired by a single image than an important subject. It´s not the subject that´s important, it´s about how you tell it.

Are there bad ideas for a film? What do you think doesn't work?

A lot of documentaries are still made by people who are more interested in journalism than filmmaking. This is an important way of making documentaries and people should continue doing it, but I have never been interested in doing that myself. I am interested in film as an emotional medium; any film that doesn´t take this into consideration is a bad idea to me.

What do you consider to be the state of documentary in Europe?

Documentaries are more cinematic than they used to be. Documentary filmmakers seem to be more aware of the dramatic and entertaining aspects of the form. They are moving towards the conventions of fiction to tell their story, which is better if you want to reach more people and create impact. But you always have to be aware of the fine line, when you're changing reality too much to create a good drama. Sometimes I get the feeling that documentaries are struggling to get into the cinemas and will use whatever means necessary.

What are you working on now?

I am editing two documentaries for other directors, and writing a script for a short film of my own – fiction this time.

If there's one piece of advice you could give to emerging documentary filmmakers, what would that be?

Use the emotional and dramatic power of the image and the edit. Use the dramatic tools of filmmaking to make it a better film but have a reality check once in a while...

25. INTERVIEW WITH MARC ISAACS, DIRECTOR OF *LIFT*

Biography

Born very near the location of his first film, *Lift*, in London's East End, Marc Isaacs began working on documentary films as an assistant producer in 1995. He then assisted Pavel Pawlikowski on *Twockers* and the award-winning *Last Resort*. After completing *Lift* in 2001, Marc directed two further documentaries for the BBC about the sub-culture of shoplifting, both of which were nominated for a BAFTA Craft Award in the UK. His documentary film *Travellers* for Channel 4 was followed by *Calais: The Last Border*, which offers an original view of England from across the Channel. His most recent film, *Philip and His Seven Wives*, premiered at the Sheffield International Documentary Film Festival in 2005.

About the film

Filmmaker Marc Isaacs set himself up in a London tower block lift with his camera, unsure how the residents would react. They came to trust him and revealed what mattered to them in life. The result is a humorous and moving portrait of a vertical multicultural community.

Where did the idea come from and how did you get it commissioned?

I was working on *Last Resort*, and one of the locations was a tower block in Margate. It was 1998 or 1999 and there were a lot of Kosovan refugees and lots of other refugees in the town. It was Czech gypsies mainly and lots of Kurds and Iranians. Living in the tower block were English people, local Margate people, but also refugees. We were filming on the top floor so we used to go up in the lift every day. I can't remember exactly how it came about but Pawel [Pawlikowski, the director of the film] and I started talking about the lift there and how it would be an interesting place to make a film. He sort of said it flippantly and it stuck in my head. I probably forgot about it then for some time – nothing really happened.

It was two years later, when I was asked by a production company to go to Channel 4 with them. They were going to sponsor new directors for Alt-TV, a new strand. It was a £40,000 budget and I think Channel 4 put out a brief to lots of different independent producers. I was working with one company, and they suggested that I go along and pitch an idea. I didn't really have an idea and at the last minute I went along and pitched something that I wasn't really into. In the first few minutes of the pitch they said they were doing it anyway. I'd had about four or five years working as an assistant to different directors by that time, so I was quite experienced, but I'd never made my own film. And then that meeting ended and I was just about to walk out the door, and suddenly from nowhere – I didn't plan to at all really – I just said, 'Oh, I've got this other idea about a lift'. It just came back, almost out of my control. This voice just jumped out of me and said that I wanted to stand in a lift for some time and film the residents, and there were two commissioners in the meeting, Peter Dale and Adam Barker, and they were really tickled by the idea, they just started laughing to each other. And they asked, 'Well, what are you going to do there?' And I said, 'Well, I don't know what I'm going to do there. I just think it'll be an interesting situation in which to see what happens, especially in this kind of strand, it could be quite experimental'. And that was it really. I left the room.

The woman who owned the production company was having a party that evening and Peter Dale was there at the party. It was the first time I'd met him that day. I went into the toilet and started having a wee and he came in and started weeing next to me, and he literally turned around and said, 'Oh, we commissioned your film today'. And that was it. It was really bizarre: that was my first experience of the commissioning process. I remember leaving the toilet and drinking a few bottles of champagne and then waking up in the morning really panicking that shit, he really believes in this stupid idea that I've had.

Maybe it wasn't as spontaneous as I remember. Perhaps I had already been to the block I ended up filming in when I knew I had to go to Channel 4, to do some research for a day or so. I used that block because it was in a really mixed area. I grew up spending a lot of time round there as a kid so I knew the area really well.

Where is it?

Commercial Street, parallel with Brick Lane. And it's near Petticoat Lane, where I used to work in the market as a kid. I remembered the block. I didn't remember anything about it particularly but I just thought that if I was going to make a film like that I didn't want it to be white working class. I wanted it to be mixed and have a variation in characters. But I was also interested in the old Jewish people who had never moved out of the East End and I knew that some of them would still live there. And I met Lily when I turned up to do research, and as soon as I met her I was convinced that I should make the film there. But I had to make sure that there were enough interesting characters there. There are a lot of flats there so I just assumed there would be, and I hired a researcher, Andrew Hinton, and asked him to go and knock on everybody's door and speak to them. I didn't want to meet anyone before I turned up in the lift. I had this feeling that if I just turned up there, if I appeared there from one day to the next, it would give me a good starting point; something would happen. So I sent Andrew round, and he basically explained that there was going to be a film about the lift and he came back with a paragraph on each person so I had a sense of who was there, which was good because I knew about them before they knew about me, and I could prepare myself a little.

What is it that makes a good character?

In the lift it was very particular. I put myself in a situation and life came to me. In a sense, the film cast itself, because people came in and presented themselves, and throughout the filming process I decided which characters to shoot. I looked for people who intrigued me, who in one way or another had something about them that interested me. So with Lily it was the fact that she reminded me of my grandmother. She was just a very familiar character that I had... I was going to say an attraction to but that's probably the wrong word... a connection to, let's say. With the Bengali guy that comes back with the food all the time, with him I was just intrigued by his hospitality and he had a really great sense of humour, which is always something that I look for. I like to find characters with a sense of humour.

Having said that, I also get interested in tragic stories. There's the guy who talks about his parents dying. He came into the lift and I asked him some questions. One was, 'What have you been thinking about today?' and he said, 'Just watching the clock go by', and I thought that was just such a bizarre thing to say. I mean sometimes I watch the clock go by, but it just seemed so desperate. And I saw him around and he always looked slightly strange so I wanted to get to know him more. So everyone in the film had something slightly intriguing about them.

I filmed lots of people. Some didn't respond in an interesting way, and I never really followed them up. But it is different in different films. I'm working now in Barking, dealing with characters who have some really quite disturbing views about things, and it's a different relationship. There's more of a fascination than an emotional attachment, but at the same time there will be characters in the film that you feel connected to, because I think you need that. You have to have that emotional connection too for a film to be successful.

How much of the structure did you have in your head?

I went in there pretty blank to be honest, without any real sense of direction or purpose. It might sound a bit aimless, but it was in a way. I went in there knowing that the initial premise was quite strong but I didn't really have any idea of how things would develop. I had some notion that possibly I would move out of the lift and follow people in their lives. I tried that with Lily very early on and it didn't work. And I realised quite quickly that it broke the spell. The lift was a perfect space and I didn't have to leave it. Everything came to me. Cinematically, that space had its own particular thing going on. People would come in and they couldn't hide anywhere, which was a bit cruel but really interesting; whatever people would say or do was magnified because you've got their face and that's it. And the awkwardness of the space, the way the doors open and people come in, it's like a curtain, as if they're entering a stage.

Then I had to think about how the film would develop, and that only came from being in the space. After two weeks – after the initial buzz and adrenalin rush of being there and meeting these people – then I had a major crisis, because I thought, where do I take this?

After the crisis I really thought long and hard about how to develop the film. Obviously I realised that I could come back to characters and find ways of going deeper with them, or try to tell little mini-stories, like when the guy goes out in search of a girlfriend and then comes back drunk. That's a very mini-story but it's a story. And I realised that if I had enough of those happening that it would give the film a momentum. So it's not just one person after another after another, we're actually getting to know people. That's how it unfolded.

The questions came out of a different approach. I wanted the film to be really intense. I wanted to keep the dynamic of a stranger being in the lift, and people's response to that. I didn't want it to become conversational or my filming with them could become loose, fraying at the edges. I wanted it to be quite focused. So I thought of questions, the universal questions, that would give the film a sort of weight. It wasn't just about, 'What did you have for dinner last night?' It was more, 'What did you dream about last night?' or 'Have you been in love before?' All those questions came out of different things. Sometimes it was just the person's face that sparked a thought. With the dream thing, there was a sense in the plot that everybody's lives were interconnected, almost unconsciously, because people are living on top of one another. You can imagine people's dreams interconnecting, and their lives weaving in and out of each other's subconsciously. You can be sleeping and hear what's going on in their flat, what's going on next door; it's like when you leave the radio on at night and it starts to enter in your dreams. I wanted to tap into that. So we show the dog not getting in the lift, and the woman talks about dreaming about a dog that was drowning.

Sometimes the space became quite dreamlike in itself, a very unreal space in a way. Sometimes it felt a bit like an asylum.

How did you shoot for the edit?

Shooting good sequences! I didn't really think too much about how the film was going to be cut together. I realised that I was hitting upon themes – religion, love, death, illness, ageing and the multicultural stuff that was in the film. In a sense I had a faith that these themes would also shape the structure of the film somehow. In the edit, we basically cut individual character stories, their mini-stories. On the timeline we had Lily's story, Peter's [the alcoholic's] story and the Bengali man's story – Mr Quereshi. We had all their moments on the timeline. Some characters we had to dump entirely because we didn't have time to tell their stories. Others we cut down. Essentially the editing became about weaving these stories together, at the same time trying to have some thematic development. But not dealing with religion in one chunk, and then love. We had to mix it up.

So there were those two things going on, and we also had natural chronology of the filming, which was really important. I wanted to create a sense of what it was like to be there from day one, and people's strange reaction, and nervous reaction and suspicious reaction, up to the point where they become more open and I become more curious and they reveal more. Part of the narrative is about that, me getting closer to them and them revealing more, which also gives the film a momentum. So they were the three different aspects that governed how we cut the film.

Were there any compromises between you and commissioners?

The only restriction I had was that the film had to be 24 minutes. I had a cut of 32 minutes, which I was very happy with, and it was hard to lose eight minutes of the film and at the time I wasn't really aware of the festival scene. I would have done two versions but I didn't really know what would happen with the film. So I only ever cut one version. I've got a rough cut on VHS of a 32-minute version, but the rushes got dumped as well, so I can never go back. I never took them home. So I just have this 24 minutes, but a VHS with an extra few minutes on. And the other restriction was the commercial break, which I think I was aware of when I was shooting; actually I was definitely aware of it when I was shooting. So I built into the story the part where the lift breaks down as a way of getting out and coming back.

You didn't engineer the breakdown though did you?!

No, I got stuck in it and then I had to shoot around it to make the sequence work. I engineered lots of other things though. There are a lot of things that feel like they happened naturally that happened because I planned them. For example, when the guy comes in and talks about his schizophrenia. He told me that story outside of the lift first of all, so I knew what had happened to him. But because I was making the film in the lift I had to ask him when he came to the lift. I asked him if it was okay that he tell that story and he agreed. There's a lot that happened in the early part of the filming with characters and I had to bring it into the space where I was filming. For instance, the woman brings in the religious pictures and sticks them on the lift. That came about from me going into her flat and seeing the religious iconography everywhere, and trying to express what I wanted to about her story but in the space in which I was filming.

Did you make them go up and down?

Sometimes I had to keep them in the lift a bit longer, yeah. But in the editing you had to be careful because there is this inbuilt time that we have the characters because we're moving between floors, and if you stay too long you start to enter into a different film. They have to leave quite quickly for it to be believable.

What inspires you?

I think that when I started, I never knew that I wanted to do this. I wouldn't say it's something I've fallen into because it makes complete sense to me why I do it, but it's something that I never imagined doing at all. I went travelling for some years after managing to escape from England, and I always compare filmmaking to travelling. Instead of putting on your backpack and taking your clothes, you pack your camera and away you go and you have experiences. The only difference with filmmaking is that you're having to shape it into a film, whereas usually these experiences remain in your head and become part of your character in some way and inform how you see the world. I think filmmaking is like travelling, and I think that's the reason why I do it, because I couldn't face a life where I wasn't constantly having new experiences and questioning what was around me and trying to make sense of it. Having to shape it into a film is always the struggle.

It's like what I'm working on now, being in a town: how do you make a film out of a whole town? How do you structure this chaos that's outside into a coherent thing that people are going to enjoy watching, that has some shape to it? So that's the challenge every time. And the reason for it, the essential reason for me anyway, is to confront fears or anxieties, and curiosities, and to understand who we are and what makes us the people we become. Something like that. Just to understand who we are. I see the films as mirrors, to hold up to ourselves, even if you're talking to an extreme right-wing person as I've been doing in the last few weeks. These prejudices are within all of us at some level if we're honest with each other. People that try to go around saying that they're not prejudiced, I don't believe for a minute; we all have these prejudices, whether it's class or whatever. Sometimes in these extreme situations you see what we're really like, and in a way it's quite interesting to delve into those very human things.

So what kind of film wouldn't you make? What really doesn't appeal to you?

I tend not to choose films... I don't want to make films where I'm limited by the subject matter. So I wouldn't choose to make a film that was just following a character going through an experience that would make me feel limited, where I couldn't really express what I wanted to express through that situation. It's hard to name a specific subject. I wouldn't make a film about a chef opening up a new restaurant, because it wouldn't allow me to express things that I'm really interested in. The subject matter has to have some kind of transcendent quality; it has to go beyond itself. On one level you could say *Philip and His Seven Wives* was a slightly sensationalist situation – a man with seven wives – but that was the least interesting thing about it for me. It was about these characters' spiritual search and through them, especially in this situation he created, understanding power relationships. I think if the film works it works for that reason. It allows you to look at power and how power works, and the need and search for meaning. So every film has to have that otherwise it's hard for me to find a meaning in it.

What would you consider essential skills for a documentary filmmaker?

I've been teaching a lot over the last couple of years and it's something I've thought about a great deal. I don't know, maybe it's very arrogant of me, but sometimes I meet people and I just instinctively feel that they would be a good filmmaker. They may have never picked up a camera before or even watched a film before, but it's something about somebody's openness and curiosity and sensitivity. I think that they're the films I enjoy. When I watch a film where you can see the personality behind the camera, you can feel it. And I think that personality is usually someone who has quite a strong vision of the world and can translate that into film.

I meet a lot of people that are desperate to be filmmakers and desperate to make documentaries, especially now when they've become so hip, and when I meet people like that and I don't instinctively feel that they have a quality that I can relate to, it's always hard, especially as a teacher, because you're always, if I'm honest, always thinking, 'Well, what are they going to do that's really special and unique?' You can learn a lot, of course you can learn a tremendous amount, but I'm not sure that you can really teach somebody to have that approach to the world that's going to make them a good filmmaker.

There are people who are fiercely ambitious, who have had all the right education and done all the right courses, and often I can't see a filmmaker in them. It sounds an awful thing to say in a way but it's honestly how I really feel, and I don't know whether I'm always proved right in that, but it's something I feel instinctively. There are lots of people I meet who aren't filmmakers and I think that if you gave them a camera they could probably do something really interesting.

You do get lots of people that have watched every documentary ever made and every fiction film. But that doesn't mean they'll be good. They probably know too much. There's no relationship between having an amazing knowledge of film and filmmaking. I think if you have the ability to make a film you can of course be influenced by lots of different things as we all are, but because you've read every book and watched every film it doesn't mean you can make a good film. It's a mystery!

Every FourDocs thing I've seen is awful. I've seen half of one that's good. There's lots of crap out there.

Do the other people selecting for the film school agree with your opinion?

Yeah, there's quite a good consensus most of the time. Kim Longinotto and I always agree, every time we've done it. We always agree on the same people, instantly. And I find that I tend to agree when it comes to other people's films that I like. I'm involved in this project that's starting in 2008. A French producer has been going around with an idea for a series of films made in different countries about the same subject, and he's handpicked people to work from different countries. He came to me and explained who else is involved in the project and they're all filmmakers whose films I love. They're quite different films but they have the same sort of sensibility.

26. INTERVIEW WITH BEN HOPKINS, DIRECTOR OF *FOOTPRINTS*

Biography

Ben has made numerous films, including the award-winning fiction film, *The Nine Lives of Tomas Katz*, and the feature documentary *37 Uses for a Dead Sheep*. Born in the UK, Ben studied at Oxford University and in Edinburgh, where he also directed his first stage productions. During his film studies course at the Royal College of Art in London from 1989–95, he made several award-winning short films.

About the film

Filmed in Afghanistan and Laos, *Footprints* is a study of the effects of cluster bombs on people and landscape. The film takes a sympathetic look at the lives of those affected, uncovering some horrific statistics along the way, while analysing the design and military purpose of these weapons and enquiring whether they should be subject to restrictive laws.

You had a successful background in film before making *Footprints*, but hadn't made documentaries. Why did you want to move into this area and how did your experience working in drama inform your approach to making a documentary?

Footprints was a direct commission by Hans Geissendörfer, the producer/financier of my feature film *Tomas Katz*. He wanted to make a film that addressed the problem of unexploded ordnance. So – to be honest – it was Hans' idea, and it came at a time when my filmmaking career was at its lowest ebb. So I seized on the opportunity to make another film, even though it was quite different from what I had done before.

I have to say I had no idea what I was doing as a 'documentary' film-maker – I didn't have any previous experience. Neither did I have any 'theories' about what kind of documentary I wanted to make. I just went and did it, making it up as I went along. It was an intuitive process, and very unconsidered.

Where did the idea for the film come from?

It was Hans' commission; but the commission was vague – just to address the issue of unexploded ordnance. I then researched the subject, from books and the Internet, and from meeting experts in the field. Early on I hit on the simple idea of comparing the situation in the first country where cluster bombs were used (Laos) and the most recent country, which was then Afghanistan. Being a poetic kind of fellow, I was interested in the metaphor of the landscape – that these bombs transform landscape from something beautiful and life-giving, into something treacherous, dangerous and life-threatening. I gathered the factual backbone necessary to tell the story, and then brought some poetic/metaphorical ideas with me. This latter element probably comes more from my fiction/writing background.

How did you handle the inevitable danger to yourself and your crew, shooting in a war zone and around unexploded bombs?

Badly. There were just three of us – me (sound/direction), Gary Clarke (camera) and Chris Horwood (an expert in UXO). Chris, like many in his profession, simply gets used to there being mines and bombs around. We weren't, and I very nearly trod on a live bomb whilst recording sound (concentrating more on my job than on the critical danger around me). Afghanistan was in chaos then, and there was no way of ensuring your safety – you just had to be as sensible as possible, and alert for trouble. But we encountered nothing but hospitality and friendship from the local population. The US Army were less polite when they discovered what we were doing there. Laos was no problem – an organised place – and we were guests of an official organisation.

So, we all knew the project was potentially highly dangerous. We were nervous about it, but knew we had to accept the danger as part of the price of getting the film made.

How did you approach the research – finding the contributors and gaining permission to film with people clearing the mines?

In the usual way, I suppose. Chris Horwood was very helpful with permissions, as he knew most of the people in the field, and was trusted and respected – so he opened many doors, and without him I don't think we would have had anything like the access we did.

The interviewees we found on the day – travelling around to meet victims in hospitals and where they were recovering at home.

Footprints **is formally very distinctive – as is your other work. How did the style of the finished film evolve during the process of making it?**

I just intuitively shot what I felt would be useful. For instance, as the film was partly about the landscape becoming dangerous, it seemed a good idea to film hooves and feet crossing the fragile landscape, so we did many feet shots. As it turned out, these shots were very useful.

It was the first time I worked with Gary Clarke, the DP. At first I was nervous with him and told him what I wanted. But I quickly realised that he had a fantastic and intuitive understanding of the style of the film, and so increasingly I just said 'get some shots of this', and left him to it. He also shot *37 Uses for a Dead Sheep*, in which I gave him very little specific direction – he is a brilliant DP, and knows his job better than I do. My work is more to provide him with interesting situations, or interviews, and leave it to him to film them in the best way he can.

The sequences about dreams are very poignant, and also a great structuring device in a story that perhaps doesn't have an obvious beginning, middle and end. How did the narrative take shape during the various phases of research, production and post-production and how did you go about structuring the film?

Dreams are a great way of opening up interviewees, and also opening up a more metaphysical or emotional realm in a film. Again, it's my romantic/poetic side that's at work here – facts are very important for documentary, of course, but I will at least try to accommodate them within an atmospheric, emotional, or – in the case of *37 Uses* – comic context. You have to find tangential ways of interviewing your subjects, not just direct, factual ones. And dreams are just one of the easiest ways of getting a new perspective on something as horrible, concrete and physical as having one of your limbs blown away by a bomb.

We shot Afghanistan first. Edited it. Then went to Laos, and then tried to intercut the two stories. As usual, the first attempts were failures, but eventually, Alan Levy (editor) and I found a kind of dialectical structure that worked quite well.

You use music very strongly and very deliberately in the film; something that you develop to great effect, I feel, in *37 Uses for a Dead Sheep*. Would you say that this is something that is very important to your approach?

Yes, music is very important. I feel recently that I have used too much music in my work – my next feature film, *The Market*, uses very little music in comparison with my other films.

In *Footprints*, what I really wanted to avoid was the kind of soundtrack that apes the music of the country where it is shot. I hate seeing a documentary about Iraq, for example, that shows a mosque and has some wailing, Eastern voice on the soundtrack for 'atmosphere'. Why not show a mosque and some thrash metal, or some Mozart? Anything that makes you look at the world with fresh eyes, and ears. So, I asked Dominik Scherrer, who wrote the music for *Footprints*, to listen to Richard Strauss and Wagner before composing the score. I don't know why, but I felt that this later Romantic music had the right elegiac tone for our film.

What inspires you? Would you say there was an overriding ideal or theme that you're drawn to in your work?

I don't know what inspires me... inspiration comes from anywhere, or nowhere. And the only overriding theme that I detect in my work is an interest in economics.

If there's one piece of advice you could give to emerging documentary filmmakers, what would that be?

For God's sake try and do something different and imaginative, be bold and individual, idiosyncratic, even mad. There are just too many boring, standard, average films around. Even if you fail, at least you tried.

27. INTERVIEW WITH ESTEBAN UYARRA, DIRECTOR OF *WAR FEELS LIKE WAR*

Biography

Esteban is an award-winning director, editor and cinematographer of documentary films who has worked for several UK television channels, including the BBC and Channel 4. He made his first feature-length documentary, *The Light in the Dark*, while in his final year at film school. His second project was a series of six documentaries about different fiestas in Spain. One of them, *The Runner*, about the running of the bulls in San Fermin, went on to win Best International Documentary and Best Directorial Debut at the New York International Independent Film & Television Festival. *War Feels Like War* has screened in festivals and on TV channels across the world and was nominated for the prestigious Grierson Awards. His latest film, *The Battle for Saddam*, documents the trial of Saddam Hussein.

About the film

This film is the story of journalists caught up in a new era in war-reporting. In the second Gulf War, the coalition forces divided the world's media into two camps – 'embeds' and 'unilaterals'. In the making of *War Feels Like War*, Esteban Uyarra lived and worked among the unilaterals. Beginning in Kuwait City, then crossing the border into southern Iraq, we follow some of these independent reporters up to Baghdad and beyond, sharing the experiences and problems faced by those reporting on modern-day war. The film won numerous awards, including the Jury Prize at the Kino, Movie Eye Film Festival, and was shortlisted for the Silver Wolf Competition at the International Documentary Festival, Amsterdam.

Can you start by talking about the initial idea for the film, when you first set off for Iraq? What inspired it?

The first influence was Arturo Perez Reverte's *Territorio Comanche*. It's about his experiences as a war reporter in Kosovo. There is a lot of stuff in the book about the hotels that journalists stayed in and I thought I could make something like 'Fort Apache' – you're safe inside the hotel, but outside there's a hostile environment. Then I read *A Mad World* by John Simpson, which also talks about similar hotels.

The plan was to go anywhere in the world where there was this sort of hotel and make a film. Afghanistan was impossible, I couldn't afford to get there. I considered Palestine but that seemed to have been covered. Then, as the build-up to war in Iraq started heating up, I thought it might be the right opportunity. I just decided to go to Kuwait City. I went the day after the famous London anti-war demonstration, I think, about 20 days before war was declared. I had no understanding – there was no understanding – of how things were going to work for the journalists. We just hung around the American press office and were given cards that said 'unilateral journalists'. We quickly felt like bystanders who could be easily brushed off.

How did the story change once you started filming?

Originally I was going to film only the sub-society that journalists create inside their hotels as a conflict takes place outside – what takes place once the cameras are put down. But it became clear to me that Kuwait was too far from the real action for this situation of hotel/fear/claustrophobia to emerge. All journalists wanted to cross into Iraq, legally or illegally. So the new story emerges: that of a beginning where we see the chaos and anxieties of the journalist corp. as they aim at getting into the real conflict, and the reality and dilemmas that they encounter once they enter this new reality. Basically a journey from black comedy to real drama and uncertainty.

How did you fund the film?

From my own pocket. I took my credit card, borrowed a friend's camera and mic and just bought a ticket to Kuwait. I spent about $2,000 in Kuwait and then just $1,000 in Iraq. See, in a war zone you can't spend much money, especially when you are taking free rides, sleeping on the floor with other journalists, and getting free DV tapes and a free bulletproof/chemical suit from CNN and *Chicago Tribune* friends. I made it as I went, borrowing, getting free meals in the big hotels, and the rest.

Did you have a distributor or buyer in mind when you were making it?

Not at all. I wasn't even sure this film would go very far. I just needed to make a film, I was bursting inside. At that stage in your career (when you are an 'uncommissionable') there is no point in thinking about the outlet. At least that's how I feel. The main thing is to go and shoot the damn thing.

How difficult was it for you to shoot as a non-embedded journalist?

To be honest, I have been back in Iraq to make another film for the last 14 months and I look back at the invasion time with melancholy. In those days, it was pretty easy to film, provided you were as stupid and naïve as I was at the time. There weren't many restrictions once you were inside Iraq. The marines made it clear to you: 'We won't stop you but you're on your own from now on.' I think there was also a sense of pride within the army that they were doing the right thing at the time, and in that sense they let you film pretty much up close and personal (provided they had not just killed some people right there). On the other hand, you were in no-man's-land most of the time. Taking your own risks, travelling without protection and crossing a warpath that changed dramatically from one hour to the next. In my case I hadn't much of a choice, I just followed the subjects of my film, so wherever they went I went. Once in the car I was 'locked' with them.

How did you handle the inevitable danger to yourself, shooting in a war zone?

As I said, with a lot of stupidity and naivety. I did pick up some tips as I went, and I just trusted that the journalists I was travelling with were less stupid than I was. I really learned quickly to mimic what my companions were doing. But a couple of times I did jump into 'the empty swimming pool' on my own and I'm still not quite sure how I made it. I did also have a bulletproof suit (courtesy of CNN) but it didn't have a plate on the front so only my back was covered really. This played on my mind quite a bit.

Can you talk a little about your choice of style? How difficult was it to keep a distance from your subjects in a situation like that?

I had always liked cinéma vérité (*The War Room* and so on). Hand-held, on-your-feet kind of filmmaking. I am not very good at creating something out of an empty room, a person and some lights. But I did find I was quite comfortable once the shit hit the fan and everybody was running for their lives. But I think that raw cinéma vérité style I developed was also out of practical necessity. I do become impatient with ticking off the 'to do list' before going into a shoot. So I just went with no tripod or lights, just a mic on the camera and shot the whole thing on automatic. For me content is the priority. I don't think I had much of an issue with keeping an objective eye with my subjects. As the person who bought the film said once, 'you have a cold but good eye'. I don't know whether to take that as a compliment, but I guess it means I can keep a good perspective on my subject. In other words, I'm a bit cynical.

How did you approach shooting for the edit? And how did the narrative evolve?

I have been an editor myself for the last eight years, so I have a bit of an understanding of how long to hold the shot or how much coverage I need to make a scene work in the cutting room (I believe!). But I'm also a believer in letting the film grow into something else during the editing, so I didn't get too hooked up on that kind of thinking during the shooting. My main concern was to be close to any of the four characters at regular intervals. The narrative was clearly one of a journey film, from A to Z, but we tried to keep the main themes from black comedy to drama increasing. There were a couple of scenes in particular that, put in their chronological order, seemed to cancel one another out, and we were tempted to take the whole Tikrit trip towards the end of the film out, but finally we suggested swapping them around and we found that the tension kept increasing and that it was worth leaving both of them. Furthermore we wanted to make a bit of a staccato film, not too smooth at the edges, so that the audience felt a bit lost, just as I was myself. Capture that sense of uncertainty. Not knowing where they are going next. We didn't 'telegraph' any sequences on purpose, and put little information in. Hopefully no one got too lost in the plot.

With a background as an editor, what was your relationship like with Brian Tagg, and how hands-on were you in the edit?

I did create a blueprint for the film and a 20-minute pilot (so that he could see the style I was going for). We did watch most of the rushes together and discuss things during those first three days. After that I stayed 90% of the time outside the editing room. Brian works much better alone and I trust him with my film life. Only once in a while and after the first rough cut did we discuss more scenes and alternatives, but I always let him do it on his own. I'm too lazy!

What happened once you got back from Iraq: how did you sell the film, and how did it get picked up by Storyville and TV2?

By then Alison Roper from In Focus Productions had joined the production 100% and she was good at getting some attention from some buyers. She had sent the 20-minute pilot to Nick Fraser and apparently he had liked it but wanted to see more. Once Brian joined (on a deferred payment at first), Nick took even more notice, and decided to come and have a look at the first cut. He was impressed and decided to buy UK rights on the spot. After that Nick suggested Mette Hoffman Meyer at TV2 for international rights. She was very enthusiastic about the film, so she bought it and sold it to some other channels including PBS.

Why documentaries?

For practical reasons. I wanted to be the next Walter Murch but I became frustrated editing other people's material. I was editing a lot of crap, and it occurred to me I could do better than the films I was editing. But I don't have the patience for working in a big team with all the preparations that fiction requires. I'm a bit of a loner when I work so I found the idea of working alone irresistible and documentaries seemed ideal.

Also, for me it's about having a new experience entering a world that I haven't known anything about previously – whether it is a war zone or the life of lawyers, as now, with my next project. But the bottom line is to transmit something exciting and interesting to others so they can share it. Thank God, in documentary filmmaking you can do this while having a good time and the experience of a lifetime.

What inspires you? Would you say there was an overriding ideal or theme that you're drawn to in your work?

I like heroes, finding something universal and interesting about someone that not even him/her knew about. I like the idea of putting others in the shoes of someone else and seeing how they feel. I don't believe in universal truths or black and whites so I see a lot of greys in all situations to explore. I'm a bit of a 'questioner'. I question everything so I get drawn to themes/people that are happy to reflect on all these grey areas in their situations and lives.

What do you think makes a good idea?

I guess the filmmaker. Is the life of an architect or the journey of a weeping camel, or a bunch of children learning in rural France a good idea? I'm not sure. I think it is the way the filmmaker approaches the idea.

What do you consider a bad idea? What do you think doesn't work?

When the filmmaker thinks that he/she has all the answers about their theme or story before the filming starts. When it's black or white. It's not so much a bad idea as a bad approach. I think that makes a bad film.

If there's one piece of advice you could give to emerging documentary filmmakers, what would that be?

Forget about climbing the ladder. Decide when you are going to take the next holiday and swap that time and money for making a film. You will have a better time, you will learn more, will meet more interesting people and experience more situations. Just pick the camera, understand the themes you want to explore and go.

What are you working on now?

I have just finished a long feature documentary of the Saddam trial, *The Battle For Saddam*.

SECTION SEVEN

28. GLOSSARY

Below is a list of some of the most common terms you will come across when making a documentary film.

Aperture
Refers to the measurement of the opening in a camera lens (the iris) that regulates the amount of light passing through and contacting the film (or in the case of a video camera the CCD). Often measured as an f-stop.

Aspect Ratio
This is the measurement of width to height of the visual frame, expressed as a ratio, and will either be 4:3 or 16:9 (often referred to as widescreen).

Bidirectional
Refers to a type of microphone that picks up sound from the front and the back, but rejects most sound from the sides.

Boom
Usually a long, extendable pole on which a microphone is attached at the end. Used by sound recordists so they can follow the direction of the sound source.

CCD
Refers to a Charge Coupled Device, which is the digital video camera equivalent of film. Effectively, it's a light-sensitive semi-conductor chip. Most good cameras have three, whereas the cheaper consumer cameras may only have one.

Close Up
This refers to a camera shot, and is the second tightest shot in a sequence, often showing someone's face in intimate detail. Differs from an Extreme Close Up.

Cutaway
A single shot inserted into a sequence of shots that momentarily interrupts the flow of action, or 'cuts away' from the main action.

Depth of Field
The area within which objects are in focus. A large depth of field allows a great range of objects to be in focus simultaneously, while a shallow depth of field offers a very limited area in focus. Both the focal length and the aperture influence the depth of field.

Dissolve
An editing term, used to describe a transition between two shots, where the first one fades out whilst simultaneously being replaced by the second.

Extreme Close Up
This is the tightest shot in a sequence, say on someone's eyes or mouth.

F-Stop
The way in which aperture is measured. Common F stops are F1.4, F2, F2.8, F4, F5.6, F8, F11, F16, F22. The higher the number, the smaller the iris aperture and the less light falling on the CCD.

Fill Light
Generally diffused light to reduce shadow or contrast range. Used in a Three Point Lighting set up.

Focal Length
The focal length of a lens is defined as the distance in mm from the optical centre of the lens to the focal point.

Focal Point

This is the exact point at which the camera is focused at maximum sharpness. When looking into the viewfinder it is usually marked in the centre with either a circle or a set of brackets.

Focus

When the lens is able to create the sharpest image of a subject, it is said to be in focus.

Gain

A function which increases the video signal, altering contrast and brightness of the picture.

High Definition Television (HDTV)

This is a digital television broadcasting system with a significantly higher resolution than traditional formats (NTSC, SECAM, PAL).

High Definition Video (HDV)

This is an inexpensive high-definition video recording format which uses MPEG2 compression to fit high-definition content onto the same DV or MiniDV tapes originally developed for standard definition recording. It differs from HD, the latter offering slightly better quality.

Iris

A variable aperture that controls exposure or the amount of light which is entering the lens.

Key Light

As the principal source of illumination, the major function of the key light is to reveal the basic shape of the object.

Lavalier

Often referred to as 'radio mics' (which can actually refer to any microphone that is connected using a transmitter and receiver) a lavalier mic is a small microphone, which can be easily hidden in a piece of clothing so as not to be seen by the camera. Also known as a 'tie-mic' or 'lapel mic'.

Lens
Defined as one or more pieces of optical glass or similar material designed to collect and focus rays of light to form a sharp image onto film or digital camera sensor (CCD).

Linear Editing
Video editing style where a programme is edited together by moving shots from the original source tapes to a master tape, one by one. Because the assembly is linear, changes made to an earlier point of the tape result in the rest of the edited tape being reassembled.

Master Shot
Usually refers to a long shot taking in a prolonged action. The intention is to cover the scene with a single basic shot, into which other shots may be introduced to enhance more specific visual drama.

Neutral Density (ND)
A filter that will reduce the amount of light that enters the lens of your camcorder without affecting the colour of your picture. A neutral density filter is typically used in bright-light situations when your image is being blown out by the sunlight or lighting in the area. Most semi-professional and professional cameras have built-in ND filters

Noise
Unwanted electrical signals that produce spots on the image. You will most notice noise when, for example, using digital gain in low-light settings.

Non-linear Editing
This is a modern editing method which involves being able to access any frame in a video clip with the same ease as any other. Like film editing (which itself is non-linear, but involves the actual cutting of the film) we can put

frames in any order we want, and it is easily reversible and non-destructible.

Offline Editing

Historically, this refers to the process of editing the majority of one's film at low resolution, either to save on equipment costs or to conserve hard disk space. When the edit is finished, the material can be recaptured at high quality, or an EDL can be exported to recreate the edit on another system. However, today, the term offline editing is often (wrongly) used to refer to the main editing phase, before the footage is graded and exported to a master tape, even though the actual footage may have been captured at full (i.e. online) resolution.

Pan

A shot taken moving on a horizontal plane (from left to right, right to left).

Phantom Power

This is a power signal that can be used to power Condenser Microphones directly from a Mixing Desk or Camera. Many professional microphones (such as the Senheisser 416 shotgun microphone) are phantom powered, thus requiring no battery.

Point of View (POV)

Refers to shooting a camera from the point of view (POV) of a subject.

Reflector

Used when lighting a scene to reflect or deflect light.

Rule of thirds

The rule of thirds is a compositional rule of thumb in filmmaking (and indeed in all forms of photography). The rule states that an image can be divided into nine equal parts by two equally-spaced horizontal lines and two equally-spaced vertical lines. The four points where these lines intersect are the four prime locations for the centre of the subject of your frame. Proponents of this technique claim that aligning a photograph with these points creates more tension, energy and interest in the frame than simply centring the feature would.

Sequence
Refers to a collection of shots used together in order to form a narrative. There are certain rules as to what order and which shots are to be used in a sequence in order to allow the audience to perceive you are telling a story. Also refers to a collection of shots put into a specific order when editing.

Shotgun
In filmmaking, this refers to a type of microphone, most often used in documentary filmmaking. Also known as a uni-directional microphone.

Storyboard
A visual representation of the shots you will take when you film.

Three Point Lighting
A standard method of lighting for documentary filmmakers, using three lights: a key light, a backlight and a fill light.

Tilt
Camera movement in a vertical plane (up or down). You may, for example, do a pan of a building in which you might start at the bottom of the building and go up to the top.

Time code
The way in which a camera records time in frames-per-second (fps). PAL cameras have 25 frames per second, whilst NTSC cameras have 30.

White Balance
White Balance is a way of getting your camera to see white objects as truly white, not as a tint of another colour. You are, in effect, telling the camera *what is white*.

NOTES

1   There were other filmmakers from other parts of the world who were also making documentary films around this time, such as the Russians Sergei Eisenstein and Dziga Vertov, who were extending and shaping the possibilities offered by film. Eisenstein's theory of montage is still studied by film students everywhere, while Vertov's theory of 'Kino Pravda' (Film Truth) made the distinction between reality as lived, and the reality captured by the camera. His film *Man with a Movie Camera* is a manifestation of this, revealing the process of filmmaking within the film itself. Their work and theories were a direct influence on the members of Britain's Documentary Film Movement.

2   Sheila Curran Bernard, (2004) *Documentary Storytelling for Video and Filmmakers*. Focal Press: London. p.13

3   Michael Rabiger (2004) *Directing the Documentary – 4th Edition*, Focal Press: London. p. 138

4   There are some instances when you can get away with crossing the line. This is usually when, in one continuous shot, you are rotating round the action before you, and the audience sees the actual 'crossing' of the line as it is occurring.

5   There are subtle differences between the different terms used, but since they are often used interchangeably, we'll stick to clumping them all together.

INDEX

creative ESSENTIALS

DVD CONTENTS

FILMS

Boogie Woogie Pappa (2002)
35mm. 13 mins. Dir. Erik Bäfving.
Multi-award-winning film about a son and father who changes from a loving daddy who danced the Boogie Woogie into an alcoholic stranger.

Lift (2001)
DV. 24 mins. Dir. Marc Isaacs.
Filmmaker Marc Isaacs sets himself up in a London tower block lift with his camera, unsure how residents will react. They come to trust him and reveal the things that matter to them. The award-winning result is a humorous and moving portrait of a vertical multicultural community.

Footprints (2003)
Digibeta and Super 8. 43 mins. Dir. Ben Hopkins.
A film about the effects of clusterbombs and landmines on the people in Afghanistan made by award-winning director Ben Hopkins.

TEMPLATES

- Blank cost report
- Budget
- Call sheet
- Expenses claim form
- Freelancer agreement
- Location agreement
- Music master synch licence (Recording)
- Post-production script (*Fly Me*)
- Release form
- Risk assessment form
- Shooting guide
- Treatment (*Fly Me*)
- Viewing and logging rushes

Downloads can also be accessed at www.kamerabooks.com/downloads